Us Before Me

Also by Patricia Illingworth

AIDS AND THE GOOD SOCIETY

ETHICAL HEALTHCARE (*co-edited with Wendy Parmet*)

GIVING WELL: The Ethics of Philanthropy (*co-edited with Thomas Pogge and Leif Wenar*)

THE POWER OF PILLS (*co-edited with Jillian Claire Cohen and Udo Schuklenk*)

TRUSTING MEDICINE

Us Before Me

Ethics and Social Capital for Global Well-Being

Patricia Illingworth
Northeastern University, USA

First published 2012 by
PALGRAVE MACMILLAN

Palgrave Macmillan in the UK is an imprint of Macmillan Publishers Limited,
registered in England, company number 785998, of Houndmills, Basingstoke,
Hampshire RG21 6XS.

Palgrave Macmillan in the US is a division of St Martin's Press LLC,
175 Fifth Avenue, New York, NY 10010.

Palgrave Macmillan is the global academic imprint of the above companies
and has companies and representatives throughout the world.

Palgrave® and Macmillan® are registered trademarks in the United States,
the United Kingdom, Europe and other countries.

ISBN 978–0–230–31443–6

This book is printed on paper suitable for recycling and made from fully
managed and sustained forest sources. Logging, pulping and manufacturing
processes are expected to conform to the environmental regulations of the
country of origin.

A catalogue record for this book is available from the British Library.

A catalog record for this book is available from the Library of Congress.

10   9   8   7   6   5   4   3   2   1
21 20 19 18 17 16 15 14 13 12

Printed and bound in Great Britain by
CPI Antony Rowe, Chippenham and Eastbourne

For friends, and the friends of friends, and for family, and the friends of family.

Contents

Foreword	ix
Acknowledgments	xviii
Introduction	**1**
Plan of this book	5
1 Making a Difference	**12**
Bandwagons and cascades	21
Philosophers as ethics entrepreneurs	25
Nudging toward social capital	29
2 The Heart of the Matter	**32**
Social capital	34
Trust	39
Value	42
Creating social capital	46
Singing in the rain	50
Global social capital	53
3 The Ethics of Us	**66**
Making it moral	69
Solidarity rights	75
Realizing the principle of social capital	76
4 The Moral Sweet Spot	**84**
Liberty and custom	88
Happiness	92
Emotional contagion: A friend indeed	95

	Culture	103
	Better with us	111
5	**With a Little Help from the Law**	**119**
	Law as social meaning	121
	Helping strangers	126
	Destroying social capital	139
	A window of opportunity	146
6	**Giving Back**	**151**
	Sweet charity	152
	Deducting our gifts	157
	Charity without borders	162
7	**Global People**	**180**
	Global belonging	185
	Global culture	196
	Global living	199
	Global citizens	203
Notes		213
References		232
Index		249

Foreword

Important problems today – resource depletion, global warming, war, terrorism and poverty – are global in the sense that human beings must solve them together, collaborating across our conventional divisions of state, language, religion, ethnicity and way of life. People can cooperate merely instrumentally, through trades, negotiations, bargaining and compromise. But cooperation is more stable and more worthwhile when it involves mutual understanding, trust and friendship. No one can maintain such genuine cooperative relations with billions of others, to be sure. But we can collaborate through the intermediation of others. And we can work to build generalized trust: a social environment in which people can be trusted and collaborate easily.

The challenge is to build trust that transcends the conventional divisions. If trusting social environments are self-contained bubbles, they cannot facilitate global cooperation. If we form friendships only with people within our country, then such friendships cannot strengthen cooperative bonds across national borders. Conversely, if many people have just a few close relations across the conventional divisions, they can connect human beings all over the world to one another at just a few removes. The friends of my friends already number in the thousands and live in every country on earth. Add in their friends as well and you find an amazing network that reaches into all communities, cultures, social classes and walks of life. If most human beings could be centers of such networks, we would have a vastly better and more sympathetic understanding of what the world feels like from other vantage points. This would make it much easier to work together toward a livable common future on our planet – a future that, in any case, will involve an increased sharing of fates.

We can glimpse the possibilities by examining successful nations in which the older familial divisions of tribe, clan and caste have faded. If this was possible in a populous and diverse national population like that of the United States, why should an analogous fading away of *national* divisions not be possible as well? In fact, is this not what we are witnessing in Europe today?

But Europe also offers a glimpse of the darker possibilities of stratified collaboration that excludes those who have little to offer, forcing them – Africans and Turks, for instance – to adapt themselves to the crushing bargaining power of the European Union. Recent trends in inequality worldwide suggest a dark future along the same lines. The conventional group disparities – by race, sex, nationality, language, religion, parental class, sexual preference and so on – are beginning to fade, and yet raw inequality among individuals worldwide is rising relentlessly. Over a recent 17-year period, only the top twentieth of the human population achieved a meaningful expansion of its share, adding 3.5 percent of global household income to reach a record 46.4 percent. The poorest 90 percent lost ground, with the bottom quarter losing a third of its already grotesquely small share which, declined from 1.16 to 0.78 of global household income.[1]

The "Us" in the title of this book is humankind. But to achieve this "Us," to build social capital that is truly global, we must be mindful of the historically much more prominent instances where social capital was – consciously or unconsciously – built up and sustained by the edge it gave insiders over others. Clans and cities, castes and nobilities, religious orders and fraternities, clubs and professional associations, corporations and cartels, parties and lobbies – they are all more successful when they maintain tight bonds of trust among their members. And their success has typically meant additional burdens on the disadvantaged: slaves, serfs, peasants, women, workers, customers, conscripts and the unemployed. Social capital contributes to the happiness and success of those who partake in it; but it need not be truly global to do so.

What reasons can Patricia Illingworth give her more privileged readers to support her vision of truly global social capital in preference to an alternative and less remote vision of social capital, confined to the global elite who dominate politics and business, investment and finance, science and technology, education and healthcare, and the media and entertainment around the world? How can we who share Illingworth's vision argue our case to members of the global elite?

We can say that such confinement of trust and concern to the emerging global elite fits poorly with the universalistic moral thinking that has become dominant since the European Enlightenment and the American and French revolutions. Social capital fundamentally involves moral motivations and moral relations among people. Elitist solidarity is subversive to the kind of morality we now have, and its bonds will therefore be weak. When you really need them, your jet-set "friends" will throw you to the wolves. Insofar as honor is inconsistent with stealing, there can be no honor among thieves.

We can add that the exclusion of the poorer majority is costly even for the global elite. Here terrorism and piracy are often mentioned, but much greater are the costs of high fertility among the poor. While the total fertility rates (TFRs) (average number of children per woman) of roughly 100 well-to-do countries have already fallen below the crucial value of 2, the TFRs for the 50 least developed countries are still 4.4, with the poorest sporting TFRs above 7. Wherever human populations have gained basic levels of material sufficiency, including basic education (especially for girls), basic healthcare and basic provision for old age, their TFRs have fallen dramatically – for example, from 3.2 to 1.9 in Australia, from 6.1 to 1.6 in Thailand and from 6.6 to 1.3 in Singapore since the 1950s. In the same period, persistent poverty has sustained persistently high TFRs – for example, in Equatorial Guinea (from 5.5 to 5.4), East Timor (unchanged at 6.5) and Niger (from 6.9 to 7.2).[2] In Kenya, a representative poor country, the population has increased from 2.9 million in the late 1920s to 41 million today.[3] Were humanity to follow Illingworth's path, the human population, at 7 billion today, could peak in 30 years at around

8 billion. Continued deprivation of billions of poor people, by contrast, could entail a still rising population of over 15 billion by the end of this century.[4] Treating the bulk of Africa's population as merely an annoying obstacle to getting that continent's natural resources to the highest bidder will actually multiply this population and thereby magnify the obstacle.

In this context one might further point out that global inequality has become so extreme that the cost of poverty eradication is astoundingly small. For example, to reach the same level as the third quarter of the human population, the bottom quarter would need an additional 1.4 percent of global household income. If this expansion of their share came entirely at the expense of the top twentieth of the human population, this elite's share would decline from 46.4 to 45 percent – losing less than half of its 1988–2005 gain. Is the benefit of avoiding this "sacrifice" really worth the cost we impose on the poor, on future generations and on the moral value of our lives?

We are sometimes confronted with the question of whether we should give up a little of our own ample income to meet basic needs among people vastly poorer than ourselves. With just 3 percent of what we earn, we could dramatically improve the lives of a dozen poor families. Illingworth poses a question that is much easier to answer in the affirmative: should we work toward a more solidaristic, friendly, trusting and less unequal world in which the more privileged, like ourselves, would have somewhat less so that billions of poor people could meet their basic needs? Would you "sacrifice" 3 percent of your income if you knew that all other affluent people would follow your example and that this would end the extreme poverty that now blights and severely shortens the lives of billions? Of course you would! But how could this be possible?

One illustrative proposal Illingworth discusses concerns the tax-deductibility of charitable donations, which currently are overwhelmingly directed to domestic charities pursuing domestic causes. If the laws were different so that direct donations to foreign-based charitable organizations could also be deducted, then the more affluent populations could and would do much more toward protecting especially poor people around the world. Their relevant contributions would increase in three ways: some of us would give to effective non-governmental organizations (NGOs) in poorer countries funds that we would otherwise have saved or spent on ourselves; some of us would give to such NGOs funds that we would otherwise have devoted to morally less important domestic causes; and all of us would also contribute to such foreign NGOs through the tax system. (A \$1,000 gift from a person in the 35 percent tax bracket saves themselves \$350 in taxes, which essentially means that their net contribution of \$650 is matched by a \$350 contribution from the state.)

All three effects would be substantially magnified if donations from poorer people – and especially from those in the United States who do not itemize deductions on their tax return – were matched at the same rate as donations by the rich. Especially when they donate appreciated assets (thereby also saving capital gains taxes) or can deduct their donation also from their state income tax liability, wealthy Americans can reduce the private cost of their donation to about half its value, thereby obtaining a 100 percent match of their cost from the state. Itemizers in the 10 percent tax bracket, by contrast, can reduce the private cost of their donation by merely 10 percent, thus obtaining only an 11 percent ($100 per $900 net contribution) match from the state. Non-itemizers get no match at all. This regressivity of the tax code comes on top of regressivity in giving: even while heavily disadvantaged by the tax code, poor Americans give a substantially larger proportion of their income than more affluent ones. A recent *New York Times* article reports that "households earning less than $25,000 a year gave away an average of 4.2 percent of their incomes; those with earnings of more than $75,000 gave away 2.7 percent."[5] According to the *Guardian*, this disparity in giving is even more pronounced in the United Kingdom.[6]

Complementary to the tax code changes Illingworth proposes, one could also extend tax-deductibility to remittances to poor countries. Many people working hard in affluent countries are guest workers or recent immigrants who send substantial portions of their earnings to much poorer relatives in their country of origin. Christian Barry and Gerhard Øverland have discussed why and how such transfers should be made tax-deductible.[7] As with Illingworth's proposal of state incentives for volunteer work, it is not easy to assure tax payers that such rewards are not abused. But these difficulties seem solvable, and the potential gains are enormous. Even under the existing rules, Americans alone are giving some $290 billion annually to charitable organizations.[8] It is easily conceivable that better rules could raise additional tens of billions for the most vulnerable people around the world. By exploring and supporting such changes, we may be able to do what seemed impossible: to impose a small cost on ourselves for the sake of substantially improving the lives of billions.

Drawing on Illingworth's illuminating discussions, I have tried to respond to what I see as the key challenge to her vision: the objection that the global elite are better off building social capital among themselves rather than among humanity at large. This response still leaves out an important strand running through the book. It takes the ends and values of the better-off as given and shows them that they have more to gain and less to lose than they had thought from supporting efforts at broader social capital formation. Illingworth does not take the ends and values of her readers as given but offers an attractive ideal of the human beings we could be, of the lives we might lead, if we lived in a world rich in truly global social capital that we were committed to preserving and enhancing. This vision does not appeal to our capacities as rational maximizers but engages us as beings who reflectively shape our own identity, as moral beings and searchers for a worthwhile life: in art and music, in love and friendship, in responding to the infinite beauty and diversity of our world. We can shut out or deform these aspects of our humanity to enjoy the five-star toys of a predatory global elite. Or we can lead a life that is mindful of all human beings and thereby help build an ethos of solidarity, a truly global culture of understanding and trust – global social capital. Rich in a different sense of the word, these lives may be incommensurable. But this does not mean we should opt for the former, if we can, just because it is closer to hand. Another world is possible. Better institutional arrangements could further it. But we can also promote it from the bottom up by how we interact with other human beings and with the most disadvantaged in particular.

Thomas Pogge

Acknowledgments

The ideas contained in this book have been taking shape over several years. I have enjoyed countless conversations with people about social capital, charity, globalization and cosmopolitanism. I am indebted to all of those who have shared their thoughts with me about the ethics of social capital, whether at a conference, in writing, over coffee or over Skype. In particular, my colleague in the Economics Department at Northeastern University, Jim Dana, gave me very detailed comments on social capital and helped to clarify my understanding of the concept. I am grateful to Peter Berenson, Christopher Bosso, Joanne Cippola Moore, Angus Dawson, Richard Daynard, Nancy Dearman, Peter Enrich, John Kotter, Jung Lee, Hope Lewis, Stephen Nathanson, Wendy Parmet, Sonia Rolland, Bob and Susan Schechter, Rory Smead, Margaret Somerville, John Tasiuolas, Leif Wenar and Dan Wikler. Each of these people, in unique and substantive ways, contributed to my thinking about the themes in this book.

Much of the work on this project was done during a sabbatical from Northeastern University, for which I am grateful. During that time I was a visiting scholar at the Harvard University Program in Ethics and Health. My colleagues at Harvard welcomed me and gave me a wonderfully supportive and intellectually rich environment in which to work. I thank them. I must also recognize the help of three excellent and dedicated research assistants: Matthew Hewes, Taran Nadler and Christina Schlegel. They did a great job and I enjoyed working with them.

Thomas Pogge's Foreword explores crucial issues. He develops the concept of global social capital and its application to global inequality. As always, he is generous with his insight, time and support, and he continues to deepen my understanding of global justice. My gratitude to him is heartfelt. In a book in which so much is about the ethics of giving and helping the most vulnerable members of our global community, it would be remiss not to thank Peter Singer; his work on global giving has been an inspiration to me and many others. Thank you for blazing the trail.

I also want to thank my daughter, Zoe. She has been a stimulating and challenging interlocutor and a precise stylistic editor. My mother, Joan Illingworth, has always supported my work, and I am deeply grateful to her for that.

Priyanka Gibbons, my editor at Palgrave Macmillan, has been diligent, fully engaged and creative at each stage of publication. I am thankful for her expertise, care, attention and good-natured disposition. The editors and proofreaders at Palgrave were excellent. I thank them for their wise editorial suggestions and for the care they took with the manuscript.

Stephanie Zelman helped me to find the right image of "Us" for the book cover. I appreciate her time and her talent.

Sections of Chapter 6 were drawn from *Giving Well: The Ethics of Philanthropy*, a book I co-edited with Thomas Pogge and Leif Wenar (Oxford University 2010). Some parts of Chapter 4 are excerpted by permission of the publisher from "The duty to promote social capital" in *The Philosophy of Public Health*, ed. Angus Dawson (Aldershot: Ashgate, 2009) pp. 37–47.

Introduction

We do not have to look far to observe tension and conflict between and among people from different cultures. In the United States, the Governor of Arizona has all but declared war on legal and illegal immigrants. Some members of the Muslim community in New York City proposed to build an Islamic Center and mosque two blocks from Ground Zero, giving rise to a groundswell of opposition among New Yorkers, especially those who lost friends and family in the attack of 9/11. In France, President Sarkozy proceeded to expel the Roma (gypsies) in defiance of the European Union's criticism that the expulsion violated the free movement principle that underlies the Union. At other times, he has threatened to suspend the Schengen Treaty in order to restrict the influx of Tunisian and Libyan migrants from Italy. And in Germany, Chancellor Merkel declared that multicultural society has failed. At each of these moments, people cling stubbornly to their positions and the perceived interests of their respective groups, unable to trust the "other" or to find common ground. This book is about the value of "us," whoever its constituents. I believe that

1

social capital (social networks and norms of reciprocity and trust), understood as a moral principle, can help to guide people to take "us" into account. Social capital will not be a panacea, and will not override all self-interest and indifference to others, but as a moral principle it would require people to include a consideration of "us" in their moral deliberations, in addition to their personal interests and the interests of others. A first step in this direction will be to understand the value of "us." Social capital, with its emphasis on the value of social networks, does this well.

Social capital is created primarily through interactions among people. As people form social ties and networks, and become familiar with one another, trust evolves. So too does social capital. When social ties are characterized by generalized reciprocity, in which people help one another without requiring reciprocation, social capital can blossom fully. Generalized reciprocity flourishes in high trust contexts, often when social connections are long term, or have other built-in protections on which people can rely. Generalized reciprocity is not essential for social capital. But giving and helping go a long way toward creating it.

To help illustrate the contours of the concept of social capital, I will provide a couple of examples of how it is created. Locally, social capital can be built through participation in voluntary organizations, such as the Parent Teacher Association, the Rotary Club and Neighborhood Watch programs. When people are engaged in activities such as these, their interaction with others can give rise to trust, generalized reciprocity, cooperation, collaboration and social goodwill. The benefits to come from these associations

often cannot be restricted to the people who contribute to the activity. The same is true for the social
capital garnered from purely social interactions, such
as block parties. Those who organize others, bring food
and clean up cannot restrict the social capital created to those who contribute. As with other public
goods, social capital has externalities, and can have a
free-rider problem. Some of the decline in social capital about which Robert Putnam has written may be
explained by the free-rider problem. But the public
good dimension of social capital is not the only problem. Indeed, it might not be a problem at all if social
capital were not coupled with a normative predisposition toward self-interest. People may be reluctant
to contribute to public goods, such as social capital,
not only because others can free-ride on their contribution, but also because, given the predominance of
the prevailing norm of self-interest, they don't want
to appear to be "dupes." When the prominent norms
and aspirations of society revolve around individualism, autonomy and self-interest, people who act for
the sake of others, or allow others to benefit from their
actions, risk appearing to be a "dupe" or a sucker. This
is a point that Cass Sunstein has stressed.

Given the focus of social capital on "us," its benefits,
efficiency and, in some cases, its superiority over alternative moral possibilities, understanding social capital
as a moral concept seems not only an accurate char-
acterization of the concept but also important in a
world of indifference to the suffering of others and
torn apart by conflict between and among people from
different cultures, sometimes with devastating consequences. Because the concept of social capital shifts

the analysis, and focus, from individual self-interest to cooperative interest, it has the potential to introduce a new moral entity into the conversation – one with its own interests, separate and distinct from the interests of the self and others.

Social capital also has a dark side; sometimes social ties and groups can become exclusionary. This problem is exacerbated by the human tendency toward homophily: the "birds of a feather flock together" phenomenon. Despite this problem, Robert Putnam, a political scientist at the Harvard Kennedy School, is optimistic that people from diverse groups will be able to create social capital. Treating social capital as a moral principle can help to overcome its dark side because ethics would demand that we act impartially with respect to creating social capital.

Given the challenges of global living, people need to be able to cooperate with people from other cultures. Globalization has much to offer people who can navigate the world of differences. They will benefit from transnational interactions, while those who are unable to negotiate transnational living may endure losses. Sadly, there is also evidence that the people most likely to be left out of the global good life are those who most need to be included: the global poor.

Social capital can be helpful internationally, not only because of what it specifies – that is, social networks, trust and reciprocity – but also for what it does not specify. It does not identify any particular social relations. It does not say that social capital can be fostered by social ties among compatriots, or Muslims, Catholics, Jews, heterosexuals or homosexuals. Although social capital is often found among homogeneous groups, in part because of proximity, there is nothing in the concept itself that demands this. Social capital directs our attention to the value that social networks can bring. Strictly speaking, that value can be nurtured anywhere, and among many different people. This is an important virtue of social capital, especially in a global context.

Plan of this book

In Chapter 1, I describe a number of global and domestic social problems that have persisted for some time, and that highlight moral indifference and an inability to cooperate to solve urgent social problems. Because social capital is associated with concern for others, and the capacity to cooperate, I believe that it would be an important mechanism for addressing these problems. Global poverty, for example, is more likely to be addressed if people living in rich countries create networks of trust and generalized reciprocity with people in poor countries to resolve these problems. As social networks are created between those in need and those able to help, helpers will care more for those in need. By building social ties and networks where there were none, or weak ties at best, moral indifference becomes a less plausible strategy. Because generalized reciprocity includes "paying forward," the inability of the poor to reciprocate to "donors" is not an obstacle. Just as helpers are "dupes" in the context of rugged individualism and self-interest, so non-helpers are self-serving and egotistic in a world informed by trust, generalized reciprocity and cooperation. A moral principle in favor of social capital can help to create a normative world in which indifference to the suffering of others is not easily brooked.

Moral norms, such as beneficence, promise-keeping and even maximizing the general happiness, have not been adequate to address some persistent, but urgent, social problems. This may partially be explained by an overemphasis on negative liberty, privacy, autonomy and self-interest (egoism). Because some social problems, such as chronic severe poverty, have persisted long past what is morally tolerable, it is important to explore a different moral focus. This project should be understood as a form of norm entrepreneurship, an effort to change the choice architecture and, following Thayer and Sunstein, "nudge" people in the direction of creating social capital and the good things that come with it.

In Chapter 2, I describe the concept of social capital, entertain various definitions and settle upon the "lean and mean" definition, similar to that used by Robert Putnam in *Bowling Alone*, and later by Joseph Stiglitz, Amartya Sen and Jean Paul Fitoussi in the *Sarkozy Report*. I identify the various kinds of value that social capital has, ranging from happiness and health to community benefits such as a lower crime rate. I also explain why a moral principle in support of social capital is essential. First, because social capital is vulnerable to free riders and is burdened by the tendency toward self-interest, a principle with some moral bite can be effective in overcoming people's inclination to act on the basis of self-interest. Moral principles trump mere self-interest. Second, given the tendency of people to favor those who are just like them, and to exclude others, treating social capital as an ethical principle imposes on people a duty to act impartially with respect to it. I also introduce the less familiar concept of global social capital, and suggest that it is an important accompaniment to international relations, international law and cosmopolitan ethics. Although there has been some difficulty creating social capital among diverse people, social capital is extremely important in the global scheme, and is prevalent internationally.

Still, not everything can count as a moral principle, and traditionally social scientists have characterized social capital, in purely descriptive terms, as the "superglue" that holds society together. It has not found its way into our lexicon of moral tools. Therefore, the burden falls on me to show that social capital does have ethical characteristics. In Chapter 3, I sketch out the ethical dimensions of social capital. I suggest that, like the concept of liberty, social capital is an enabler concept, valuable for what it produces. Also, like the concept of liberty, it can be used for bad, as with the Taliban and the Ku Klux Klan. Social capital concerns conduct toward people. It is universalizable, and has a prescriptive capacity. Social capital is also communitarian: of the people and for the people. If we take social capital seriously, we will also need to revise our thinking about how and to whom we ascribe responsibility. Some things for which we now hold individuals responsible might be better ascribed to social networks. Good health, for example, seems to have a lot to do with how much social capital individuals have available to them. Finally, I take a look at solidarity rights and argue that it is difficult to make sense of these rights without a robust notion of social capital.

Social capital fits nicely with utilitarian ethics. John Stuart Mill has an appreciation for people's social nature, and appears to believe that the "social feelings of mankind" are the foundation of utilitarian ethics. In other places, he talks about the need for secondary principles to supplement the principle of happiness. In Chapter 4, I discuss some of the social science findings that suggest social relations and social capital are an important source of well-being and happiness. Many social scientists think that good and meaningful social relations are central to human happiness. If so, the principle of social capital may be a fruitful secondary principle for utilitarian ethics. Social capital is also important for utilitarianism because of the phenomenon of emotional contagion, according to which people's happiness is related to the happiness of their friends and the friends of their friends. Therefore, social capital is important for individual happiness and collective happiness. If we do not promote social capital, we forfeit a significant opportunity to maximize the general happiness.

One of the benefits of social capital is that it may ground individual identities. In some philosophical quarters, cultural identity is treated as an essential ingredient of liberal societies. Unfortunately, cultural identity is a double-edged sword. Culture may serve to launch identities and promote trust, but it can also give rise to intercultural conflict, violence, aggression and sometimes genocide. I argue that social capital is a morally preferable alternative to cultural identity. It can ground identities, satiate the need to belong and nurture trust, without the unfortunate, and sometimes tragic, harms that follow in the wake of cultural affiliation. Some people have identified a similar problem with social capital, pointing out that it can give rise to insularity and exclusivity. Although insularity can occur with bonding social capital, there is nothing about social capital per se that breeds insularity. If people are mindful of the *moral* obligation to promote social capital, they would also be obligated to act impartially with respect to it.

Law can also play an important role in building and sustaining our reservoir of social capital. Many laws already do so. Laws that stress inclusion and equality, such as affirmative action, disability law and same sex marriage law, all help to create social capital. In Chapter 5, I look at examples of how the law can build and destroy social capital: duty to rescue law and termination at will. Although my analysis is primarily illustrative, I suggest that we use social capital as a principle or canon of law. Judges, legislators and practitioners could think about the impact of the law on social capital. Social capital also plays an important role in international law where negotiation, agreement and consent are important components of the law. After all, it is primarily through consent that countries are bound by international law.

Because giving and helping can be important steps in the cultivation of generalized reciprocity – a key ingredient in social capital – I devote Chapter 6 to an analysis of law that affects giving, namely the charitable tax deduction. I argue that the charitable tax deduction has an impact on people's giving practices, and that we ought to be especially mindful of social capital when we think about it. I develop this insight further by showing that water's edge policies, which restrict the charitable deduction to charities organized or created in the tax payer's country, will have an adverse impact on our reservoir of global social capital, and will undermine cosmopolitan aspirations.

If we can find meaningful ways to create global social capital, it will be an invaluable tool for global living, peace and sustainable environments worldwide. Moreover, global social capital will provide the glue that brings people from around the world together and increases both their concern for distant others and their willingness to help them. In many respects, social capital and its sister concept, global social capital, are moral concepts of the future. By emphasizing *together* over autonomy, and us before me, social capital paves the way for more complex living arrangements in which transpatriates negotiate their lives in multiple countries. Because Thomas Pogge has proposed a format for such living, I use the term "Pogge's global people" to refer to these global actors. By focusing on the value of "us" social capital shifts our moral attention away from me, and you, to *us*. In a world where it is crucial that we find ways to solve apparently intractable problems between and among peoples from different countries, cultures and religions, the capacity to shift to an inclusive perspective is enormously valuable while the contrary carries frightening prospects. In the last chapter, I focus on how social capital can help global people, such as Pogge's people. I also look at the role of international service in creating global social capital.

Focusing on social capital's moral dimensions may be especially fruitful today and in the coming decades as governments in countries such as Britain, France and Canada begin to re-evaluate their preoccupation with gross domestic product (GDP) in favor of a wider lens that includes well-being. In a speech at the Google Zeitgeist Europe Conference, the Prime Minister of Britain, David Cameron, underscored the importance of the role that social relations play in well-being.

> Wellbeing can't be measured by money or traded in markets. It's about the beauty of our surroundings, the quality of our culture and, above all, the strength of our relationships. Improving our society's sense of wellbeing is, I believe, the central political challenge of our times.[1]

This recalibration of political purpose reflects a new zeitgeist. It deserves and needs a moral principle that can complement it. Social capital reflects the spirit of our times and it deserves a chance to blossom.

1

Making a Difference

Chronic, severe poverty is a global problem of enormous magnitude that causes suffering. According to the World Bank, 1.4 billion people live on $1.25 or less a day. Not only is there extreme poverty worldwide, there is also vast inequality. The wealthiest 20 percent of the world's population control 76 percent of the world's goods while 80 percent have what remains. There is adequate wealth available to alleviate the suffering that exists.[1]

According to the United Nations Children's Emergency Fund (UNICEF), 22,000 children die each day because of poverty. There are 2.2 billion children living in the world. Of that number, roughly half live in poverty. In the developing world there are 1.9 billion children. One in three of those children live without adequate shelter, one in five without access to safe water and one in seven with no health services. In 2003, 10.6 million children died before they reached the age of five and 1.4 million die each year from unsafe drinking water and poor sanitation.[2] At present, 40 million people live with HIV/AIDS. In 2004, 3 million people died from AIDS. There are 350–500 million cases of malaria in a year and 1 million deaths in a year worldwide. African children account for 90 percent of these deaths. Over 1 billion people in developing countries have inadequate access to water and 2.6 billion lack basic sanitation.[3]

There is global homelessness as well. There are over 26 million internally displaced persons living in about 52 countries across the globe. Some live in camps, huts and so on – the outcasts from conflict and natural disasters. In addition, there are over 10 million refugees.[4] In a world of plenty, persistent homelessness and poverty indicate that many people do not care enough about other people to provide for their basic needs, despite the existence of human rights to food, shelter and medicines.[5]

Indifference, and an inability of some nations to cooperate with other nations, may be at the heart of the failure to create effective policy. The failure to reach a binding agreement at the United Nation's Copenhagen Summit with respect to global warming is a good example. China and the United States account for about 40 percent of the world's greenhouse gas emissions, and these emissions may cause serious harm to people in poor countries who can least afford to endure the harmful effects of global warming. Still, there is no binding agreement to accept emissions limitations.[6] These harmful effects include extreme weather, such as hurricanes, cyclones and drought, and the destruction they bring, as well as a reduction in the size of glaciers and the deaths of both people and animals due to changes in the environment and food supply and the prevalence of disease.

In November 2002, the Chinese government suppressed information about the outbreak of a respiratory disease in Guangdong province, placing people at great risk. Despite the efforts of China to maintain secrecy, the information leaked through various internet sources. On 11 February 2003, after being approached by the World Health Organization,[7] China disclosed that there was an outbreak of severe acute respiratory syndrome (SARS) in Guangdong province, which had resulted in about 300 cases and five deaths. Between February and April 2003, although the government acknowledged the outbreak, they tried to cover up its prevalence in the community. Among other things, they prohibited state-controlled media from reporting on the outbreak. Again we can see how a failure of global trust and cooperation can put lives at risk.

In 2009, between 2.5 and 3.5 million people were homeless in the United States; about 38 percent of them were children. There are many more homeless people in the United States than there are available shelters.[8] Although there was a global recession in 2009, these statistics are not significantly different from earlier years. Many of the homeless also suffer from mental illness. When there are no shelters available, homeless people live on the street, under bridges, near warm vents and in abandoned cars. In 2009, in an article aptly entitled "Frozen in Indifference: Life Goes on around Body Found in Vacant Warehouse," it was reported that a body had been found embedded in three feet of ice in a Detroit warehouse:

Sure enough, in the well of the cargo elevator, two feet jutted out above the ice. Closer inspection revealed that the rest of the body was encased in 2–3 feet of ice, the body prostrate, suspended into the ice like a porpoising walrus. The hem of a beige jacket could be made out, as could the cuffs of blue jeans.... What happened to this person one wonders.... Stone-cold dead.

The article reported that the body was found in an old warehouse that served as home to a number of homeless people. Some people had seen it but didn't think to call 911; others reported having more urgent concerns such as keeping warm.[9]

People turn a blind eye to the suffering of others on a regular basis. In 2009 it was reported that the bodies of 11 women were found in the Ohio home of Anthony Sowell. No one had called 911 to report suspicious conduct during the years preceding his arrest. Instead the bodies just seemed to accumulate over time. This case has come to be called "The House of Horrors,"[10] but what is particularly worrisome is that no one was involved in the life of Anthony Sowell enough to be concerned about the stench of rotting flesh that came from his apartment. Unfortunately, incidents such as this may reflect the moral indifference that is at the heart of so much suffering and our tolerance of it. Sometimes, people don't help others because no one else is helping. At other times, they may not want to help because they don't want to be considered "suckers" or "chumps."

As people worldwide are left to suffer by those who could help, there is good reason to believe that suffering, especially in the case of global poverty, is a result of our violation of a negative duty to not cause harm to others. Thomas Pogge, a philosopher at Yale University, has argued in *World Poverty and Human Rights* that:

> ... most of us do not just let people starve, but also participate in starving "them" because we do nothing to change the institutional arrangements and structures that cause and perpetuate global poverty. If these arguments are right, and I believe they are, it is not only the case that we ignore the suffering of others, which is problematic enough. It is also the case that we caused the very suffering that we now walk away from.[11]

In other words, in a world in which global systems and structures are present, not only are we indifferent to the misery of other people, but we are also the source of their misery. This only underscores the moral urgency of global poverty, and the need to consider a new ethical approach to the suffering of others.

Other examples can be given of indifference to both local and distant suffering. Very often, people are aware of the suffering that exists. Sometimes, however, they don't help others because they think it is morally wrong to do so. Some people believe they shouldn't help because it is not their responsibility to help; it is the responsibility of another person. Or they may believe that people should take personal responsibility for their own misery. Some people, such as those with "donor fatigue," are weary of helping. But very often people don't help others because they are indifferent to the suffering and misery of other people or are simply preoccupied with their own affairs. They don't care. Princeton philosopher Peter Singer has argued for the need to create a culture of giving: one in which people would give enough to the distant poor to relieve their misery.[12] Caring about others would be a prerequisite for such a culture.

It would be wrong to suggest that people never help others. People are especially attentive to their families, friends and – sometimes – communities. In some jurisdictions, people are required by law to help those with whom they have a close relationship, such as a child or spouse. As we see in the media, people come to the aid of others when there is a highly publicized disaster. There was an outpouring of help for the people of Haiti following a massive earthquake on 12 January 2010. Soon after, however, when monsoon rains came to Pakistan causing the worst flooding in its history and a humanitarian crisis, donor fatigue set in and aid was slow to arrive.[13] Given the persistence of severe poverty, there is much more that people could and should do, given our participation in an international system that creates and sustains this suffering, and the enormous available wealth.[14] People need to *care* more about others. Unfortunately, care and concern for others is not the kind of emotion one can produce at will, or upon command.

Caring behavior seems to arise among people who interact with one another. There is plenty of evidence that social capital, understood as social networks and norms of reciprocity and trust, gives rise to more socially engaged behavior. I will argue that including social capital among our moral principles would increase caring behavior such as sharing, giving and helping. Social capital understood as a moral norm could diminish the prevalence of self-interested behavior and replace it with a willingness to help others. One of the core values in social capital is generalized reciprocity, according to which people help others without demanding immediate or direct reciprocation, satisfied that they will benefit, and content for them to reciprocate by paying forward. Some people have called this paying forward. When generalized reciprocity is present, giving and helping are uninhibited.

In *The Life You Can Save*, Peter Singer makes an interesting observation about Americans: although Americans give to charity, they rarely discuss their giving publicly. Singer found that even when people in the United States act altruistically, they justify their actions on the basis of self-interested reasons. For example, people who volunteer rationalize helping others with reference to the way it filled their day and "got [them] out of the house." They do not say, "I wanted to help."[15] According to Singer, "the norm (of self-interest) is self-reinforcing and yet socially pernicious, because if we believe that no one else acts altruistically, we are less likely to do it ourselves; the norm becomes a self-fulfilling prophecy."[16]

Singer recommends, for upper-income Americans, giving based on a fixed percentage of income, scaled up as incomes increase, along with publicizing the gift and advocating that others give. On this approach, the norm of self-interest with respect to charity will slowly give way to a norm of giving. But whatever progress is made, it may not come soon enough to alleviate worldwide suffering and the moral urgency created by our complicity in creating the conditions of poverty and human suffering. Supplementing Singer's approach with a moral commitment to promote social capital can create an environment in which a culture of giving can flourish. Social capital is culturally non-specific, and when universalized could override the bias in favor of compatriots, and the exclusivity of groups. As a *moral* norm, social capital could override self-interest – a mere non-moral norm.

To build concern for others, the norm of self-interest needs to be counteracted with a new norm that shifts the focus from "me" to "us." As the normative world now stands – in the West, at least – liberty, autonomy, self-determination, privacy, self-interest and sovereignty come together to shield people from the harm they cause others, directly and through their institutions, making them morally complacent and indifferent. To create Singer's *culture* of giving, and Pogge's global justice, pro-social norms are needed to transform the current culture of self-interest and indifference to one committed to helping others. Helping others, whether it consists in shoveling an elderly neighbor's snow, donating money to Oxfam, inventing drugs for neglected diseases or working with AIDS patients in Africa, needs additional support from ethics. Ethics brings two important features to the concept of social capital that are not supplied by descriptive explanations of it: (1) moral concerns trump non-moral concerns, and (2) the moral point of view imposes a requirement of impartiality. In practice, these turn out to be very important.

Social scientists, psychologists, policy practitioners, governments and non-governmental organizations

(NGOs) include social capital in their deliberations as a way to increase solidarity and cooperation. Although social capital can be used for bad – as can liberty – it is widely recognized as a social good. Ethical conduct, such as truth-telling and promise-keeping, helps facilitate trust, which is a crucial component of on-going social relations and, in turn, social capital. Similarly, the principle of beneficence promotes kindness toward others. But these norms have not been adequate to meet human need, especially given the allure of self-interest. To create social capital, one also has to cultivate social relations and face-to-face interactions. People need to be encouraged to spend time with their neighbors, volunteer at the local hospital, interact with diverse groups and, for the sake of global social capital, travel globally, give globally and volunteer globally. Social capital can be fostered by governments, businesses, individuals, law and ethics.

As we shall see in upcoming chapters, social capital is a valuable social good, associated with benefits that are important for our community and globe. Although controversial, there is evidence that in the United States social capital is on the decline. Robert Putnam has found a substantial reduction in most indices of social capital, such as socializing with neighbours, voting and participating in campaigns.[17] Studies show that trust, an important measure for social capital, is declining.[18] To make matters worse, the social factors that have contributed to the apparent decline in social capital, such as long commutes, stressful living, work and excessive television watching, persist.[19] A moral principle that favors social capital can boost our levels of social capital, and sustain them, as it overrides the norm of self-interest. Investing in social capital for moral reasons will not only build our fund of social capital, but will also help to counteract some of the dark side of social capital – the inclination toward homophily and exclusion.

Bandwagons and cascades

Moral norms are not path-dependent. They change all the time and people are often the agents of change. Norm entrepreneurship, a term coined by Cass Sunstein, refers to efforts to actively change norms. The definition of "norms" varies widely. In general: "Norms are informal obligations or social rules that are not dependent on government either for their creation or their enforcement. They can be both descriptive and aspirational, as they portray how people behave and also prescribe how they should behave to conform to community expectations."[20] Sociologist Karl-Dieter Opp identifies four characteristics of norms: (1) oughtness, (2) conditionality, (3) behavior and (4) individuals.[21] The first, oughtness, implies that norms create an expectation that the behavior ought to be performed. This puts norms in the domain of ethics. The second characteristic, conditionality, means that the dictates of norms are contingent upon the circumstances and agents. Third, although some norms also refer to beliefs and some carry sanctions, norms are generally accepted prescriptions about behavior. Fourth, norms usually apply to individuals. According to Opp, norms are instrumental and emerge when they are in the interest of collectives. Some norms emerge through human design, such as the law, while others emerge spontaneously, for example the norm against smoking, from the ground up.[22] Norms against junk food, obesity and bullying also seem to be rising from the ground up. Norms work by influencing behavior. Internal norms exist when people believe they have a personal obligation to do something even if others will not reward the action.[23] At present, charitable giving and filial duties are examples of internal norms. In contrast, external norms are reinforced through gossip, shaming and ostracism, and compliance is rewarded with praise and inclusion.[24] Not all norms are moral; it would be difficult, for example, to construe the norm of tipping a waiter as a moral norm.[25] But many are.

Norm creation and change can occur internationally, and international norms can have an impact on national law. Few countries failed to recognize that the United States was the only wealthy Western country in the world that did not have universal access to medical care, and this omission was, for many in the United States, a global embarrassment. Internationally, there was a universal-access norm, while the United States was a normative outlier. Importantly, when it comes to norms, law says as much by what it doesn't do as it says by what it does do. If the law systematically reinforces individual liberty and rarely reinforces social solidarity, this speaks volumes about its approval of the former and disapproval of the latter. Norms that are no longer in the community's interest can be replaced with new norms; they fade as new norms take their place. Norm entrepreneurs make it their business to change norms. Governments, lawyers, philosophers, activists and NGOs have all been norm entrepreneurs.

Some social conditions are more fertile for norm-change than others. Cass Sunstein has the following to say about windows of opportunity for norm-change:

> People's private judgments and desires diverge greatly from public appearances. For this reason, current social states can be far more fragile than is generally thought – as small shocks to publicly endorsed norms and roles decrease the cost of displaying deviant norms, and rapidly bring about large-scale changes in publicly displayed judgment and desires. Hence societies experience *norm bandwagons* and *norm cascades*. *Norm bandwagons* occur where the lowered cost of expressing new norms encourages an ever increasing number of people to reject previously popular norms, to a "tipping point" where it is adherence to the old norms that produces social disapproval. *Norm cascades* occur when societies are presented with rapid shifts toward new norms.[26]

Sunstein's point is that new norms can surface gradually or rapidly as old norms become fragile or forgotten, and the costs associated with breaking them dissipate. Peter Singer may have been observing just such normative dissonance when he noticed that Americans give quite generously, but don't acknowledge publicly that they are doing so. Rather, they prefer to characterize their actions in terms of the prevailing norm of self-interest, without bringing attention to their kindness. This dissonance may suggest that significant normative change, amounting to a bandwagon effect, is possible, or even underway, with respect to our charitable duties, especially to the distant poor.

Law can supplement norm entrepreneurship in an effort to change behavior, or it can remain silent and neutral with respect to the new norm. Sometimes corporations will anticipate norm shifts and initiate change, as Pepsi did when it voluntarily removed its soda from American schools, in order to avoid the public backlash against childhood obesity. John Ruggie, the United Nations Secretary-General's Special Representative for Business and Human Rights, is in the process of changing global norms with respect to multinational organizations and imposing on them obligations of due diligence for human rights.[27] Paul Hunt, former Special Rapporteur for the Right to Health, began a similar undertaking with respect to pharmaceutical companies and the right to health.[28] There is a great deal that can be done to create, maintain and sustain social capital. In Chapters 5 and 6, I will have more to say about how the law can be used to this end. But since norms are a powerful mechanism for change, and social capital has a normative component, it is also important to consider ways in which we might tinker with our normative world, with an eye to overriding the destructive effects of the norm of self-interest. A little norm entrepreneurship is in order. With respect to the norm of social capital, there is work to be done by both moral philosophers and the legal community. Norm-change is easier when the law reflects the shift in norms as it does, for example, with the norm against smoking and bans against smoking in public places.

Philosophers as ethics entrepreneurs

In recent years, with the rise of public philosophy, moral philosophers have become increasingly engaged in advocacy. Many philosophers have acted as ethics entrepreneurs with respect to cosmopolitan norms.[29] Thomas Pogge, Peter Singer, Amartya Sen and Martha Nussbaum, for example, are not simply describing an existing ethic, but are shaping a moral framework that can supplement the activism of NGOs and human rights activists. They may draw upon great thinkers toward this end, but their goal is to transform the way we think about global moral duties. They are ethics entrepreneurs.

Us Before Me is a project in ethics entrepreneurship insofar as it is an attempt to replace an old norm with a new moral norm. If people spend time together, care about each other and see others as deserving of their trust, they are more likely to help others without regard to reciprocation. When giving and helping are uninhibited and there is no expectation of direct reciprocation, the scope of beneficiaries changes likewise. This is called generalized reciprocity. Global poverty, global warming, Bad Samaritanism and corruption exist at least in part because of moral indifference. Some of this indifference has to do with the prominence of the norm of self-interest. By requiring people to create social networks, trust and generalized reciprocity, the principle of social capital fosters an environment in which moral conduct toward other people can flourish. By shifting the emphasis from individuals to relationships, away from me and to us, it enables social goods that are more easily achieved through solidarity. It extends the scope of our moral world to embrace not just individuals but also networks of people. The social relations that are enabled by a pro-social norm trigger our concern about others in the same way that the moral norms of liberty and privacy trigger self-interest. Social capital, like liberty, is an enabler concept.

People who are interested in creating a better world for all should be interested in social capital. Today, more than ever, moral philosophers pay attention to the *implementation* of moral goods when, for example, they make policy recommendations: Thomas Pogge's Health Impact Fund,[30] Peter Singer's www.TheLifeYouCanSave.com and the University of Oxford's Toby Ord's www.GivingWhatWeCan.org. A moral principle focused on social capital would facilitate pro-social behavior and minimize indifference to others. I have so far suggested that norms do change and that they often do so with the help of norm entrepreneurs. This leaves unanswered the question of whether it is morally right to change them. In some quarters, people believe that norm creation can interfere with individual liberty, and that governments and law should not be in the business of creating norms. This is often explained in terms of the desirability of neutrality among conceptions of the "good." I will address this concern as it relates to the law in Chapter 5. Briefly, however, since I propose supplementing the current norm landscape with another moral norm, I am adding a new option and thereby enhancing the range of moral considerations. If anything, introducing the moral principle of social capital would seem to add to our autonomy and liberty.

Currently in the United States, and elsewhere, norms favor individualism and autonomy. For many people, rugged individualism is a normative aspiration. This emphasis on individualism, paramount in Western psyches, may overwhelm the interest in social solidarity.[31] In wealthy Western countries, dependence on others – or the potential for dependence – can signal weakness and vulnerability. It is not surprising that new enhancement technologies are aimed, not at making us more social, kinder and better team players, but instead at making us smarter, stronger and more focused, with better memories; that is, the aim is to enhance our competitive qualities as individuals, not our collaborative ones.

Although the last several years have witnessed a greater interest in pro-social behavior and social qualities in general, the preoccupation with individualism is still prominent in Western culture, history and law. It is in part because of the historical overemphasis on individualism, self-reliance and self-interest, combined with the failure to value social relations, that a reinvigorated or new moral norm is necessary. With a moral commitment to build social capital people may come to be more fully engaged in local and global communities. They may be less tempted to analyze their generosity in terms of self-interest, but might instead celebrate it as an example of their desire to help the less fortunate and build strong communities. Additionally, if the data of social psychology is accurate, they will probably also be happier. Indifference to the suffering of others may be easier to overcome if the social virtues have an independent and strong normative foundation.

There is no getting around norms; they are part of social life. Not all norms are good, however. The norm of self-interest has consequences that are not good for either individuals or communities. Public goods, which are vulnerable to free-rider problems, may also be susceptible to remedy through norm entrepreneurship. According to Sunstein, studies show that people who contribute to public goods, and refuse to free-ride, are more numerous than one might imagine. Apparently, people are willing to cooperate and to solve collective action problems if they believe that most people are cooperators. When most people are cooperative, the social meaning of non-cooperation is greed and selfishness. The reverse is true when most people are free riders. People who cooperate when most people are free riders can see themselves as "dupes" or "suckers."[32] In Sunstein's words: "the desire to contribute to a collective good is probably a function of social norms. If social norms do not lead most people to contribute, contributors decrease steadily and drastically."[33] One wonders if the explanation for the dissonance between people's giving practices and their explanation for those practices, noticed by Singer, is their concern with being viewed as a "sucker." Social capital also has free-rider problems, and is therefore vulnerable to being set aside in favor of other norms. It is precisely because of this vulnerability that a moral norm is needed to protect and promote it. Given the existence of such a strong norm of self-interest, and its moral perniciousness, there surely is good reason to minimize its impact with an alternative emphasis on "us."

Nudging toward social capital

I argue in favor of treating social capital as morally important in our individual conduct, our social policy and sometimes in our law. My hope is that when people come to value social networks, reciprocity and trust, at least as much as they do self-interest, they will be more inclined to help others. I will have a lot more to say about this throughout this book. For now, I want to keep my remarks brief. Acting for the sake of social capital can mean, for example, that people consider the effect of their actions not only on specific others but also on networks and their ability to achieve joint ends. Providing people with opportunities to gather together repeatedly and over time will help. Being inclusive of others facilitates social capital. And when those others are diverse, or strangers, acting on the basis of social capital contributes to build much needed bridging social capital – an important resource in a multicultural and global world. Simply understanding what social capital is, putting it in the public discourse, and in the global public domain, will contribute to building it. It is also important to protect existing social capital.

With respect to the law, I suggest including social capital as a principle or canon, one that invites judges and law makers to consider the impact of their decisions on social networks, trust and reciprocity. This might mean changing some laws that favor market principles instead of social capital, or national interest instead of global ties. In a now well-known book, *Nudge*, Richard Thaler and Cass Sunstein argue that we sometimes ought to engage in choice architecture to help people make decisions that will improve their health, wealth and happiness. That is, we ought to guide their decisions while at the same time providing them with liberty. For Thaler and Sunstein "a nudge... is any aspect of the choice architecture that alters people's behavior in a predictable way without forbidding any options or significantly changing their economic incentives. To count as a mere nudge, the intervention must be easy and cheap to avoid."[34] Moral norms are a piece of the choice architecture that people use in making choices and acting on them. A new moral norm that identifies social capital would nudge people in the direction of social ties, trust and reciprocity.

Thaler and Sunstein support "nudges" for a variety of reasons. Human beings make mistakes; they are often overly optimistic. They mindlessly err on the side of the status quo, and act to their detriment, often unwittingly. Today, social science can provide us with more guidance about how people make choices, and what kinds of choices make them happy. Thaler and Sunstein refer to their approach as "libertarian paternalism" and advocate "...self-conscious efforts, by institutions... to steer people's choices in directions that will improve their lives. In our understanding, a policy is 'paternalistic' if it tries to influence choices in a way that will make choosers better off, *as judged by themselves.*"[35] Thus the kind of choice architecture recommended by Thaler and Sunstein is actually liberty-preserving even though people's choices are being manipulated.

For the most part, *Us Before Me* advocates a nudge. Social capital has been shown to be good for both individuals and communities. By including a principle of social capital in our moral repertoire, my hope is that people, institutions and organizations will include a consideration of social capital in their deliberations about how they ought to act and what they ought to do. More often than not, this would not remove any choices, although hopefully the preoccupation with other norms, such as autonomy, self-determination and economic efficiency, would diminish as people begin to make choices that support social capital. By introducing another moral principle into the array of moral norms, we increase the likelihood that social capital will be cultivated, and other values, such as self-interest, will not. This in turn would increase social capital and, as I will argue, happiness and global well-being. Given the considerable benefits associated with social capital, and its neutrality with respect to *specific* social relations, including it on our moral palette can contribute to global well-being. Finally, a moral principle in support of social capital can overcome social capital's dark side, the tendency of people to create networks of like people and to exclude others, leaving them to endure network poverty.

2

The Heart of the Matter

Before turning to the main argument of this book, it will help to have a good understanding of what social capital is and what it brings with it. This is easier said than done. There is no single definition of social capital. Deservedly, it has been the subject of study by researchers and practitioners from a variety of fields, each with their own focus. Although traditionally a political, sociological and economic concept, more recently social capital has been the focus of the field of public health. It has also been embraced by government, practitioners in management and development. In the first half of 2011, the Organization for Economic Cooperation and Development (OECD) included social connections and civic engagement – both associated with social capital – among the key indicators of well-being for people living in developed economies and some emerging economies. For the World Bank, "social capital is a concept that has significant implications for enhancing the quality, effectiveness and sustainability of World Bank operations, particularly those that are based on community action."[1] In this chapter, I will say a lot about what social capital is, what it has been observed to do and what it might do. Although I opt for what has been called the "lean and mean" definition (social networks and the associated norms of reciprocity and trust), I also recount some of the other definitions on offer. Toward the end of the chapter, I give an account of global social capital, using the lean and mean definition to guide the way.

There are different kinds of capital: financial, physical, human and social, to name a few. Physical capital refers to an asset made by people, such as a tractor, a food processor or a shovel. These assets can be used to produce something of value. Tractors have multiple purposes in agriculture, including preparing the soil for seed. Food processors also serve multiple purposes: kneading dough for bread, chopping fruit and mixing cake batter. Human capital is most often associated with skills acquired through training or experience, but can also include intellect, creativity and other skills or talents. Like physical capital, these skills and abilities are used to create something of value. Human capital, unlike physical capital, is inseparable from the individual who owns it. People write books and songs, create software and cure diseases. Here they use their skills to produce something of value. Social networks and the norms that facilitate them also have value. In its simplest terms, social capital refers to social networks and the value they create.

Social capital

When people come together they create trust, reinforce pro-social norms such as generalized reciprocity, help one another and in the end create value together. Let's consider a variety of definitions of social capital. The concept of social capital has a long and distinguished history, beginning in the early twentieth century when education reformers used it to encourage participation in schools. According to sociologist James Coleman:

> Social capital is defined by its function. It is not a single entity, but a variety of different entities claiming two characteristics in common: they all consist of some aspect of social structure, and they facilitate certain actions of individuals who are within the structure. Like other forms of capital, social capital is productive, making possible the achievement of certain ends that would not be attainable in its absence.[2]

Coleman is not the only social scientist to define social capital in terms of the value it creates. Like physical capital, social capital can be understood as an input into the value creation process. Social epidemiologists Lisa Berkman and Ichiro Kawachi have noted that social capital is social in that it is "a feature of the collective (neighborhood, community, society) to which the individual belongs,"[3] and is a public good that should be viewed as a "byproduct of social relationships."[4] Political scientist Dietlind Stolle gives the following account:

... Social capital is conceptualized as a societal resource that locks citizens to each other and enables them to pursue their common objectives more effectively. It taps the potential willingness of citizens to cooperate with each other and to engage in civic endeavors collectively. As such, it has proved influential as a means of countering the strong emphasis on the atomized individual.[5]

This account underscores the role social capital can play in democratic societies. Because social capital increases citizen participation in community affairs, it enhances democracy. This is one reason it is a social good, but is not only a good for the community. Individuals also benefit from social capital. Social capital creates the possibility of productive, cooperative activity.

In recent years, Francis Fukuyama and Robert Putnam have popularized the concept of social capital.[6] According to Fukuyama, social capital is "a capability that arises from the prevalence of trust in society."[7] It is facilitated by the shared norms permitting "regular and honest cooperative behavior."[8] In Robert Putnam's early work he defined social capital as the "networks, norms, and social trust that facilitate coordination and cooperation for mutual benefit."[9] The earlier definition has since been revised slightly, and has come to be called the "lean and mean" definition. I use the revised version, in part because it appears in recent high-profile documents, such as the *Sarkozy Report*.[10] For the lean and mean definition, social capital consists in "social networks and the associated norms of reciprocity and trustworthiness."[11] I use trust and trustworthiness interchangeably. I also prefer the revised version because it omits "for mutual benefit," an unnecessary complication. It isn't always true, for example, that people act for mutual benefit when they act on the basis of generalized reciprocity. Definitions that list more items, such as safe neighborhoods, happiness and good health, are simply including greater detail and additional examples. For Putnam, social capital creates value for the people who are connected and at least sometimes for bystanders.[12]

Social ties are at the heart of social capital. People with extensive social networks can advance professionally and socially, and can protect others more efficiently. Because networks convey the message that people can be "relied on" for kindness, they also create social capital for the community.[13] People within networks help one another attain their goals – often collective goals. In this respect, networks contribute to the conception of people as kind and helpful. Networks give rise to generalized reciprocity in which people give to others time, gifts or help, without anticipating immediate or direct reciprocation. Instead they are content to know that others will benefit and that they may one day be a recipient, perhaps from another person, or not at all. Generalized reciprocity is a form of uninhibited giving which, as I mention in Chapter 1, is sometimes referred to as paying forward.

Following a somewhat different path, Robison and Flora define social capital as "sympathy toward another person or group that may produce a potential benefit, advantage, and preferential treatment for another person or groups beyond that expected in an exchange relationship."[14] Although this account differs from the lean and mean definition, some of the characteristics identified by Robison and Flora are important for creating networks and social trust. They list sympathy as a component of social capital, and sympathy and empathy are emotional goods that facilitate social connections. Without them, there would be little that is social in social capital. As with Putnam, Robison and Flora underscore the value created by social interaction. Robison and Flora's definition illuminates why social capital can be useful in overcoming indifference to others. When social capital is present, people are more likely to care about others.

These various definitions are not incompatible with one another. Each emphasizes different aspects of social capital. Some definitions, such as Coleman's, focus on the productive capacity of social networks; others, the benefits to participants; and still others, such as Robinson and Flora, the emotional dimension. I opt for the lean and mean definition because of its simplicity and currency in a variety of contexts. But it is consistent with more nuanced definitions on both the social and value side. It is also worth keeping in mind that there are two different types of social capital: bonding and bridging. *Bonding* social capital is created in relatively homogeneous groups, such as fraternal organizations and church groups. It reinforces the inward perspective of a group, and allows the group to cooperate in order to achieve certain ends.[15] Historically, it has been facilitated by the "thick trust" of face-to-face interactions within primary relations.[16] Unlike bridging social capital, social capital of this kind can breed exclusivity within relatively insular groups.

Here lies the dark side of social capital: the tendency of people toward homophily and exclusivity.

Bridging social capital, facilitated by "thin trust," is the glue that links people within groups to people in other groups. Thin trust fosters a willingness to trust people outside of our immediate circle.[17] Bridging social capital is valuable precisely because it builds bridges between groups and enhances the willingness of people "to give most [people] – even those whom they don't know from direct experience – the benefit of the doubt."[18] Because bridging social capital promotes tolerance and empathy, it is particularly important in diverse societies and in the global scheme.[19] But as valuable as it is, it is also a relatively scarce resource.

Research on social capital within diverse groups is at a nascent stage, but it suggests that cultivating social capital among diverse people is challenging. People tend to like people who are similar to themselves. Network theorists have found a trend toward homophily in networks. Research shows that people's personal networks are homophilous with respect to sociodemographic, behavioral and intrapersonal characteristics. Homophily with respect to race and ethnicity is the most common. Age, religion, education, occupation and gender follow them in that order of strength.[20] Because the benefits of social networks are great and homophily can serve as a mechanism for excluding others, many of whom are already marginalized, we need to be sensitive to the moral implications of homophily. We'll look at this more closely toward the end of this chapter, and again in Chapter 7.

Social capital has also been associated with cohesion and social solidarity. According to the World

Bank, trust and solidarity go hand in hand, and both enhance social cohesion and collective action. In their words, cohesion "mitigates the risk of conflict and promotes equitable access to development by enhancing participation of the marginalized."[21] They also point out that "information and communication breaks down negative social capital and enables positive social capital by improving access to information."[22] The World Bank is interested in social capital because of the promise it has for development. Economic development is strengthened through transactions among individuals, groups and households in poor countries.

The mutual trust created by networks facilitates collective decision-making and can supplement legal mechanisms such as laws, rules and elections. When social capital is present in a community more people are engaged in, for example, the democratic process. Social capital reduces opportunistic behavior.[23] Although the World Bank's focus on solidarity seems to be a departure from the lean and mean definition's emphasis on social networks and associated norms of reciprocity and trust, closely knit networks in which there is social capital are cohesive.

Trust

Because networks and social ties are a component of social capital and they hinge on trust, we can also say that trust is part of social capital. Trust has the potential to transform self-interested and self-seeking actors into collaborators and cooperators. Because of the role that trust plays in social connection, the amount of trust present is treated by Putnam and others as a measure of the presence of social capital. Trust facilitates generalized reciprocity, which takes interpersonal relations outside of a tit-for-tat exchange in which people require an immediate and direct return on their "gifts." When social interactions are informed by generalized reciprocity, social capital flourishes.

For reasons that are not altogether clear, social interactions facilitate trust and generalized reciprocity. Recent studies involving the "trust game" suggest an interesting neurobiological explanation for trust, involving the peptide oxytocin (otherwise referred to as the bonding peptide and the trust hormone).[24] Study subjects were paid $10 for an hour and a half of their time. They were given an opportunity to share none, some or all of the money with another unknown subject who might or might not return some portion of the money to them. The money that was transferred was then tripled and added to the second subject's $10. The willingness of people to send money to the other person signaled their trust, and the willingness of recipients to send money back was a sign of their trustworthiness. The entrusted subjects sent money back, and were found to release increased amounts of oxytocin.[25] In fact, subjects with the highest oxytocin levels sent the most money back and when the initiating subjects were given synthetic oxytocin they were willing to share more of their money. The researchers believe that a social interaction in which giving is involved signals trust, creates positive feelings and trustworthy behavior in the second subject.

This study involved non-face-to-face interactions between two strangers, in which one chose to give the other money.[26] The act of giving created both

trustworthy behavior and reciprocation. The reciprocation reinforces the first subject's trust, and the back-
and-forth exchange exemplifies trust and cooperation.
The study suggests that giving is itself a mechanism
that creates trust and social capital. Interestingly, from
the perspective of global social capital it suggests that
the trust that is essential for social capital does not
need to be garnered from face-to-face interactions, but
could be secured from other sorts of interactions in
which people signal trust.[27] Still, caution is in order
because even if subjects are willing to send strangers
money, and to trust them, they may have presuppo-
sitions about who these strangers are. They may, for
example, put the strangers in the class of "research subject just like me," minimizing difference while facilitating trust. Nonetheless, the study has interesting
implications for global social capital.

Trust, like social capital, is a social good. According
to Sissela Bok, "trust is a social good to be protected
just as much as the air we breathe or the water we
drink. When it is damaged, the community as a whole
suffers and when it is destroyed, societies falter and
collapse."[28] Although there are different accounts of
trust, each focusing on different variables as the source
of trust, there are two main ones. In one, qualities
of the individual are stressed, and in the other social
context is emphasized.[29] According to personality theory, trust is among core personality traits that include
optimism, a belief in cooperation and confidence that
differences can be resolved. For this account, optimism
and a belief in one's capacity to control events in the
world are key.[30] In a variation on this approach to
trust, the focus is on the unique vulnerability of the

poor. While all trust is risky, the poor are especially vulnerable to trust loss. Study after study supports the observation that the rich are more trusting than the poor.[31]

Social theories focus on the role of social context in creating trust. Here trust is not understood as a characteristic of individuals, but rather of cultures. Cultures and institutions are thought to foster the development of trusting behavior. When people are surveyed about trust, their answers reflect how successful their respective societies are in creating the condition of trust. With this approach, some factors are more important for creating trust than others. Putnam, for example, believes that voluntary associations are most important while others focus on close contact with other people. For network theory, the close associations of everyday life, friends, family and neighbors are thought to be essential for building social trust.[32] Although these approaches to trust have different emphases, they are not mutually exclusive.

Given the centrality of trust for generalized reciprocity, and, in turn, for social capital, it is important to understand that trust consists in both social factors and personal ones. In trust-risk communities (a neighborhood in which there is considerable violence, for example) we might need to develop social support that can compensate for trust deficits that are based on personal experiences.

Value

Just as one skill can be used to create multiple products, so social capital has varied and wondrous rewards – some of which we are unaware.[33] Individuals with social capital stand to benefit, but the group also benefits. For example, if everyone on Lexington Avenue takes time to know their neighbors, and attends their annual photo shoot, each person will benefit from the social ties created, as each person has the pleasure of the event and takes home a photograph. But the street as a whole will also be safer as people recognize one another. Real estate values may rise accordingly. In this way, both individuals and the neighborhood benefit. The value associated with social capital is enormous and varied.

People rich in social capital are happier, healthier and safer. They may also be more productive and wealthier. Because social capital is associated with "mutual support, cooperation, trust and institutional effectiveness," these people may be better friends and better citizens.[34] Social capital has been found to be important for preventing delinquency, improving education and the quality of community life and in crime prevention.[35] I will have more to say about the connections between social capital and happiness in Chapter 4.

Children seem to thrive when social capital is present. Babies are born healthier and teenagers show lower rates of suicide, pregnancy, school drop-out and crime. In states with high levels of social capital, children flourish.[36] They benefit not only from supportive neighborhoods, but from their parents' social capital. Schools are also better in social capital rich environments, and students perform better on standardized tests.[37] Poor families without access to financial and educational resources are also more dependent on social capital.[38] With respect to both children and poor families, social capital can soften some of the blows of life.

Investing in neighborhood social capital is especially important because of a phenomenon called "neighborhood effects." Social scientists have found that a person's behavior depends not only on her personal qualities, but also on the characteristics of those around her,[39] including neighbors and playmates. If children who live in social capital poor neighborhoods are at greater risk of failing to flourish than those who live in social capital rich neighborhoods, improving neighborhoods could have an important impact on the welfare of the poor. According to Putnam, "...because poor people (by definition) have little economic capital and face formidable obstacles in acquiring human capital (education)...social capital is disproportionately important to their welfare."[40] Of course, some countries make it easier to acquire human capital than others by providing excellent state-supported schools, from grade school to higher education.

Social capital also contributes to economic prosperity. It is well known that social networks are valuable for securing jobs. Because of this, networking opportunities abound at professional schools. There is also lots of evidence that a cooperative approach to business – one that is informed by generalized reciprocity – leads to better economic performance.

The health benefits associated with social capital are well documented. One of the earliest studies showing a connection between social capital and health was done in Roseto, Pennsylvania.[41] Beginning in the 1950s and conducted on a small group of Italian Americans over a period of 40 years, the study found that members of Roseto had half the heart attack rate of people in neighboring communities. The usual physiological explanations, such as diet, exercise and smoking, could not explain the difference in heart attack rates. In fact, researchers noted that people from Roseto often had more unhealthy behaviors than those in neighboring towns. But the people in Roseto were a cohesive group, with lots of social capital and little display of wealth. Unfortunately, as these social conditions changed over time, so did the heart attack rate.[42] Social capital is thought to promote health in a few ways. Social networks provide people with support. They can provide money, transportation and help with taking medicines. People within social networks reinforce healthy behavior. Studies show that socially isolated people are more likely to smoke, drink and overeat than socially integrated people. There is some evidence that social capital affects people's immune system, helping them to fight disease and manage stress more effectively.[43] Social capital is good for our health and in terms of cost, less expensive than medical solutions. Unfortunately, low levels of social capital can be fatal for some people.

Traditionally, social capital has been associated with good citizenship. Putnam points out that successful democratic societies require citizens to perform public duties and be involved in civic groups. People embedded in groups are a more powerful force, and can press their agendas more efficiently. Together they are able to increase their chances of being heard and of participating effectively. They are also better informed because they access information through their social ties. Participation in voluntary groups and community activities teaches people civic virtues and gives them an opportunity to understand the views of others in the community.[44] In this way, group participation can also promote tolerance.

Creating social capital

There are many ways to create social capital. But social interaction and social networks are crucial for social capital. Much of the literature on social capital, including literature on the sources of social capital, is based on measurements of the presence of trust in societies. Because social capital is difficult to measure, trust has served as a proxy for it. Ronald Inglehart's World Value Survey, conducted since 1981, questions people about trust, among other things. In particular the survey asks: "Generally speaking, would you say that most people can be trusted or that you need to be very careful in dealing with people?" On the basis of this, researchers were able to determine the level of trust in communities. There are high-trust and low-trust societies, and there is evidence that in societies where trust is high " ... social interactions are relatively rich, community problems can be solved, relationships between citizens and politicians seem relatively healthy, and the economy is blossoming."[45]

Early research on social capital emphasized the importance of voluntary associations, such as the Parent Teacher Association, and helping at the local hospital as sources of social capital. Political engagement is also useful for creating social capital. The values learned in these associations find their way back into the community at large. People are thought to be more trusting, cooperative and civic-minded as a result of their experiences in voluntary associations. The special emphasis on voluntary associations has since been replaced with the view that social interactions and social networks are themselves valuable, and that the social connections needn't occur in the context of voluntary associations in order to contribute to social capital reservoirs.[46] Social networks of all kinds are now thought to be valuable sources of social capital: family, work, voluntary associations, religious affiliations, friendships, neighborhood groups and community arts projects. It would seem then that whatever we can do to nurture social interactions, especially interactions that are inclusive rather than exclusive, will be important for creating social capital.

The poor are especially vulnerable to network poverty.[47] They may work so much that they don't have time to build social ties. Networks may be easier to create when people have money to spend on socializing. Volunteering and gifting, for example, can involve outlays of money that the poor may not have. Some networks are inherited through family ties and expectations, both of which middle-class and wealthy families have a greater supply.[48] The wealthy are also able to send their children to private schools and excellent colleges, and enhance their access to valuable social capital once there. Unfortunately, the poor often find themselves with fewer ties to pass on to their children, or to use in supporting them.

Many people don't have the skills to interact socially and build social networks, or the skills to sustain them. Providing students with an education that will give them the skills they need to develop social networks would be valuable. Although social interactions come easily to some people, they are very difficult for others. In *Better Together*, Putnam and Feldstein recommend encouraging civic pride and community spirit through education. They also suggest that smaller schools and classes are preferable to larger ones, and that after-school programs be given additional funding.[49] Community groups could also be encouraged to invite young people to participate on their boards and committees.

Some communities are better at creating and sustaining social capital than others. Putnam and Feldstein point out that Portland, Oregon, for example, was experiencing a "civic renaissance" as the rest of the United States was becoming isolated and passive.[50] There are a variety of reasons for this. Portland has a history of effective activism. It has many small neighborhoods, each with its own downtown area. It is, relatively speaking, egalitarian and has numerous small houses on small lots, encouraging social interaction among neighbors. The city was attractive to environmentalists because of its natural beauty. Local government has been very responsive to the requests of the activist community, thus encouraging them to continue their activism. It is also a relatively homogeneous population. Portland's high level of social capital has benefitted from an altruistic population, effective government and strategic urban design.

Business can contribute to the creation of social capital by encouraging employees to spend time with their families and communities. Flexible hours and expanded leave are also ways of doing this. Because religious organizations are the source of a substantial amount of social capital, *Better Together* also recommends that support be given to faith-based organizations.[51]

Notably missing from the various suggestions for creating social capital is a proposal to treat social capital as a moral principle. Reluctance to focus on the ethics of social capital may be based on the intuition that, for reasons to do with liberty, it is wrong to interfere with people's morals. Sometimes this is expressed in terms of a concern with norm manipulation. But as Sunstein and others have pointed out, people choose and act on the basis of whatever norms are present. If the existing norms are counterproductive, undermine important social goods and leave people to suffer from chronic poverty and homelessness, there is surely no reason to assign them a morally privileged status simply because they exist. Thayer and Sunstein call the inclination to defer to existing norms a *status quo* bias.

Social capital is valuable and it is relatively cost-effective, in part because of its "rainmaker effect" which results in good things for people outside the group. In addition, this may be a propitious time to promote social capital. Governments such as France, Germany, Norway and the United Kingdom have recognized the need to promote well-being, and social capital is part of well-being. There is a virtual explosion of service tourism for people who want to help others, including global others. Billionaires such as Bill and Melinda Gates and Warren Buffet have taken the philanthropic lead with the Billionaire's Club and the Giving Pledge. And network theorists are finding ways to map networks and use them for good. If we are in the midst of norm change, a bandwagon may be underway.

Singing in the rain

People who contribute to the creation of social capital are not the only ones to derive value from it. Social capital can sometimes be a public good. Public goods are non-excludable and non-rivalrous. Social capital is non-rivalrous in the sense that it can be used by more than one person. One person's use of it doesn't deprive others from using it as well. It can also be non-excludable. Considerable effort is needed to exclude people from accessing some social capital.[52] Public goods give rise to free riders: people who enjoy the good but don't contribute to its creation. Put differently, social capital has externalities or a rainmaker effect. Because of this, it can create opportunities for people completely unaffiliated with the group. If a neighborhood is rich in social capital, everyone in the neighborhood enjoys the available social capital. If the streets are safe because most neighbors are vigilant, that safety cannot be restricted to those who participate in neighborhood watch. Even those who never attend a neighborhood potluck or participate in the neighborhood photo shoot will enjoy a safe neighborhood. This is the characteristic of social capital that gives rise to free riders, a problem that can be addressed by tweaking social norms.[53]

Social capital's externalities and vulnerability to free riders can wreak havoc on the willingness of people to engage in activities that will generate social capital. Coleman observed:

> ... because many of the benefits of actions that bring social capital into being are experienced by persons

other than the person so acting, it is not to that person's interest to bring it into being. The result is that most funds of social capital are created or destroyed as a byproduct of other activities. Much social capital arises or disappears without anyone's willing it into or out of being . . . .[54]

Whether or not people realize it, social capital has enormous – even if not exclusive – benefits for the people who create it. Coleman's words highlight vulnerabilities for social capital: its value is not always evident to people, and it is non-excludable. People who enjoy good health, for example, don't attribute it to social capital. Instead, they credit good genes and a healthy lifestyle. Yet studies show that people with social capital have better health outcomes.[55] People may be predisposed to ignore the contributions of social capital because of their preoccupation with individualism and the idea of health as a personal responsibility.[56] But some of this reticence also has to do with a lack of basic knowledge about social capital.

When people realize that the social capital they create benefits others but fail to see that it also benefits them, they may withdraw from the activities that create it, especially if they also subscribe to the norm of self-interest. People who endorse pro-social values would not be bothered by so-called "free riders." With a moral foundation, social capital could counter the norm of self-interest and address the free-rider problem. The bias in favor of self-interest can undermine social capital because it can dictate that *only* the self should benefit while social capital often benefits many, including the self.

Our preoccupation with self-interest is not conducive to building social capital. Coleman gives the example of stay-at-home mothers who commit time and effort to sustaining extracurricular activities at their children's schools. Other parents and their children, who are unable to make the same contributions to the school, benefit from the time commitment of those who do contribute. It may make sense for one or more parent contributors to take a part-time job and stop contributing time and effort to the school. The loss from her departure would be experienced by all of those who depend on her contributions and their loss may be significant.[57] If the dominant norm is one of self-interest, with little counterbalance from prosocial norms, it is more likely that she will opt for the self-interested option, especially, since to underscore Sunstein's point, she might otherwise feel like a "dupe," or be concerned, in a society that prizes self-interest, that she appears to be so.

From a moral perspective, it isn't obvious that there is any morally relevant reason for excluding people from the good things created by social capital simply because they didn't contribute to its creation. In the absence of the norm of self-interest, it is difficult to see why people would object to others enjoying the fruits of their labor or social contribution. Indeed, many people would consider this a virtue of social capital, something to sing about. Instead of regarding people who benefit from a fund of social capital, to which they have not contributed, as free riders, we might well consider them "happy followers," people singing in the rain.[58]

In the absence of a moral commitment to invest in social capital, cooperative interests may not be taken into account. Given the obligatory quality of the moral over the non-moral, highlighting the ethics of social capital would result in an increase in our stocks of social capital. Although social capital is valuable – both individually and collectively – and efficient, it is often set aside in favor of other forms of value, and often unwittingly, without any attention to the loss. If we underscore the moral dimension of social capital, we encourage people to engage socially, even when they cannot exclude others, and we will, in turn, begin to weaken the considerable grip self-interest has on us, and build social capital reservoirs. Rainmakers have been celebrated by groups as diverse as Native Americans and corporate law firms, both of which have appreciated the value of singing in the rain.

Global social capital

It is especially challenging for social capital to flourish among diverse people. Global – or transnational – social capital may be similarly vulnerable. Global social capital is simply social capital that takes place between and among people from two or more countries. It might be more accurately referred to as "transnational social capital," but for stylistic reasons I use the term "global social capital." Very little has been written about global social capital and most of what has been written is to be found in literature on globalization and immigration. Global social capital can also be understood using the lean and mean definition as a guide.

As the world becomes more accessible, through frequent travel for business and leisure, rapid and instantaneous internet telecommunication, global financial interdependence and global governance organizations, people from different countries will have more frequent interactions. With these increased interactions and new networks will come a sense of familiarity that didn't exist in the past, and that can nurture trust and generalized reciprocity. Cosmopolitan obligations will help to cement transnational relationships. Social capital takes time to build and repeated contact to maintain. As I discuss in Chapter 5, a serious effort to integrate people from diverse groups has been present in the United States, at least since *Brown v. Board of Education*[59] when "separate but equal" was overturned. Efforts continue today. Many school-age children now study with a diverse group of students, and they are, in turn, familiar with a wide array of cultural practices. Although efforts to integrate people from diverse backgrounds within one nation are not what we would think of as global social capital, relationships with "strangers" down the street will affect the relations we have transnationally. The same is true for transnational networks and their impact on social ties amongst diverse people locally.

According to John Helliwell, migrants and refugees possess a considerable amount of social capital.[60] The definition of social capital that Helliwell uses, which is drawn from the OECD, is similar to the lean and mean definition: "networks, together with shared norms, values and understandings that facilitate cooperation within and among groups."[61] He believes that "migration creates both challenges and opportunities for the development and maintenance of social capital, while the quality and nature of a community's social capital will largely determine the success of migration."[62] Migrants use their networks, relationships and knowledge of their home country to build trade relations with new countries.[63] Devesh Kapur makes a similar point about India, suggesting that recent immigrants from India to the Silicon Valley used their "reputational intermediation," with trust and networks in both places to build "...globe-spanning networks that permit Bangalore to solve problems while Silicon Valley sleeps."[64] The trust-based networks created by migrants make these exchanges possible. Migrant-driven trade networks "...open up international trade possibilities for small firms as much or even more than for large firms, permitting an international version of the small-scale trust-based networks of family enterprises."[65]

Migrants often use bonding social capital to help them move to a new country. As they tap into the community of their sending country in their new country, they establish themselves in a new nation. Some people are concerned that this use of bonding social capital from the sending country will preclude the cultivation of bridging social capital in the receiving country. But Helliwell found that people with more bonding networks also had more bridging networks. He concluded that bonding ties complement rather than compete with bridging ties. If this is so, it is good news for global social capital. It suggests that trade-offs do not have to be made between local and global social capital, or bonding and bridging capital.[66] Social capital, even bonding social capital, can travel, and it can be maintained both at home and in the country to which people migrate. Trust and social ties are used to move, to set up a new life and to build businesses. Because both bonding and bridging social capital can coexist for migrants, there is reason to be optimistic that once people learn that some people are trustworthy, they can see similar virtues in diverse others that allow them to trust "strangers." This can, in turn, facilitate the creation of generalized reciprocity among diverse people. But the migrant experience is not the only source of global social capital.

There are global organizations of all kinds. Transnational organizations have a global agenda and reach. There are also NGOs that have a global scope, such as those that target global AIDS, global malaria and global warming. There are global governance mechanisms, such as the United Nations, with its commitment to universal human rights. There is an emerging global culture, and for that matter a vibrant global counterculture. In each of these instances there are global norms that correspond to global aspirations. There are also plenty of international service opportunities and internships.

For these international organizations to operate at all, the people within them must interact with people globally. Some of these networks have existed for some time, and are likely to involve generalized reciprocity, which itself requires significant transnational trust and cooperation. NGOs are a good example of organizations that have created global social capital, as they engage worldwide to make the world a better place.

There is also transnational reciprocity, and it is very often generalized reciprocity. International service is a good example. People worldwide spend considerable time and money helping people in poor countries build their homes, farm their land and heal the sick. Out of these interactions, social networks evolve among people from different countries. There is also enormous value from the social capital that is created through transnational service. The people served by volunteers benefit, but there are also benefits for the volunteers and those close to them. I will have more to say about this in Chapter 7. But briefly, transnational service creates networks for information flows, crosscultural knowledge and transnational opportunities for cooperation and collaboration. It also facilitates tolerance of cultural difference. These benefits are conferred not only on the people of the countries directly involved but also on those indirectly involved.

There are also global norms. The Universal Declaration of Human Rights sets universal standards for all people. In Chapter 1, I mentioned several philosophers who are engaged in formulating a cosmopolitan ethic with the goals of achieving global social justice and eradicating global poverty. We can also infer the existence of norms of reciprocity from the existence of extensive global networks. Transnational business would be impossible without social capital. In addition to human rights, there are basic norms of truth-telling, promise-keeping and transparency that allow transnational business to occur.

Social capital, generalized reciprocity and the trust that makes them possible are important for global justice. Wealthy nations may be more willing to give to people in poor countries if transnational social capital can be cultivated. It bears repeating that people need to care about other people if we are ever to make progress toward realizing their human rights.[67] Since social capital is associated with matters of the heart – concern and care for those within the network – it can play an important role in ensuring that the obligations to respect, protect and fulfill human rights are met. Generalized reciprocity is especially relevant to global justice because people in poor countries cannot reciprocate in kind. Even if we recognize our justice-based obligations to help people in poor countries,[68] global social capital can help us to realize those obligations by facilitating cooperation with other countries to meet them.

As important for global justice as global social capital is, there are obstacles to acquiring it. Ethnic and religious diversity make it difficult to cultivate social capital. Studies show that civic engagement (which, according to Putnam, is an important index of social capital) is lower in diverse communities. Homogeneity appears to enhance civic participation.[69] Costa and Khan provide the following explanation:

> Diversity...imposes costs. Whether in choosing a college roommate, a residential community, or a place to pray, people tend to self-segregate. They prefer to interact with others like them because of shared interests, socialization to the same cultural norms, and greater empathy toward individuals who remind them of themselves...[70]

When individuals are involved in groups and are mindful of group interests, they may exclude those who do not belong to the group. No doubt some of the same problems will surface when the diversity is created by a global community. Although the research on social capital and diversity is at a nascent stage, Robert Putnam has some preliminary findings that include the observation that within ethnically diverse communities people engage in "hunkering."[71]

> Diversity does not produce "bad race relations" or ethnically-defined group hostility . . . Rather, inhabitants of diverse communities tend to withdraw from collective life, to distrust their neighbors, regardless of the color of their skin, to withdraw even from close friends, to expect the worst from their community and its leaders, to volunteer less, give less to charity and work on community projects less often, to register to vote less, to agitate for social reform more, but have less faith that they can actually make a difference, and to huddle unhappily in front of the television. . . . Diversity, at least in the short run, seems to bring out the turtle in all of us.[72]

Despite the tendency toward homophily and the inclination to hunker, the proliferation of transnational organizations and international volunteerism suggests that, although social capital among strangers may be difficult to acquire, it is not impossible. Putnam's research shows that social capital in diverse communities (and his research does not posit global diversity) may require refashioning social identities to embrace diversity.[73] To this end, people may need to locate their identities in larger, perhaps global communities. New social identities could focus on the norms of cosmopolitanism, or membership in the group that enjoys universal human rights. Public philosophers, such as Thomas Pogge, Martha Nussbaum and Peter Singer, have devoted considerable thought to our understanding of the "global citizen."[74] Pogge has the following to say about citizenship in a cosmopolitan-informed world:

> Persons should be citizens of, and govern themselves through, a number of political units of various sizes, without any one political unit being dominant... And their political allegiance and loyalties should be widely dispersed over these units; neighborhood, town, country, province, state, region, and world at large. People should be politically at home in each of them, without converging upon any one of them as the lodestar of their political identity.[75]

For Pogge's global people to disperse political loyalties and allegiances more expansively, and to feel at home in each, people would need varied and diffuse social capital. In the remainder of this book, I use the term "Pogge's global people" as a quasi-term of art to refer to people who live transnationally with widely dispersed political loyalties and cultural identities.

Homophily is understandable. People are drawn to those whom they perceive to be similar to themselves. People may feel safe with like people. Trust is strengthened when there are frequent face-to-face interactions. It is also not surprising that social capital flourishes in homogeneous communities since, driven by homophily, many people gravitate to communities where there are like people. Proximity helps here. But surely with rapid transit and communication, it is now possible to encourage face-to-face interactions among people from many places. Although many people are drawn to those who appear to be like them, many others seem to be drawn to the exotic and unfamiliar. Social capital may be associated with social cohesion, and the latter with insular groups (the dark side of social capital), but there is nothing about social capital per se that mandates this. Social capital is neutral with respect to which people should be networked.

The potential to forge a new "global" identity may be aided by changing demographics. There is growing evidence that racial, national and cultural classifications are changing, and that a mixed race identity is far more common than in the past.[76] In the United States, for example, the number of Americans who count themselves as mixed race is changing dramatically due to an increase in immigration and intermarriage over the last two decades. At present, one in seven marriages in the United States is either interracial or interethnic.[77] Universities in the United States now have the largest group of mixed race students they have ever had. This trend is expected to either continue or to accelerate. Many students with mixed backgrounds have a "fluid sense of identity," and reject the idea that they must choose one racial identity over another. In the past, different forms, such as the census form, required people to check only one box indicating race, directing them to regard themselves as only one race – be it African American, Caucasian, Asian,

Hispanic and so on. But beginning in 2000, the Census Bureau gave Americans the opportunity to mark more than one race. In the 2000 census, 2.4 percent of the population marked more than one race. Since then, however, the mixed race population has grown by more than 35 percent.[78] It isn't clear yet how this change in demographics will alter how people identify themselves. But for many, given a multi-racial background, it becomes difficult to choose a single race or ethnicity. For others, it is irrelevant. As demographics change, the problems diversity poses for social capital will also change, and perhaps fade away. When a person recognizes the multiple races within, he or she may be far less likely to find "strangers" unfamiliar and instead may welcome them as "family."

The Iranian protest in 2009, also called the Twitter Revolution, is a good example of how transnational social capital can be spontaneously created. At the time of the protest, the US State Department negotiated with Twitter to ensure that its service was available to Iranians protesting against the results of the election. Information that was useful to protestors was tweeted, and when the Iranian government blocked the IP addresses that were delivering tweets to protestors, twitter users worldwide intervened with alternative proxy network addresses so that the protestors' tweets could be communicated during the protest.[79] This is a good example of how international networks can be built through helping, and how governments can facilitate the creation of social capital or – in the case of the Iranian government – destroy it. It also reflects considerable generalized reciprocity; it is difficult to imagine that the people helping through social-networking sites expect any kind of direct reciprocity. Twitter users across the globe mobilized to help the Iranian protestors. Perhaps not surprisingly, given the close connection between social capital and democracy, transnational social capital surfaced in the name of democracy, and these social networkers served as good global citizens and global justice activists. A similar phenomenon took place in Egypt in 2011; however, President Mubarak had the Internet turned off. Here again we may be witnessing an important norm bandwagon as people view themselves as global activists, helping "the people" globally. Transnational social capital can play an important role in fostering global justice.

Both international personal relationships and international business relationships create and depend on global social capital. Individuals have international friendships and family and may belong to international organizations. International business networks are widespread and growing. They include not only transnational enterprises but also contractual and commercial networks. Unfortunately, they also include international criminal networks used for smuggling, drugs, prostitutes, sex-trafficking, gems and money laundering. Finally, global governance organizations such as the United Nations, World Bank, International Monetary Fund, General Agreement on Tariffs and Trade and World Trade Organization all create and rely on extensive global social capital, as do the countless number of NGOs that exist worldwide. Most of these networks involve face-to-face interactions at least some of the time, and trust evolves over time. But internet networks and email are often used to sustain social capital in transnational interactions. As we saw in the Twitter Revolution, face-to-face interactions are not essential.

A great deal of transnational social capital is already at work in the global public domain. John Ruggie, a professor at Harvard University's John F. Kennedy School of Government, defines the global public domain:

> ... as an institutionalized arena of discourse, contestation and action organized around the production of global public goods. It is constituted by interactions among non-state actors as well as states. It permits the direct expression and pursuit of a variety of human interests, not merely those mediated – filtered, interpreted, promoted – by states. It "exists" in transnational non-territorial spatial formations, and is anchored in norms and expectations as well as institutional networks and circuits within, across and beyond states.[80]

The global public domain is the locus of activity for multiple, interconnected transnational and national actors from a variety of sectors. Various actors come together to create, implement and monitor policy that affects development, human rights, the environment and global public health. The global public domain reflects the existence of global social capital, for without it the domain could not exist. But at the same time the global public domain, with its many networks of transnational and multi-sectored actors, is a massive source of global social capital, a virtuous cycle demonstrating the regenerative capacity of social capital.

Social capital's global dimension is enormously important. Today, more than at any other time in history, international relations have the potential for great benefit, especially for the most vulnerable people in the world. If we can create global social capital and harness it to inspire and enable people to help those who are worst off, global social capital will be well worth the investment.

Despite the value associated with social capital, it is not an unalloyed good. Sometimes social capital will have negative externalities, such as when people are excluded from joining a tightly knit group in which bonding social capital is present. And sometimes social capital has positive rainmaking externalities – if we could only recognize them as such. The ethics of social capital can be helpful in diminishing the harm associated with bonding social capital. Building global social capital will require effort to create the sorts of values, networks and norms that will allow social capital to transcend the barriers created by ethnic and cultural affiliations. But, as I will show in the next chapter, the moral dimension of social capital can help with this.

3
The Ethics of Us

Communities are cohesive, generous and safe when social capital is available. Children do well in school and on standardized tests. People are healthier when there is adequate social capital. Despite these benefits, the persistent need for it and worldwide deprivation, social capital may not blossom fully. Because some social capital has public good characteristics, it can suffer from a free-rider problem. In a society governed by individualism and self-interest, the non-excludability of social capital (its rainmaker effect) can discourage people from acting in ways that would build social capital reservoirs. If people don't have a way to exclude others from benefitting from the fruit of their activities, and they are motivated primarily by self-interest, they may be unwilling to contribute to the social capital reservoir. Indeed, even if people are not motivated by self-interest, if they live in a society in which the prominent norm is self-interest, they may not want others to free-ride on their contributions.

Although social capital may be the proverbial win-win, those under the spell of self-interest may not view win-win scenarios as worthwhile.

If social capital were recognized as among the goods that a person is *morally* obligated to take into account, its non-excludability would not count against it. Self-interest is not a good reason for not performing one's *moral* duty. Also, people who act in order to promote social capital, and not self-interest, are less likely to be disturbed by so-called "free riders," and are more likely to be content that there are "happy followers."[1] In view of the benefits associated with social capital, and its vulnerability to free riders, it behooves us to make it part of our moral lives. Yet even if social capital did not have free-rider vulnerabilities, its considerable benefits, including importance for well-being, should be enough to put it on the moral map. If there were a moral obligation to take social capital into account, people would, for example, consider the effects of their actions not just on themselves as individuals, nor on the other as an individual, but on their capacity to form relationships, reciprocate, cooperate and create trust. The ethics of social capital brings a new entity into the moral mix. In what follows, I shall set out the reasons for thinking that social capital has the characteristics needed to function in this way. My view is that social capital has a moral dimension which can be teased out of it, highlighted and then placed in the public's moral discourse.

For the most part ethics is concerned with our conduct toward people, animals, the environment and future generations. To say that a concept or principle is ethical is to say that it is generally regarded as good, is worthy of pursuit and that it would be better to have than not to have. Although I argue in the next chapter that social capital is the moral sweet spot, it is not my intention to say that it is *the* most important value. As with other ethical principles, there may be times when social capital conflicts with other values – all morally worthwhile pursuits – and we will sometimes need to make choices among them. The ethics of social capital is best understood as a moral principle that should be taken into account when it is relevant. It provides people with reasons for acting one way rather than another; it carries some moral weight, but is not all or nothing.[2] The obligation to promote social capital requires us to consider the consequences of our actions, policies and law on social capital, and where possible to act to foster and protect it.

It bears repeating that social capital is like the concept of liberty: it is an enabler concept, valuable for what it enables. Liberty, as we know from John Stuart Mill's discussion in *On Liberty*, is important because, among other things, people know themselves best and should be given the liberty to choose their life plans.[3] Mill seems to believe that if we want to maximize happiness, it is best to give people freedom. Here liberty is not valuable for its own sake, but for what it can enable. Similarly, when there is abundant social capital people are in a better position to secure the benefits that accompany social networks, trust and reciprocity, both for themselves and for others. Because social capital also inheres in collectives, the community enjoys it as much as individuals. But these are not the only beneficiaries of social capital. As I discussed in Chapter 2, social capital has a rainmaker effect which results in good things for people outside the group of people who create it.

Making it moral

The concept of social capital meets the standard criteria for an ethical concept. First, as I mentioned earlier, ethics usually concerns conduct toward others.[4] Baron, Field and Schuller make the point that "One of the key merits of social capital is the way it shifts the focus of analysis from the behavior of individual agents to the pattern of relations between agents in social units and institutions."[5] Since social capital evolves from the relationships between and among people, it easily satisfies this criterion of the moral. Generalized reciprocity also reflects a concern with other people. Simply focusing on reciprocation itself is a step away from the self and toward others. Generalized reciprocity is an additional step. The values inherent in generalized reciprocity imply that people ought to give to others even when they cannot anticipate immediate and direct reciprocation from the recipient. It counts as reciprocity because the giver trusts that reciprocation will take place, even if someone other than the original giver is the beneficiary. Paying forward counts as reciprocation.

Second, ethical judgments and decisions are universal: if a judgment is an ethical one, then what it dictates will be true for everyone.[6] Universalization can be understood in a number of ways. The concept of liberty can again be instructive. As with liberty, social capital seems to be important for everyone. Though people possess different amounts of social capital (as they do liberty), and different psychological capacities to take advantage of it, access to social capital seems to be universally valuable. There is another sense of universal, according to which we should treat people impartially. With respect to creating social capital, impartiality would require us to fashion norms and networks impartially, without regard to race, gender, religion and other personal characteristics. This is crucial for the ethics of social capital and is one of the strongest reasons for treating social capital as a moral concept. Because of homophily, people tend to associate with people who are just like them. The preference for people similar to oneself can lead to prejudice and discrimination against other people. In turn, social capital reservoirs can be concentrated within homogeneous groups which exclude "strangers." When we understand social capital as a moral concept, the option to favor those who are similar to oneself is a violation of impartiality, and therefore morally wrong. Generalized reciprocity is similar to the Golden Rule. It states simply "give even when you cannot anticipate immediate reciprocity," or simply "give." Here, giving should be understood broadly to include not only giving money, but also giving time, consideration and other forms of help.

Third, ethical statements are prescriptive. If a concept is an ethical one, then to say that it is ethical is also to say it is good, or go ahead and do "it." Social capital also satisfies this condition. Although social capital may have a dark side (excluding others in the case of bonding social capital), overall it is a good thing, and it is regarded as such. Social capital is a form of capital; it is productive of goods that we value.

Fourth, ethical statements are also normative. They are not descriptive statements, but state what ought to be the case. Insofar as social capital is used to promote good ends (and not, for example, to promote the racist goals of the Ku Klux Klan), it makes sense to encourage it. One might take the position that social capital used for bad ends should not qualify as the kind of social capital that is morally valuable. For my purposes, only social capital that is used for good falls within the moral domain.

Social capital also has some important substantive moral qualities. It is communitarian or social. It is *of* the people, and *for* the people. Social capital cannot be produced by one person; it is not the stuff of rugged individualism, but rather the stuff of social relations in which people act for each other and together. A society with a strong commitment to negative liberty may find it difficult to cultivate social capital. Social capital needs to be nurtured at the very least by putting people together. As we saw in the last chapter, communities interested in cultivating social capital have community get-togethers, such as block parties and photo shoots, and create green spaces. Without these opportunities to engage with others it is difficult to create social capital because social capital is most easily facilitated by *face-to-face* interaction. But participating in such activities takes effort, some human capital – including certain social skills – and above all adequate regard for the other. When people value social capital and view its creation as morally important, they are more likely to promote it even when they may not feel inclined to do so, or are tempted to act in self-interest.

Social capital carries with it a particular vision of responsibility. Consider again a comparison with the concept of liberty. Individual liberty implies that *individuals* are responsible for their actions. This is encapsulated in the notion of personal responsibility. Social capital seems to suggest that many outcomes that we typically associate with individual action may be understood more accurately as the result of collaborations or cooperative actions. For example, the good health that some people experience may be the result not only of individual lifestyle or genetic makeup, but also of the social networks available to them or the green environment they have collectively created. Similarly, if global warming were to be reduced, it would be the result of collective action. To have a substantive impact on greenhouse gas emissions, people need to change their behavior, and if they do change it, it will be in part because others have done so. This is one way that social capital shifts the analysis from "me" to "us."

A deep understanding of the role of social capital in community life may lift some outcomes out of the moral paradigm of individual and personal responsibility and place them in the paradigm of collaborative or collective responsibility. Were we to take social capital into account in policy, ethics and law, some of our assumptions about causation and responsibility might be challenged. In tort law, for example, causation is primarily analyzed in terms of "but for" causation; "but for" a particular action, a particular injury or harm would not have taken place.[7] This causal framework is better suited to individual events and actions than to collective ones. In fact, it invites the finder of fact to distinguish one event or action from all of the others that may play a causal role in an outcome.

In the economic sphere, Nobel Prize winner Herbert Simon made a similar point in his essay entitled, "A Basic Income for All." There he argues that an important source of the difference in incomes, both within a single society and between societies, is the presence of and access to social capital. By "social capital" Simon has in mind "knowledge and participation in kinship and other privileged social relations."[8] Peter Singer in his book *The Life You Can Save* makes this point as well. When we include social capital in our conceptual repertoire, it will often be more accurate to use "we" where we now use "I." Interestingly, the widely used expression "giving back to the community," used by donors to explain their giving and by fundraisers to solicit it, may signal an appreciation for the role that social capital plays in personal fortunes, and of the consequences of that insight for giving. Generalized reciprocity makes more sense than *quid pro quo* exchanges when we recognize the impact social capital has on various kinds of benefits we enjoy. Social capital highlights the fact that benefits as wide-ranging as human happiness, good health, good government and safe neighborhoods are associated not with the activities of individual people but with social networks, cooperation and pro-social norms, such as generalized reciprocity and trust.

Social capital is also important for justice, which is concerned with the distribution of burdens and benefits in society. Social capital is both a benefit to be distributed and a mechanism for distributing prized benefits. As Putnam points out, those with a more extensive Rolodex enjoy greater social capital and the benefits it creates. Because of the substantial gains associated with social capital, and the dependence of the poor on it as a means to secure many benefits, it is important, for the sake of justice, to be mindful of the impact of policy on social capital. Indeed, a Rawlsian commitment to equality of opportunity and to benefit the worst off might well dictate such a distribution.

Social capital is such a valuable resource in terms of individual growth and well-being that its absence could leave people at a distinct disadvantage socially and economically. This inequality is exacerbated by the fact that wealthy people have more social capital than poor people while the poor appear to need it more than the wealthy (since they do not have access to mechanisms that might compensate for its absence). By treating social capital as a moral concept, greater care will be exercised with respect to who has access to networks. In this way, we can protect people from the harsh consequences of "network poverty." Because, in general, social capital cannot be bought and sold but is "free," it is an essential resource for the poor. Wealthy people also compensate for low social capital. They can gate communities to ensure their safety and employ lawyers to protect their agreements, instead of relying on trust. For those who have neither money nor social capital, the losses can be substantial. Social capital is particularly important for the most vulnerable members of our community, both locally and globally.

Solidarity rights

Social capital needs to be invoked in order to make sense of some rights, such as solidarity rights. Karel Vasak, a French jurist, identified three classifications of rights. First-generation rights are civil and political. They can be found in the Universal Declaration of Human Rights (1948). Second-generation rights can be found in the United Nations International Covenant on Economics, Social and Cultural Rights and include the right to health, medicines, food and shelter. More controversial are third-generation rights, the so-called solidarity rights. Solidarity rights include the right to self-determination, right to development, right to peace, the right to a healthy environment and the right to intergenerational equity. Unlike first- and second-generation rights, these rights belong to collectives. Although third-generation rights have been recognized by the United Nations, they need wider recognition and acceptance. But progress has begun. Africa, for example, has enacted the African Charter of Human and People's Rights (1986), which includes some third-generation rights. Articles 1 to 24 recognize the rights of peoples. Article 20 states "all peoples shall have the right to existence" and Article 21 states "all peoples shall freely dispose of their own wealth and natural resources." In Article 22 it is stated that "all peoples shall have the right to their economic, social and cultural development with due regard to their freedom and identity and in the equal enjoyment of the common heritage of mankind." Article 23 gives to peoples " ... the right to national and international peace and security ...." These rights belong to groups.[9]

Consider the right to peace: war is sometimes against nation states and sometimes against peoples within nation states. But war is always against collectives and the obligation is owed to the group. Similarly, the right to sustainable development requires that some peoples be allowed to develop even if they are not a nation. The right to a healthy environment is another good example: all humanity shares the environment and if we are to enjoy a healthy environment it will require cooperation among all peoples.

If there are solidarity rights, then there must be "collectives," and there cannot be collectives without social capital. For the right to a healthy environment, for example, people must change their conduct, and in some cases, they must do so for the sake of peoples in other countries. A healthy environment requires an enormous amount of cooperation among people transnationally. Solidarity is not always welcome. Governments can try to undermine group solidarity by attacking the mechanisms that foster social capital, such as political gatherings. This may be what happened during the massacre at Tiananmen Square. But there cannot be "solidarity rights" without solidarity and there cannot be solidarity without social capital. Social capital is at the heart of these up and coming rights.

Realizing the principle of social capital

To assign moral importance to social capital is to say something about its place both among other moral goods and non-moral goods. Social capital understood as a moral good would take precedence over non-moral goods, aesthetic considerations and mere social convention. If there is a moral duty to promote social capital, it can be taken into account at both individual and institutional levels. Social capital can be considered in our deliberations about what actions we ought to perform, and what policies our institutions ought to adopt. Countries such as Britain, Ireland and Canada already consider the impact of policy on a community's social capital. The World Bank has a social capital assessment tool. But if social capital is to become part of the public discourse, it needs to be operationalized. Applied ethicists and social and political philosophers, among others, could begin to incorporate an analysis of the implications of policies on social capital reservoirs. Some philosophers have already assigned cooperation a special status. For Rawls, justice as fairness involves a society of free citizens, with equal basic rights, *cooperating* in an egalitarian system.[10]

It makes little sense to identify the concept of social capital as a moral one, unless one can state upon whom the obligation would fall. Who would be responsible for promoting social capital? Individuals could fulfill their obligation to cultivate social capital just as they do many other obligations: they are mindful of the principle in their daily interactions and in the way they choose their life plans. When neighbors ask for small favors, such as watering plants and feeding pets, a consideration of the principle of social capital might sway an otherwise ambivalent neighbor into one who helps. Similarly, joining civic organizations such as the Parent Teacher Association would be valuable not only because it would benefit the volunteer's child but also because it would build social capital for the community. A reluctant parent would participate even though his own child may be "golden" and not need the benefit of a community. There are countless instances when individuals can act in the service of social capital in their daily lives.

Actions that might be rational from a self-interested perspective, and not be proscribed on the basis of any other moral principle, might fall within the scope of social capital. For example, in my hometown of Cambridge, Massachusetts, it is common practice following a heavy snow storm to place a chair on a public parking space from which one has shoveled snow to signal "ownership" of this space. Cleared-off parking spaces can sit for hours, with only a chair occupying them, while neighbors search for places to park. As an expatriate of snowy Canada, I was astonished at this self-interested "taking" of public space. If the shoveler were to consider this practice in light of social capital, she would probably not participate in the chair norm. Instead, she might help to clear the snow from other needed spaces. The chair norm is opportunistic and pits the interest of individuals within a neighborhood against one another, instead of finding a way that helps the collective. Rather than negotiate an agreement that would work for everyone, unused spaces are held captive with only a chair, while some people must park miles away. Social capital as a moral imperative would trump the self-interest that lies behind the chair norm.

But is it social capital that does the work here or some other principle? Certainly, the chair norm undermines social capital. It favors self-interested and personal benefit over any consideration of others, but doesn't target particular others. It creates unnecessary antagonism among people. Were people to consider the impact of the act on social trust (a key component of social capital), they would be discouraged from hijacking public spaces in this way. The chair norm encourages people to compete for limited spaces instead of working together to find a way to share spaces. If people acted on the basis of generalized reciprocity, they would simply clear off spaces, trusting others to be similarly generous in the future. The moral duty to promote social capital would easily override the non-moral preoccupation with self-interest. In some cases, although there may be an overlap between the demands of social capital and those of beneficence, the reasons and analysis underlying each would be different.

Consider another example. Bridging social capital within diverse groups is a scarcer and more valuable resource than common bonding social capital. In view of this, there may be a moral obligation to break down social barriers in one's friendships, befriending people from whom one would ordinarily shy away. If creating social capital were regarded as morally important, then spheres which we often consider purely private, such as who we befriend, would have a moral aspect to them. A consideration of social capital would dictate that we form social ties impartially, giving all people the benefit of the doubt. We would be morally required to include people from diverse groups within our networks in order to create bridging and global social capital.

The point to keep in mind about social capital understood as a moral norm is that in deliberations about what we ought to do it would carry greater weight than considerations of etiquette, narrow self-interest and opportunism. It might not be weightier than all moral norms, but it would be weightier than some norms, and certainly weightier than non-moral norms. In the case of other moral norms, such as liberty, autonomy and beneficence, for example, it might well carry equal weight. But the greatest advantage of focusing on the moral dimensions of social capital is that it increases the moral weight social ties have in a world currently preoccupied by individuals and self-interest.

There are, without a doubt, other norms to think about and to include in deciding what one ought to do, and sometimes those values will override the value of social capital. Liberty and privacy are two obvious ones. At other times, consideration of social capital would serve as a reason to help a stranger, or advocate for a fellow employee, or to remain at one's current post. It might help to resolve a dispute between Muslim New Yorkers and non-Muslim New Yorkers about where to build a mosque. It may dictate that we spend our summer helping the people of Haiti, or studying the culture of India.

At the same time, given the moral value of social capital, it might be morally wrong in some cases to exclude people from activities and opportunities in which they could either build social capital or benefit from it. When female members of President Obama's White House team complained that his basketball games omitted women, they were concerned about access to valuable social capital. In this case, it is arguable that President Obama's failure was a moral failure. Had there been a moral principle in support of social capital, President Obama might not have been so neglectful.

Institutions, such as state and federal governments, NGOs and the judicial system, both domestic and international law, could also promote social capital. Organizing schedules and designing physical locations to facilitate interaction among people will be helpful. Enacting laws that encourage people to care for others would promote social capital. Disability, affirmative action and same sex marriage are all examples of areas where law could, and in some cases does, foster social capital as it integrates people into the community. Implicit within such law is the assumption that participation and inclusion in the community are valuable. I'll have more to say about the law and social capital in Chapters 5 and 6.

Creating global social capital, to be used transnationally by people and by business and government, will require a paradigm shift – one that embraces the values of ethical and cultural cosmopolitanism in which people (not nations) are the relevant category. Because social capital is neutral with respect to specific social relationships, it can help to realize transnational and cosmopolitan perspectives.

Martha Nussbaum believes that headway can be made toward cosmopolitanism by concentrating on solving problems that require international cooperation. Efforts to solve global poverty or global warming require " ... global planning, global knowledge, and the recognition of a shared future." In her words, "to conduct this sort of global dialogue, we need knowledge not only of the geography and ecology of other nations – something that would already entail much revision in our curriculum – but also a great deal about their people, so that in talking with them we may be capable of respecting their traditions and commitments. Cosmopolitan education would supply the background necessary for this type of deliberation."[11] Nussbaum is right; knowledge about other cultures is important for global dialogue, and to solve urgent global problems. Recognizing our shared future is essential, but we must also recognize that in order to create a shared future we must forge transnational social networks and create global social capital. Only with abundant global social capital can we realize cosmopolitan aspirations.

As we come to understand our shared humanity, for example, through our shared vulnerability to environmental hazards, contagions such as SARS and avian flu, or our shared vulnerability to the global economy, we may also forge greater trust among diverse communities. Increased travel and Internet use may enhance interactions among people from different nations, and at the same time create global social capital. Promoting global social capital as an ethical concept will help to realize cosmopolitan values. But there is a virtuous cycle here because supporting social capital through ethics will increase social networks, foster trust, pro-social behavior, and diminish the inclination to exclude strangers. At the same time support for cosmopolitan values will also increase face-to-face contact with diverse people, and may contribute to global social capital and, in turn, global justice.

By understanding social capital as a *moral* norm, we thereby diminish its dark side because people will then be bound to universalize social capital and to act impartially toward others with respect to it. Homophily, like aggression and self-interest, is a tendency, which, though common and perhaps natural, is best subordinated in the service of other goals. Ethics can be an effective mechanism for achieving this end.

4
The Moral Sweet Spot

Social capital seems to make people happy. Because of this, it can be important for utilitarian ethics. In this chapter, I describe some of the social science findings with respect to social capital, happiness and well-being. For these purposes, the terms happiness and well-being are used interchangeably. Subjective well-being refers to a person's own appraisal of their happiness and well-being. It turns out that social relations are important, not only because people are happier when they have good, meaningful ties with others, but also because of the phenomenon of emotional contagion. Happiness spreads through social networks; so too for other emotions such as depression. Social capital may be the moral sweet spot, an effective mechanism for maximizing happiness, overriding self-interest and overcoming homophily – social capital's dark side.

Social capital is also essential for thriving cultures. In some philosophical quarters, culture is associated with important values, such as individual identity, trust and the human need to belong. Without social capital, culture would be impossible. Yet culture can come with costs, sometimes tragic ones, such as war and genocide. Because of this, whatever benefits cultures have, it may not make sense to protect them unless those benefits are greater than the costs. If one of the costs is cultural conflict, sometimes fraught with violence, or the expulsion of people for cultural reasons, then the benefits of protecting cultures will have to be considerable indeed. My view is that culture is not essential for individual identity, for trust, nor to satisfy the need to belong. Social capital may be an adequate and morally preferable alternative to culture, at least as a mechanism to launch individual identity, ground trust and, as I will show in Chapter 7, satisfy the need to belong.

If individuals and institutions are mindful of social capital, there will likely be greater happiness. In *Utilitarianism*, John Stuart Mill advocates the "Happiness Principle," according to which morally right actions are those that maximize the general happiness – each to count for one, and none to count for more than one.[1] Happiness consists in pleasure and the absence of pain. He also believes, however, that the principle of utility can be effective as a moral principle, because people have a natural basis of sentiment for utilitarian morality which consists in their social connections with others.[2] Consider the following passages from *Utilitarianism*:

> ...there is this basis of powerful natural sentiment; ...when once the general happiness is

recognized as the ethical standard, will constitute the strength of the utilitarian moralists. This
firm foundation is that of the social feelings of
mankind – the desire to be in unity with our fellow
creatures....[3]

Later in *Utilitarianism*, Mill says:

... they are also familiar with the fact of cooperating
with others and proposing to themselves a collective, not an individual, interest as the aim ... of their
actions. So long as they are cooperating, their ends
are identified with those of others; there is at least
a temporary feeling that the interests of others are
their own interests. Not only does all strengthen-
ing of social ties, and all healthy growth of society,
give to each individual a stronger personal interest
in consulting the welfare of others, it also leads him
to identify his feelings more and more with their
good....[4]

Although Mill recognizes that society affects people's
ability to realize the social sentiments, he also believes
that people want "harmony between their feelings and
aims and those of their fellow human beings."[5] Mill
believes social sentiments constitute the foundation of
utilitarian ethics.

For Mill, people have an interest in the welfare of
all because, given the social feeling of mankind, they
believe their own interests are tied to those of the collective. Thus Mill appears to take the view that because
people identify their happiness with their social ties,
we can be confident that by turning to their wishes and

desires in order to maximize happiness, we will find desires that harmonize with the general happiness. Because the happiness of individuals is tied to others, they will not veer too far from the interests of others.[6] Mill seems to be including something very much like social capital in the utility calculus when he maintains that individual happiness depends on the social sentiments. His emphasis on the role of social feelings and cooperation for individual happiness could be well served by social capital. Since, for Mill, happiness is maximized by consulting people's desires, the fact that people connect their interests with the interests of others will, he believes, ensure that collective interests are included when maximizing the general happiness. For Mill, social capital (social ties, trust and reciprocity) is simply a fact of human life to be relied upon by utilitarians.

As I mentioned in Chapter 2, Robert Putnam found that social capital is declining in the United States. He attributes this to increased time pressure, work obligations, excessive television watching, suburban sprawl and the gradual replacement of a civically engaged generation with a disengaged one.[7] If Putnam is right, the social inclinations that "constitute the strength of the Utilitarian moralists" may also be threatened. Given the importance of happiness for ethics, and Mill's views on the need to maximize happiness (pleasure and the absence of pain), it is worth considering what social scientists have to say about happiness. Does liberty make people happy? How about rugged individualism? Do pleasurable sensations make them happy? Do autonomy, money and good health make people happy? Or was Mill on the right track when he looked to people's social feelings? Fortunately, social scientists have been spending considerable time and effort answering these questions. Less fortunately, we can consider only the most salient of their findings.

Liberty and custom

Before turning to the recent research on happiness, let's look more closely at Mill's views. Although different philosophers have been concerned with happiness, utilitarianism continues to have considerable currency in the policy arena, both in the form of cost bene-fit analysis and law economics. Additionally, France, Bhutan and Britain, to name a few, have included happiness and well-being as indicators of societal health and as a policy goal. As we saw, Mill identifies the happiness of individuals in part with their ties to other people.[8] Although he recognizes the significance of social connections for human beings, he may not reconcile this with the role that custom, and to some extent law, can play in facilitating those very social relations. If the "social feelings of mankind" are to do the job Mill has given them, they may need to be nurtured. Mill supports a wide sphere for liberty, protected from the intrusions of law, because he seems to believe that individualism (unlike social inclinations) is at risk.

The principle of utility is only one mechanism Mill used to ensure the general happiness. In his introduction to Mill's *Principles of Political Economy*, Stephen Nathanson remarks that Mill believed that secondary principles could supplement the principle of utility.[9] In Mill's words, "The proposition that happiness is the end and aim of morality, does not mean that no road ought to be laid down to that goal, or that persons going thither should not be advised to take one direction rather than another."[10] According to Nathanson, Mill offered the principle of liberty (the view that the only time the state should interfere in individual liberty is when a person's act can harm others) as a key secondary principle, but extended an invitation to moral and political reformers to discover other ways to implement the principle of utility.[11]

When we compare Mill's view in *On Liberty* with some of the recent findings of social science, there are some interesting differences. MIll celebrates liberty and individuality because "...it brings human beings themselves nearer to the best thing they can be."[12] In *On Liberty* he defines "individuality" as development and states, "...that it is only the cultivation of individuality which produces, or can produce, well-developed human beings."[13] Individuality holds a cherished place in Mill's view of human nature and well-being, and he takes the promotion of individuality to be a driving force behind the design of law. Indeed, Mill's harm principle was crafted to protect a sphere in which individuality could flourish.[14] According to the harm principle, liberty can be interfered with only when individual conduct harms others, and interfering will maximize happiness.[15] Consider the following passage from *On Liberty*:

> Where, not the person's own character, but the traditions or customs of other people are the rule of conduct, there is wanting one of the principal ingredients of human happiness, and quite the chief ingredient of individual and social progress... If it

were felt that the free development of individuality is one of the leading essentials of well-being; that it is not only a coordinate element with all that is designated by the terms civilization, instruction, education, culture, but is itself a necessary part and condition of all those things; there would be no danger that liberty should be undervalued.[16]

From this passage we can see that Mill values individuality because of the role he assigns it in well-being. Mill points to custom as a significant obstacle to individuality. In another famous passage in which he celebrates autonomy, he also criticizes those who defer to custom.

He who does anything because it is custom, makes no choice.... He who lets the world, or his own portion of it, choose his plan of life for him has no need of any other faculty, than the ape-like one of imitation. He who chooses his plan for himself, employs all of his faculties.[17]

Although I share Mill's appreciation for autonomy, and his concern for its oppression, some studies on well-being suggest that even if autonomy is important for well-being, it is not nearly as important as Mill believes it is. Other research shows that people flourish when they are part of a network of people, including friends, colleagues, partners and neighbors.

A recent groundbreaking discovery suggests that part of what allows people to flourish in social contexts are mirror neurons which give them the capacity to mimic others – the very capacity that Mill criticizes when he mentions the role of the "ape-like" quality of imitation. As it turns out, mirroring the actions of others is one of the primary mechanisms human beings have to empathize with others and to establish social connections. According to neuroscientist Marco Iacoboni, "... it seems as if our brain is built for mirroring, and that only through mirroring – through the simulation in our brain of the felt experiences of other minds – do we deeply understand what other people are feeling."[18] Studies also show that the more people like others, the more they imitate them. Mirroring may help to establish trust among people. Deference to custom may be "mindless" and ape-like imitation, but it may also be pro-social and a way that people connect with one another. No doubt Mill had nothing like mirror neurons in mind when he critiqued the "ape-like" quality of imitation, and it is slightly unfair to take him to task for this. Nonetheless, he seems to underappreciate the role of imitation in social relations and happiness.

In *Utilitarianism,* Mill expresses an appreciation for the importance of social relations for human well-being and the utilitarian agenda. Social inclinations may be compromised in contemporary, fast-paced, 24-7 society. People may need the benefit of "nudges," to use the Thaler-Sunstein terminology, to help them connect with others, especially when there are so many opportunities to disconnect: the stress of making ends meet, both parents working, television, the Internet and the norm of self-interest to name a few. In the next chapter, I argue that some laws acknowledge the need for affiliation and social connection, and can promote social capital. Mill may lament such laws on the grounds that they violate the harm principle. Yet, in the end they may be just what we need for the general happiness.

Over the last few years happiness and well-being have been the subject of extensive empirical study. This research shows that social relationships are crucial for happiness. This body of research is vast and unfortunately I cannot address most of it here, but instead summarize some of the well-established findings.

Happiness

Social relationships are crucial for happiness. The only external factor distinguishing people who are very happy from those who are less happy is that the former have "rich and satisfying social relationships."[19] To dispel a myth, money does not buy happiness. Studies show that at low levels of economic development income does predict subjective well-being, but at higher levels it does not. More evidence for this comes from the observation that, although per capita incomes have quadrupled in the last 50 years in advanced economies, aggregate levels of well-being are unchanged. Studies also show that people are concerned not with absolute income but with relative income. And people like to compare favorably to others.[20] So money can buy happiness for some people, but not for others. Deaton and Kahneman found that there was not much more happiness to be had from an individual income over $75,000 a year.[21] Social relationships are important for happiness and they are at the heart of social capital. There is some evidence that social capital flourishes in environments of relative equality or where there is the appearance of equality.

In social capital rich Roseto, which we discussed in Chapter 2, there were few public displays of wealth. It may turn out that economic inequality makes social connection among people difficult, and in this way compromises social capital and, in turn, happiness.[22] Kawachi, Kenard and Lochner, for instance, found that income inequality leads to disinvestment in social capital and increased mortality.[23]

Marriage, race, level of education, employment and income are all social status factors that affect well-being. Age has been positively correlated to well-being, especially for the young and the elderly; the middle-aged tend to be less happy.[24] Not surprisingly, unemployment is especially destructive to subjective well-being.[25] There may be a variety of reasons for this, but loss of social ties may figure importantly here. Although education is associated with greater levels of subjective well-being, the benefits decline with greater education. Better-educated people may be more adept at socializing, given their access to wider social networks.[26]

Faith and church attendance are also positively associated with well-being. According to Helliwell and Putnam, people who go to church or who belong to more community organizations are more likely to believe that others can be trusted. Curiously, people who have a strong belief in God are also less likely to believe that people can be trusted. Helliwell and Putnam speculate that trust in God and trust in others may be substitute beliefs for people.[27] Nonetheless, frequent social interaction in church and community increases the tendency of people to think that others can be trusted, and in this way enhances their subjective well-being. The social interaction that takes place at church may be responsible for the increased well-being that church attendance brings, rather than the belief in God.

Interpersonal relationships are by far the most important factor for well-being. "People who have close friends and confidants, friendly neighbors and supportive co-workers are less likely to experience sadness, loneliness, low self-esteem and problems with eating and sleeping."[28] Family-level social capital is also connected to increased well-being. Recent studies conducted in the United States and Canada show that people who see family frequently have greater well-being. This body of research counts marriage as a social relationship: being married increases life satisfaction and happiness, especially when the alternative is being separated or divorced. Thus family social capital is important for well-being.[29] Helliwell and Putnam find that people who believe they live in high-trust communities also report higher levels of life satisfaction and happiness. Community involvement is conducive to higher levels of trust. Some of the benefits of community-level participation flow through the trust that is generated by community participation, and trust may be a function of how egalitarian a society is or appears to be. Eric Uslaner found that societies that are more egalitarian are more trusting.[30] As I mentioned in Chapter 2, trust is understood to be a proxy for social capital.

Not only is there evidence that social relations are good for people, there is also strong evidence that isolation and loneliness are bad for them. Human beings are social animals. Researchers believe that people have varying degrees of need for connection and social intimacy, some of which depend on genetic and environmental factors. In their work on loneliness, Cacioppo and Patrick found that social isolation gives rise to medical problems: "Once we see loneliness on the list of serious risk factors for illness and early death, right alongside of smoking, obesity, and lack of exercise, that context should heighten our motivation to improve our level of social satisfaction, both as individuals and as a society."[31] For these researchers, social isolation is a high-risk factor for illness and early death.[32] Putnam's, Kawachi's and Berkman's research on social capital and health confirm that social capital is good for health. The benefits of social interaction, however, do not lie with the duration of those interactions, but instead with how meaningful the social interaction is. But social capital is not only important for individual happiness and well-being. It is also good for the general happiness.

Emotional contagion: A friend indeed

A person's happiness is related to the happiness of his friends, his friends' friends and the friends of his friends' friends. Nicholas Christakis and James Fowler found that social networks have clusters of happy and unhappy people. According to their analysis, a person is 15 percent more likely to be happy if he has a direct connection to a happy person with one degree of separation; with two degrees of separation (friend of a friend), he is 10 percent more likely to be happy; and with three degrees of separation, only 6 percent. In addition, the clusters of happy networks are at the centers of the other clusters. This phenomenon is called emotional contagion and refers to the process by which emotions spread from person to person.[33] For Christakis and Fowler, "happiness...is not merely a function of personal experience, but also is a property of groups. Emotions are a collective phenomenon."[34] It is not clear why happiness spreads through networks. Some of the spread may be explained by proximity. Christakis and Fowler speculate that happy people may be more generous with others financially, emotionally and practically. They may be kinder to people in their networks, or their emotions may be contagious.[35]

These findings have a number of important implications for us. First, the study confirms that social networks are important for happiness. It also suggests that some social connections are more important for happiness than others. Social ties between and among happy people are especially valuable because they are the networks through which happiness is conveyed. If social ties contribute to happiness and happiness spreads, making some people happy will be an efficient mechanism for making others happy. Because of this, social networks provide a good venue through which to increase happiness. By increasing the happiness of one, we are increasing the happiness of others. Happiness, as well as other emotions, is both a collective and individual phenomenon. The phenomenon of emotional contagion also suggests that Mill was right that the "social feelings of mankind" are the foundation of utilitarian moralists.

For utilitarians, it would be close to impossible to maximize the general happiness without social capital.

The social networks through which happiness spreads are crucial and social capital can supply those networks. Social capital is important, then, not only because it is a source of numerous social benefits, but also because the networks that constitute social capital are pathways through which happiness travels to others. From a policy perspective, utilitarians need to ensure that social ties are bountiful. Given Mill's interest in maximizing the general happiness, and his openness to new principles, the obligation to promote social capital may well be a secondary principle that he would welcome.

The research on social capital and happiness, along with Mill's comments about the social nature of human beings, suggests that Mill appreciates the need for social connection. People enjoy relationships with others, and they benefit enormously from those relationships. Meeting our moral obligations with respect to social capital will go a long way toward maximizing the general happiness. Despite Mill's appreciation for the social nature of human beings, his emphasis on autonomy in *On Liberty*, combined with his come-what-may approach to people's social needs, suggests that he may have too much confidence in the ability of people to establish the social relations that he believes are essential for the general happiness.[36]

Mill leaves individuals a wide berth, eschewing paternalistic use of the law that would direct them to act for their own benefit and happiness. He reasons that individuals themselves are best equipped to make these decisions. And even when they are not, there is virtue in having them make choices.[37] Unfortunately, studies show that people are actually poor judges of what will make them happy. They are not good at predicting for how long an event will make them happy. They overestimate the effects of an event on their happiness, and seem unaware of how soon they will grow accustomed to the change.[38] Most Americans seem to believe that more money will make them happy yet, as we know, this is simply not true.[39] When Mill wrote *On Liberty* in 1859 and *Utilitarianism* in 1861, he did not have access to the abundant findings of the social sciences. But if Mill's assumptions about the ability of people to know what will make them happy are wrong, a nudge in the direction of social capital and social ties seems consistent with his concern for people's happiness.

Richard Wollheim ascribes to Mill the view that people need liberty to choose and actualize a life plan in order to find real pleasure and happiness.[40] On his reading, providing them with a wide sphere of liberty is consistent with utilitarianism because only if people find a life plan that suits them and actualize it will they find happiness. According to Wollheim, people need autonomy and self-determination for happiness. Although Diener and Seligman found a connection between autonomy and happiness, it comes with qualifications. Their research shows that there are three paths to happiness: the pleasant life, the good life and the meaningful life. Pleasant moments, such as sitting with a good book and sipping a fine port, can provide contentment. But Diener and Seligman found that people become bored with this. In the second, people are engaged with life, spending time with friends, family and a project. In the third, the most effective path to happiness, people use their own unique personal strengths in the service of something important.[41] Diener and Seligman believe that happiness endures longer after altruistic acts than after pleasant ones. Happiness, on this approach, calls on people to identify their unique strengths and use them for something higher than their own interest. In this way, it recognizes the importance of self-determination and authenticity. But Diener and Seligman have a narrow view of self-determination, since only certain kinds of life choices will lead to happiness – namely, life choices that support giving and altruism.

People lack good judgment about their well-being and development. If their happiness and well-being depend entirely on their own judgment, they may never find happiness. And if they don't find it, their friends may never find it, nor the friends of their friends. If we value autonomy, as Mill does, we might compensate for this deficit in judgment with education that increases people's knowledge about what makes people happy. But poor judgment and an information deficit are not the only impediments to happiness. People also have psychological, neuropsychological and psychiatric deficits. In the United States the Surgeon General stated that 28–30 percent of the population have either a mental or addictive disorder. In a given year, 19 percent of adult Americans have a mental disorder, 3 percent have both mental and addictive disorders and 6 percent have only addictive disorders. Anxiety disorders, such as phobias, social phobias and agoraphobia, among others, constitute about 16 percent of cases. Mood disorders such as depressive episodes, bipolar disease and schizophrenia affect about 7 percent of American adults between the ages of 18 and 54. About 20 percent of children and adolescents suffer from mental disorders with at least mild impairment caused by anxiety disorders, mood disorders and disruptive disorders. Among those over 55 and the elderly, roughly 11 percent suffer from anxiety disorders and 4 percent from mood disorders such as depression.[42]

Few people in the United States are untouched by psychiatric problems, whether personally or through a friend, child, sibling or parent. Although the Surgeon General's report uses a conservative definition of mental disorder, these statistics are startling. Antidepressant and anti-anxiety medications are also widely used. But depression is also a global problem. Studies show that globally one in five people suffer from depression over a lifetime; it was the fourth greatest contributor to the global burden of disease in 2000.[43] Between 1995 and 2002, the use of antidepressants rose by 48 percent. According to the Centers for Disease Control in the United States, adult antidepressant use tripled between the periods of 1988–94 and 1999–2000. Ten percent of women over 18 and 4 percent of men take antidepressants. They are the most commonly prescribed drug in the United States. Even if antidepressants are overprescribed, these statistics show that many people in the United States are unhappy enough to seek or be offered antidepressants.[44]

Most people who suffer from a mental disorder are perfectly competent decision makers when evaluated for legal competence. But their judgment may not be what it would be if they did not suffer from depression or anxiety. Paul Biegler points out that depression impairs autonomy "...through the negative information-processing biases that skew judgments towards pessimism."[45] People who suffer from depression may not be fully autonomous. Their autonomy may be compromised and their subsequent judgments may only worsen their depression. A similar analysis would be true of many other decision makers who suffer from mental illness. For example, those who have post-traumatic stress disorder, bipolar disorder and obsessive compulsive disorder may not be fully autonomous. If we take into account the predisposition of ordinary people to make poor judgments about what would make them happy, and combine it with a consideration of all the people who are affected by one kind or another of mental disorder, there isn't reason to be optimistic that people are the best decision makers about their happiness. If we add to that the likelihood that people don't have general knowledge about what kinds of things make people happy, the prospects for good individual decisions about personal happiness are not great.

Because of the phenomenon of emotional contagion, if we do not advance norms and policies that contribute positively to happiness, such as the principle of social capital, we forfeit a valuable opportunity to maximize the general happiness. Mill's harm principle cautions us not to interfere with people's self-regarding actions for their own sake and advises that the only time that government can interfere with people's actions is when individual actions would harm other people. But Mill seems to believe that liberty and autonomy will make people happy overall because they will ensure "free development of individuality."

It seems, however, that at this time in history, a secondary principle promoting social capital would be more promising. An ethical principle that highlights social ties, trust and reciprocity would help to lift people out of loneliness and forge social ties that would not only contribute to their own well-being but would serve double duty and contribute to the well-being of those with whom they are connected.

Some people believe that if a person can avoid a harm to self yet nevertheless chooses it, it should not count as a harm. This is captured in the phrase: "To one who consents, no harm is done." If this were so, it might show that people consent to harm, such as depression, that they encounter through their networks. Put differently, they assume the risk of harm when they interact with others. But people are social beings who need to be connected to others. It is unlikely that they could choose otherwise. Isolation comes at too great a cost. Because being in networks is important for people, it is also important to ensure that those networks are as good as they can be. The studies on emotional contagion show that within the emotional sphere our sadness and happiness are *not* self-regarding. The phenomenon of emotional contagion lifts emotions out of the self-regarding category and puts them in the other regarding one.

Mill's beliefs about the social nature of human beings are supported by recent research. But it isn't clear how important autonomy is for well-being. In practice people's judgment abilities and mental health undermine the overall effectiveness of Mill's harm principle. Unfortunately, if we base policy and law on a fiction about autonomous and self-determining agents, without regard for the many psychological, physical and informational vulnerabilities people have, we may inadvertently hurt them. Given Mill's concern with human happiness, he should welcome the findings of social science, as well as a secondary principle that supports social capital. There is reason for optimism. Acknowledging the ethical dimensions of social capital and promoting it as a secondary principle fits nicely with Mill's overall goal of maximizing happiness, and will help to minimize some of the problems raised by social capital's non-excludability. Given the high regard in which Mill held the social sentiments of mankind and the need for cooperation, it is difficult to imagine that he would not welcome a secondary principle that supports social capital.

Culture

"Belonging" matters to people. They find gratification in belonging to communities and professional groups, and some may ground their identities in belonging to cultures. Understanding what can meet the need to belong is important because it helps to frame the scope of our obligations to people. Several philosophers have contributed substantially to our understanding of the role culture plays in the lives of people. Will Kymlicka, a philosopher at Queen's University in Canada, argues, for example, that individuals are embedded in their cultures, and they create their identities within a culture.

For Kymlicka, a societal culture is "... a culture that provides its members with meaningful ways of life across the full range of human activities, including social, educational, religious, recreational, and economic life, encompassing both public and private spheres. These cultures tend to be territorially concentrated, and based on a shared language."[46] Societal cultures share memories, values, common institutions, practices and an "everyday vocabulary of social life, embodied in practices covering most areas of human activity."[47] Culture gives rise to the need for a high degree of solidarity within modern democratic states, and solidarity requires citizens to have a strong sense of common identity. Kymlicka believes that a common identity needs a common language and history.[48] To his mind, culture is morally important because it provides a rich array of options from which individuals can make choices that are meaningful to them. Choice is at the heart of individual freedom and freedom is morally and politically important for liberal philosophy. For now, let's assume that Kymlicka is right about the moral importance of societal cultures and the role of solidarity for these cultures.

In other philosophical quarters, special value is assigned to culture because it "provides the spectacles through which we identify experiences as valuable."[49] Because culture is the mechanism through which meaningful options are identified and realized, it is protected by those who value liberty. Margolit and Raz believe that culture is crucial for people's well-being because it determines "the boundaries of the imaginable" and affects how others perceive and respond to us. According to them, "...our own identity depends on criteria of belonging rather than on accomplishments. Secure identification at that level is particularly important to one's wellbeing."[50]

Culture has figured importantly in the work of other philosophers. Yael Tamir suggests that belonging to a culture adds meaning to our actions. She underscores that when institutions are informed by a culture they promote trust and participation in public affairs. For Tamir, this fosters a sense of belonging and relationships of mutual recognition and mutual responsibility. David Miller places special value on trust, and ties it closely to nationalism. Miller has the following to say:

> I take it as virtually self-evident that ties of community are an important source of such trust between individuals who are not personally known to one another and who are in no position directly to monitor one another's behavior. A shared identity carries with it a shared loyalty, and this increases confidence that others will reciprocate one's own cooperative behavior.[51]

He also believes that nation states are essential for trust. In his words:

> For democratic decision making to work successfully, each participating group must be willing to listen to opposing points of view, and be willing to moderate its own demands in order to reach a compromise that everyone can accept. Equally when a decision has been reached, those who find themselves in a minority...must be willing to comply with the outcome, knowing that their point of view

has at least been taken seriously, and that on future occasions they may find themselves on the winning side. All of this requires confidence in, and understanding of, those one disagrees with politically. Trust of this kind is much more likely to exist among people who share a common national identity, speak a common language, and have overlapping cultural values.[52]

Miller is probably right that trust is more common among people with a shared language and overlapping culture, but that may be the result of proximity. It may also be a variation on homophily. And, of course, it may not be morally desirable. Trust comes about for a variety of reasons: fiduciary duties can create trust by reassuring those protected by them that their interests come first; giving can create trust even among strangers; and it appears that repeated contact in long-term relationships can create trust, as people act in light of future interactions. Future ties create trust as people recognize that others have a shared interest in the continued relations. Miller may confuse the activities that create trust with the context in which it typically occurs. As the oxytocin study described in Chapter 2 showed, giving can create trust even among strangers. Cooperative activity and collaborations give people repeated contact, much in the way that a common nationality does. The prospect of future interactions serves as a guarantee that people will be trustworthy because they have an interest in maintaining ties. But it is the repeated contact that enables trust. Fortunately, repeated intercultural contact is possible, and when multicultural societies are successful, it is prevalent. Trust needn't be nation bound. In addition, as we saw in Chapter 2, people's identities change as demographics change. Although race and culture are not identical, there is often an overlap. People with more fluid racial identities may find it easier to trust people from other countries, and to identify more widely.

Moral value is attributed to culture for a cluster of overlapping reasons. It is thought to ground individual identities, satisfy the need to belong, determine what is meaningful and create an array of possibilities from which people can choose. Culture is also thought to be important because it fosters trust, loyalty and cooperation. Culture can bring meaning to our actions, and it is valued for the role it plays in well-being. For these reasons, some philosophers consider culture morally significant and worthy of protection.

Although culture can be an important source of these benefits, it is not the only source. Nonetheless, it is worth noting that if culture is important in any of the ways mentioned, then social capital is as well. Without it, cultures would not exist. But, the question needs to be asked whether, given the problems associated with culture, there is a better alternative to it. Culture may provide all of the benefits listed, but may also create social problems such as exclusiveness and xenophobia, which may become more acute as our day-to-day experiences become global. If social capital is a moral principle and requires us to act impartially toward social ties, rigid and culturally grounded ties would be morally problematic. Although this may strike some as counterintuitive, it is no more so than the idea that people deserve to be trusted because of their cultural affinity. Is it morally, or practically, desirable to trust a practice, or a person, because of their culture?

Studies show that people give preferences to those within their groups even when the factors that constitute the group are trivial. Unfortunately, conflict is thought to be inherent to categorization of the self into groups and is a feature of group identity. I'll have more to say about this in Chapter 7. Although culture is lauded for its trust-building qualities, it may also create the impression that the *only* people who can be trusted are one's compatriots. This strikes me as morally problematic under any circumstance. In a global era, people need to be able to trust and cooperate with people who are unlike them and they need to be able to do this both at home and when they go abroad. Similarly, culture is important as a backdrop against which life choices can be made, but in a global context our choices far exceed the nation state. Neither nationality nor culture are good reasons in and of themselves to trust others. Trust should be based on whether someone is trustworthy, and whether or not they are depends in part on what is at issue, because we trust people for particular matters and what assurances there are in the context to support one's trust. For example, are there relevant norms in place and is there a long-term cooperative relationship?

Given some of the social costs of culture, it is worth exploring whether we purchase the benefit of grounding identity on national culture at too great a cost. If there were an alternative to culture that could achieve the same ends, but without the costs, that would be appealing. Social capital can do much of the work of culture, and does not give rise to the serious problems that accompany it. In a global context, tying one's identity to national culture is too restrictive. Indeed, some people may be significantly disadvantaged because they hold steadfastly to a culturally determined identity as others reach globally for something more fluid. Exclusive focus on one's own culture as a way to frame one's options is also far too restrictive in a global context. Indeed, some cultural practices, such as female genital cutting, constitute violations of human rights. Surely, in these cases, people ought to draw on worldwide cultural knowledge in framing their choices and practices. People with a transnational perspective are able to evaluate practices within their own communities in a way that people who don cultural blinders are not. Pogge's global people, for example, are likely to draw on knowledge and experience from several political units in framing their possibilities and life choices. If anything, this would ensure that transnational people make better informed choices and more authentic ones.

Cultures may be spectacles, or blinders, as the case may be. Many cultural norms and practices are in transition because of global challenges to them. Laws banning the burka have been enacted in Australia, France, Belgium and Quebec, Canada. Regardless of how one feels about the burka, intercultural comparisons can facilitate norm change. Similar global challenges have been under way for some time in the global public domain with respect to female genital cutting. In a global context, there is no real reason why people could not choose from a palette of cultural practices. Why should they be restricted to those that are nearby, some of which may not suit their personalities, may be harmful to them or may narrow their perspective? Although there may have been a time when culture determined the "boundaries of the imaginable," that time is no longer. Today, with rapid transit and high speed communications, boundaries are now unimaginable for many. If culture isn't important for other reasons, it should not be prized because of the role it serves in framing possibilities. If anything, when the possibilities are global, as they are for many, and will be for many more, restricting people's perspective to their national culture is liberty-limiting. For those who embrace culture for liberty-based reasons, the enhanced choices of a global perspective are significant. The argument from choice highlights the role of culture in molding choice, yet from a global perspective a nation-based culture narrows those choices dramatically and unnecessarily.

Is culture important for trust and cooperation? I don't think so. That seems to be furnished by social capital. The "trust game" which was discussed in Chapter 2 shows that exchanges can contribute to the creation of trust and increased oxytocin even between strangers. As I have suggested, trust is a complex matter. Who we trust may largely be a matter of who we encounter and with whom we have long-term interactions. For many, that may be people within one culture, and for many others, people from multiple cultures. Social connections are important, and people seek ties with other people. That much is clear. For the sake of trust, there is little evidence that the ties that bind need to be cultural ones. Although culture-based ties may be an easy and convenient way to meet these needs, it is not the only way to do so. Many other features that are ascribed to culture may be true enough, but could just as easily be true of a global culture. Transpatriates, for example, might find people with a global moral vision more trustworthy than those with a narrow cultural vision. Social capital may itself provide people with a sense of belonging and social identity.[53]

There is an emerging global identity as more people view themselves as transpatriots, and begin to value that as an identity. Since the mid-1990s Oxfam, for example, has been involved in an effort to educate people about global citizenship.[54] To respond to the need for a global workforce, many new businesses have surfaced, with the purpose of providing the international workforce with a global mindset and cultural competence. Although cross-cultural training of this sort is new to business, it has been used by the military and foreign service for some time now. Companies such as Culture Wizard pave the way for the international workforce and their families.[55] Reverting to cultural identities when there is a possibility of a global identity would be regrettable, especially for those who might thereby miss global opportunities and those who depend upon global others for their very lives.

Better with us

The connection between social capital and culture is complex. Francis Fukuyama believes that culture is necessary for social capital.[56] Cultures that foster norms and values consistent with trust and cooperation are useful for the creation of trust and social capital. But some cultures, such as the culture of the mafia, and cultures in which competition and/or corruption are prevalent, might actually discourage cooperation and encourage suspicion and distrust. Similarly, some cultural practices might induce fear and shame, especially for some members of the culture, such as women living amidst the Taliban. Robert Edgerton makes this point:

> Humans in various societies, whether urban or folk, are capable of empathy, kindness, even love, and they can sometimes achieve astounding mastery of the challenges posed by their environments. But they are also capable of maintaining beliefs, values, and social institutions that result in senseless cruelty, needless suffering, and monumental folly in their relations among themselves as well as with other societies and the physical environment in which they live.[57]

To understand the connection between culture and social capital, it will be helpful to consider some of the work from social psychologists. According to Chi-yue Chiu and Ying-Yi Hong, culture is both a collective and individual phenomenon. "It consists of a set of shared meanings, which provide a common frame of reference for a group to make sense of reality, coordinate their activities in collective living, and adapt to the external environment."[58] Cultural knowledge is shared knowledge and concerns common knowledge about thinking, feeling and interacting among people.[59] A culture has different networks for sharing knowledge; some are straightforward, such as important documents (for example, the Bill of Rights), and others are ideas that are diffused more broadly, such as secular values. People participate in the creation of culture both by adapting to their environment and creating culture in the process, and by communicating culture intergenerationally. Culture revolves around shared meanings and it "emerges because there is a need to coordinate the activities of interdependent individuals."[60]

Fukuyama believes that social capital, "... the crucible of trust and critical to the health of an economy, rests on cultural roots."[61] For Fukuyama culture consists in "inherited ethical habits, such as an idea or a value." Interestingly, too, for Fukuyama social capital appears to be restricted to those norms that actually promote social cooperation. "The norms that produce social capital ... must substantively include virtues like truth telling, meeting obligations, and reciprocity."[62] But the interplay between social capital and culture seems to go both ways. Culture relies on social capital, for without the interactions among people there would be little culture, especially if culture is understood as subject to change and transmission. For culture to exist people need to interact and in the process they create social capital. At the same time, they typically interact toward some end, and very often those ends are supplied by culture. People gather to celebrate a cultural event, or they may share cultural practices such as shaking hands or a friendly greeting – both of which facilitate the kinds of interactions that create social capital, trust and the capacity to work cooperatively and create value. But culture is constantly changing and the social networks of social capital are one of the mechanisms of change.

When culture facilitates social networks, it isn't always a matter of national culture. It could be "Deaf culture," "activist culture," "hippie culture" or "green culture" and these cultures are very often transnational. I believe that what in some quarters is attributed to culture could be more accurately attributed to social capital. When David Miller, for example, refers to the "ties of the community" and the importance they have for trust, it might be more accurate to look to social capital than culture, because social capital includes the ties that facilitate trust. On the lean and mean definition of social capital, social ties and the norms of trust and reciprocity are key. To ground trust we need go no further than social capital. Culture may be the by-product of social capital, but some cultures, such as the culture of the mafia, have little to do with trust. Other cultures, such as the "green culture," and global culture, have little to do with national cultures.

The happiness research weighs in favor of social relations as a primary source of happiness. Culture may be one source of social relations, but it is the relations themselves that contribute significantly to well-being. For those who believe that culture is morally important because it is the background against which people create their identities, I suggest that multiple affiliations and global culture could do the same. Moreover, insofar as the multiple affiliations of Pogge's global people also promote tolerance and respect for difference, multiple affiliations are morally preferable. I will say more about global culture in Chapter 7.

Some studies show that people have a preference for people who are like them, and that in the face of diversity people withdraw from social life.[63] Being faced with the unfamiliar is often frightening. But given that social capital is most easily (though not necessarily) created by face-to-face interactions, there is no reason to think that it must inhere in a national culture rather than in, for example, a global culture, human rights culture or just among a network of people. If we cling too rigidly to culturally based identities, we place unnecessary obstacles in the way of bridging social capital.

For now, I have shown that social relations are important for well-being and utilitarian ethics places high value on well-being. I have also shown that there is a close connection between social capital and culture, and that if culture is morally prized so too should social capital. Regardless of where one stands on the moral value of culture, it is clear that social capital is integral to culture. I have also argued, however, that social capital may be doing much of the work that is now attributed to culture, and that it does this without the risks associated with national culture.

How we create social identities is a matter of choice. Just as we *choose* to build social cohesion around 4 July or May Day, we could choose to build it around Earth Day (22 April), International Women's Day (8 March) or the day the Universal Declaration of Human Rights was enacted (10 December). Were we to move in the direction of global culture or multiple political units, diversity may be less troubling for people and social capital easier to create both within diverse communities and globally.

Human beings have a deep need to belong. But in some quarters it is assumed that the need to belong is best satisfied by a national or social culture, tied together by practices, traditions and language. One reason nations are attractive as objects of belonging is because they are responsible for protecting the rights and entitlements of their citizens. In the current nation state context, the absence of a state to protect people is an enormous liability. The plight of over 26 million internally displaced persons is good evidence of that problem. Some of the importance assigned to culture might be a result of the legal protections nations afford people, and not qualities of the state itself. When people are unable to take care of themselves, or in the case of children when their parents are negligent, states have *parens patriae* duties. Were we to substitute another mechanism for protecting those same legal rights, perhaps through global governance organizations, nation states might not figure so importantly in the belonging calculus. Or, if global governance mechanisms could provide greater protection than nation states, as they sometimes do in conflict ravaged communities, norms, networks and trust might revolve around them, and identity might follow suit. Even at this time in history, with respect to some global public goods, such as the environment, NGOs working in the global public domain may be doing more to protect human rights than nations are doing.[64]

According to Baumeister and Leary, "humans have a pervasive drive to form and maintain at least a minimum quantity of lasting, positive, and significant interpersonal relationships."[65] There are important psychological and evolutionary explanations for the human need to establish a sense of belonging across the spectrum of life experiences, which we will consider closely in Chapter 7. There are also strong social universals that turn humans into belonging seekers. Giddens, for example, believes that humans share a universal desire for certainty and ontological security in a world of risk, uncertainty and unpredictability.[66] It isn't clear, however, that national culture is the locus of ontological security.

If a sense of security could be provided through other means, those means could also serve as the source of identity. For some people that might be the nation state, and for others it might be the United Nations or some abstract notion of global citizenry. Some people might find it within themselves or their social networks. When entire countries are ravaged by disasters, as Japan was when it was struck by an earthquake registering nine on the Richter scale, then by a tsunami, then by nuclear mishaps, the country itself must reach beyond its borders for help. The international community is often the source of help, and may over time come to ensure security for many peoples. Today, people are more mobile than they were 50 years ago, and they will be more mobile still in 50 years' time. With the expansion of rapid, effective and inexpensive telecommunications, cooperation across continents has become easier than ever before. This trend is expected to continue long into the future. The various relationships that transpatriates cultivate globally could serve to ground their identities, and perhaps meet their need for ontological security.

It would be regrettable if we embraced rigid cultures in order to ground identities, when all that was really needed were social networks and social capital.

National culture comes with costs, and those costs can be xenophobia, hostility to strangers and sometimes genocide. For others, it might only narrow the scope of their expectations from a global village to a village. If national identities were no longer the distinguishing factor among peoples, and people interacted more widely across cultures, with a number of different groups, they might be more content, and we might not have the kind of conflict often associated with cultural belonging. Glen Hutchins, co-founder of a private equity firm, describes it this way:

> Beijing has a lot in common with New York, London or Mumbai. You see the same people, you eat in the same restaurant, you stay in the same hotels. But most important, we are engaged as global citizens in cross-cultural commercial, political and social matters of common concern. We are much less place-based than we used to be.[67]

The life of Glen Hutchins is not defined by geography and culture but by his interests and activities, and they span the globe. Although he has wealth on his side, his experience may nonetheless foreshadow a time when interests and activities are more important for identity and belonging than geography and culture. It is urgent that we act now to ensure that global living, and the global social capital needed to facilitate it, are accessible to all people, and especially to the most vulnerable and marginalized members of the global community.[68]

5
With a Little Help from the Law

We can do a lot to create and protect social capital. Treating social capital as a moral principle will do an enormous amount to override our inclination toward self-interest, address the free-rider problem that exists with some social capital and, in the end, build our social capital reservoir. The moral requirement to act impartially will counter the tendency toward homophily, diminish social capital's dark side and contribute substantially to our reservoir of global social capital. But we can also use the law to bolster social capital. Doing so would constitute more than a mere nudge, since the penalties associated with violating the law would reduce people's options. Nonetheless, given the value of social capital and the harms associated with its deprivation, we need to take seriously the potential role that law can play in creating and preserving social capital. In this chapter and the next, I look at the impact of the law on social capital. Law affects trust, generalized reciprocity and social capital. It can do so either positively or negatively. If, as I argued in Chapter 3, social capital is morally valuable, we should consider fashioning law to ensure that we don't destroy social capital, and instead increase it. This is not to say that anything that is morally good should also be legally obligatory. There is an important difference between law and morality. But in light of social capital's moral dimension and abundant benefits, we should also consider the implications that the law has for it. The law's effectiveness rests, in part, on the presence of social capital, and on the willingness and ability of people to cooperate with it even when they are not being monitored. Cooperation is also important for international law.

When the law doesn't take social capital into account, it can unintentionally send social capital spiraling downward. Although my focus is on the American legal context, there is no reason to think that this analysis would not apply to other legal systems, though many would surely fare better than the United States with respect to how the law nurtures social capital. Underlying my analysis is the view that law can be used to create social capital. In this, I differ from legal scholar Richard Pildes, who supports the idea that law ought to be mindful of social capital, but is against crafting law for the purpose of enhancing social capital in the absence of harm to others.[1] Because law says as much by what it doesn't do as it says by it what it does, law that ignores social capital may indirectly undermine it.

After discussing how law can affect social capital, I look at two laws. Duty to rescue law, which imposes a duty on people to help strangers, is likely to build social capital. Its absence runs the risk of undermining social capital. Termination at will – law that allows employers to fire employees at will and for no cause – undermines social capital. Many different laws have the potential to build social capital. My analysis is intended only to illustrate how law can create or destroy social capital. In the next chapter, I look at the charitable tax deduction, with a special focus on global giving. In my overview of the law and social capital, I include a consideration of not only the expressive content of the law but also the expressive content of the absence of law, and I will also say something about the special role of social capital in international law. Let's begin with a more general discussion of how law creates meanings in society.

Law as social meaning

According to an influential group of legal scholars – Robert Cooter, Lawrence Lessig, Rick Pildes, Cass Sunstein and others – law has social meaning and can serve an expressive function. In addition to controlling behavior through admonitions and prohibitions, and facilitating agreements with contract,[2] law serves to express social value, encouraging some norms and discouraging others.[3] Laws can "make a statement about how much, and how, a good or a bad, should be valued." They create and affect "social meaning, social norms, and social roles."[4] According to Sunstein, laws that have important expressive functions can be justified on that ground alone. They are valued in virtue of their ability to affect social norms and to shape behavior in the desired direction.[5] Laws that regulate euthanasia are a good example of law that has abundant expressive content. Here, courts are often concerned with the meaning and value assigned to life, and with the potential for a "slippery slope" – not only with the actual consequences of the law for patients. A couple of remarks about the expressive function of law will be helpful. First, on this view, one of the functions of the law is to shape social norms. Second, it is also clear that some law has expressive content that can become tired, outdated and inconsistent with current knowledge and norms. Law prohibiting sexual relations between same sex couples is a good example.

Law creates, sustains and destroys norms. It can facilitate trust by ensuring, through contract for example, that life is predictable, and the possibility of recourse to the judicial system allows trust to develop. People know that if they are faced with a breach of contract they can turn to the legal system. Law can affect social capital directly. To paraphrase Pildes, law can:

(1) Destroy social capital indirectly by destroying the structures that facilitate cooperation. Zoning laws that fail to accommodate gathering places would be an example.

(2) Undermine norms of reciprocity. Were the government to fail to compensate people for taking private property they would undermine reciprocity.

(3) Fail to recognize that by incorporating the substance of social norms into coercive state regulations, it may compromise the norms that are enforced socially rather than through law. Mandating the publication of the names of men who

solicit prostitutes can force wives to divorce their husbands to protect their good names.[6]

Law can also foster social capital. The Takings Clause, which requires just compensation when the government takes private property for public use, may maintain social trust by requiring compensation even though such compensation typically falls below market value.[7] "Compensation is socially perceived as an acknowledgment that government is overriding valid claims, and a sign of respect for the harms inflicted."[8] Here the norm of reciprocity is sustained by government. I will suggest in the next chapter that the charitable tax deduction does the same.

For the most part, laws that foster generalized reciprocity will be helpful in sustaining social capital. When generalized reciprocity governs interactions, people are willing to give to others without exacting immediate return. When law encourages people to act for the sake of others, it nurtures social capital. When it encourages them to act for people who may not reciprocate, it nurtures generalized reciprocity. Given the role of social networks in social capital, law that facilitates social interaction will foster social capital. When the law encourages inclusion rather than exclusion, integration rather than segregation, as it does in *Brown v. Board of Education*,[9] it creates the social structures necessary for social capital. Law that fosters interaction among diverse people enhances scarce, and valuable, bridging social capital. Some law fosters helping behavior. Consider the Americans with Disabilities Act (ADA). It not only builds networks by ensuring that people with disabilities can participate in important life activities, but also promotes generalized reciprocity. With respect to the ADA, Congress states the following:

> (1) Physical or mental disabilities in no way diminish a person's right to fully participate in all aspects of society, yet many people with physical or mental disabilities have been precluded from doing so because of discrimination; others who have a record of a disability or are regarded as having a disability also have been subject to discrimination.

> (2) Historically, society has tended to isolate and segregate individuals with disabilities...such forms of discrimination against individuals with disabilities continue to be a serious and pervasive social problem....

> (3) The Nation's proper goals regarding individuals with disabilities are to assure equality of opportunity, full participation, independent living, and economic self-sufficiency for such individuals.[10]

People with disabilities are entitled to accommodations, such as ramps for wheelchair access and interpreters for the hearing impaired. Here the law requires people to help people with disabilities, even though it is unlikely that the recipient of accommodation will directly reciprocate. The ADA expresses the values of helping, caring and inclusion. In part, the goal of the ADA is to ensure that people with disabilities are able to participate in society and are not isolated because of their disability. In this way, it creates the conditions necessary for social networks to flourish.

By extending these protections to people with disabilities, the ADA also expresses a pro-social message about helping people who are different in some way. The obligation to accommodate falls not only to the state but also to the employers. The ADA demonstrates state support for the value of generalized reciprocity and requires people and institutions to help even when they cannot be assured of in-kind reciprocity. The ADA also helps people with disabilities access valuable social capital, which they might otherwise be unable to do. It protects them from network poverty. Of course, the networks created have the potential to benefit everyone in the network, and not only people with disabilities.

Law promoting affirmative action (*Regents of the University of California v. Bakke*)[11] and same sex marriage (*Goodridge v. Dept. of Health*)[12] are also good examples of how the law can encourage values at the heart of social capital. In these areas law recognizes the importance of inclusion in a community, whether it is a community of tradesman, law school students or a community of people who share in a fundamental social institution, such as marriage. Such law creates the conditions necessary for social connection to thrive, whether they are connections between and among the able and disabled, black and white, or same sex lovers, and the community at large.

Some people would argue that using the law to deliberately create social capital is morally wrong because it manipulates norms, and is arguably inconsistent with liberalism and the spirit behind the distinction between morality and law. Whether we actively promote certain norms or not, the norms that are present guide and inform the law.[13] But having demonstrated that social capital is morally valuable, it would be a mistake not to promote it simply because another norm preceded it. Indeed, if a new norm is morally superior to an old norm, surely there is a moral obligation to try to replace the old norm with the better one, or to supplement the old norm with the new one. In the United States, for example, the prevailing norm with respect to healthcare has been one of individual responsibility, thus leaving an estimated 50 million Americans without health insurance.[14] That norm is changing as the United States embraces healthcare reform, and replaces the old norm with a new healthcare-for-all norm. Despite the fact that the old market-based healthcare norm was the first, the consensus of the world is that healthcare-for-all is the morally preferable norm. The human right to health, as enunciated in Article 12 of the International Covenant on Economic, Social and Cultural Rights, takes just this position.[15] The decision about what moral norms we should use to guide our lives and law should be based on the merit of the norm, and not on its seniority. As we discussed in Chapter 2, norms can change when they are no longer in the collective interest, and norm bandwagons can form. Let's turn to a specific example of law that can create social capital.

Helping strangers

Too often onlookers stand by and do nothing to help as strangers face life-threatening emergencies. Social psychologists call this bystander non-intervention. In 1964 young Kitty Genovese was stabbed to death as a reported 38 onlookers stood by and did nothing, not even make a phone call to the police. Although some of the facts of this case are disputed, third-party non-intervention is common. Situations of this kind are puzzling. It is difficult to understand why people fail to help even when it would be of little risk to them. Duty to rescue law can require people to help strangers. At present, however, such laws are rare in the United States (and elsewhere) and some jurisdictions have laws that leave helpers vulnerable to legal suit if something goes wrong in the midst of helping. Hurricane Katrina brought to light a similar set of problems for medical and non-medical volunteers who wanted to help, but were confounded by the law. Some volunteers were sued. After having traveled some distance to help the victims of Katrina, many volunteers found themselves unable to do so for fear that they would be sued. Since then, some laws have been changed to address this vulnerability.

Public response to breaches of the expectation to help have been volatile, and may reflect a norm change. At the heart of the reluctance to enact robust duty to rescue laws is the norm that people are under no obligation to help strangers. In the absence of such law, we risk deepening an entrenched ethnocentrism in a world that calls out for wider cosmopolitan duties and the willingness of people to help distant strangers. It is unlikely that we will ever convince our compatriots that "global strangers" ought to be helped, if we are unable to convince them that the stranger down the street deserves their aid. Unfortunately, the absence of duty to rescue laws, when there is a need for rescue, can convey a message to the community that strangers don't warrant their care.

In general, Good Samaritan laws protect medical rescuers from liability should something go wrong while they are helping. In contrast, duty to rescue laws impose a positive duty on bystanders to help those who are at risk of harm even when the bystander has done nothing to cause the harm. Common law countries, such as the United Kingdom and the countries it colonized – including the United States – are reluctant to include a duty to rescue as part of their penal code, while civil law countries do.[16] Countries such as France, Italy, Germany and others in Europe have a general penal law to rescue.[17] The statutes differ with respect to which dangers trigger the duty and on whom it is imposed. Penalties vary, but have included fines, detention and imprisonment. Common law countries tend to have specific duties to render aid, but rarely general ones. For example, parents have a duty to feed their children and doctors to care for their patients.[18] Some European private law also posits a duty to rescue, often ignoring the difference between acting and failing to act.[19]

Duty to rescue laws reflect generalized reciprocity because they impose a duty on bystanders to help strangers even though it is unlikely the rescuer will receive in-kind reciprocation, or for that matter any reciprocation at all. In view of this, both duty to rescue and Good Samaritan laws are an important mechanism for promoting the very values on which social capital relies. They encourage people to help strangers even when there is little chance of direct reciprocation and they reinforce generalized reciprocity. Regrettably, such laws are scarce in the United States.[20]

Social psychologists believe one reason people don't help strangers is because of uncertainty about their responsibility, especially when there are other bystanders present. People may assume that if there were a serious threat someone else would help, or they may think helping is not their responsibility. Unfortunately, reluctance to help strangers may be exacerbated by an absence of duty to rescue laws. Laws can signal to bystanders that the responsibility falls on them to help. In the absence of such laws, and given the expressive function of the law, people may believe that the state does not support helping strangers. This inference is all the more likely given the presence of laws that require people to help those with whom they have a close connection (spouse, child and so on). People may wonder why the latter, but not the former. It is not simply that there is no obligation to help in the absence of having caused the harm, because there is a duty to help those with whom we have special relationships even when we are not the source of the harm. Because the law selects special relationships for "helping," it cements and supports close and special ties, leaving strangers to fend for themselves.

The moral and legal vacuum left in the wake of this lacuna could not be more evident than in the Sherrice Iverson case. This case is startling, not only because of the events that took place, but because of the narrative surrounding them. In 1997, Leroy Iverson took his seven-year-old daughter Sherrice to a casino in Nevada. Sherrice was playing hide and seek with a stranger, Jeremy Strohmeyer, while her father was preoccupied gambling. She was seen on a security camera going into the bathroom followed by Strohmeyer. Later, Sherrice was found thrown over a toilet seat, sexually molested and dead. Strohmeyer was convicted and sentenced to life in prison. At the time of the murder, David Cash, Strohmeyer's friend, stood by, watched the crime and did nothing to prevent it. In Cash's words:

> It's a tough thing, an innocent bystander lost her life, a very tragic event. But the simple fact remains that I do not know this little girl – I do not know dark children in Panama, I do not know people that die of disease in Egypt. The only person I knew in this event was Jeremy Strohmeyer... and I'm sad because I lost a best friend.[21]

Because of the absence of either a civil or criminal common law duty to assist, Cash could not be held liable for failure to help Sherrice. Nor did he fall within the scope of accessory to a crime, or conspiracy. Cash's words are repugnant. He is smug about his loyalty to Jeremy, and equally convinced that he had no obligation to help Sherrice, a stranger to him, and African American.[22] Ideally, Cash would have intervened and stopped Jeremy from killing Sherrice. Rather than analogize Sherrice to distant strangers and negate his duty to her, he might have acknowledged a duty to help strangers, and in turn a duty to help this young stranger, Sherrice Iverson. Rather than send trust and social capital spiraling downward, he might have nurtured social capital by helping Sherrice. Had his actions been governed by the ethic inherent in generalized reciprocity, rather than a perverse version of the principle of loyalty to friend, he might have helped Sherrice and saved her life. Had there been a law in place requiring a rescue, one that expressed general community intolerance for Cash's failure to help, the community would have had a mechanism to hold Cash accountable for his inaction and express its moral outrage.

The expressive content of law can serve as a way for legal institutions to influence conduct, and for the community as a way to express its response to conduct. Let us consider the Iverson case in light of its expressive content. Pildes does a nice job of defining expressive harms:

> An expressive harm is one that results from the ideas or attitudes expressed through a governmental action rather than from the more tangible consequences the action brings about. On this view, the meaning of a governmental action is just as important as what that action does. Public policies can violate the constitution not only because they bring about concrete costs but because the meaning they convey expresses inappropriate respect for relevant constitutional norms.

> Expressive harms are therefore social rather than individual. Their primary effect is not the tangible burdens they impose on individuals, but the way in which they undermine collective understandings. Public action and collective understandings mutually influence each other. Government action shapes and reconstitutes them.

Governmental actions can express and perhaps sustain a rejection of these norms.[23]

For Pildes, expressive harms are the consequence of government *action*. Yet we can see from the Iverson case that expressive harms are just as likely to be the consequence of government *inaction*. When the government fails to act in a manner people expect, social meaning is created just as much as if government were to have acted. In terms of expressive harms, there is no reason to think that government inaction will cause less expressive harm to the common social good than government action.

Let's return to the case of Sherrice Iverson. Although the public was furious with both Strohmeyer and Sherrice's father, the bystander – David Cash – was also the target of public rage. In the end, Cash's failure to help led to the enactment of the Sherrice Iverson Child Victim Protection Act which requires witnesses to report sexual or violent crimes against children under 14.[24] Community outcry against Cash centered on the failure of both Cash and the state. From the perspective of the community, there was a social harm, and one that needed to be redressed with government action.[25] The student body at the University of California, Berkeley, where Cash was enrolled as a student, were especially outraged. The student senate convened to decide whether or not Cash should be expelled from the school. People were concerned about their safety and didn't like the idea that Cash received a state-sponsored education.[26] Not only did Cash voice the view that he had no obligation to help Sherrice, repeating in different words that his obligation was to his friend, he also bragged that he would make money with his new notoriety and found it easier to "score" with girls. One CNN article subtitled one of its sections: "Intangible Anger in Absence of 'Good Samaritan' Law."[27]

If there is one thing that the Sherrice Iverson case shows, it is that government inaction can express meaning. Here there was a social harm precisely because people believe that the state should have taken action, perhaps that justice demanded it, and it failed the community by not doing so. People were struck by the fact that the state appeared to reward Cash with a state-sponsored education. If expressive harms are to be understood as social harms, then Nevada's failure to enact duty to rescue law qualifies on that count. Community outrage, anger and a desire for revenge are present. People mobilized to advocate state action in the face of government impotence. Some of the outrage consisted in objections to Cash's ethical world view: that he owes nothing to a stranger.

For many people, Cash's views were morally outrageous. Yet David Cash invoked a moral principle in support of his conduct – he favored loyalty to friends over helping strangers. Cash may have been a moral monster, or he may simply not have understood the moral urgency of the situation. Duty to rescue law can play an important educative role. Laws that support helping strangers can overcome some of the cognitive dissonance that surfaces when bystanders do nothing to help. If bystander non-intervention studies are correct, many people don't help strangers, and often because they don't know that it is their obligation.[28] The absence of other bystanders makes Cash atypical, yet under the circumstances his remarks about loyalty to his friend reveal a cognitive deficit.

Curiously, Cash offers an alternative moral principle to justify his failure to help Sherrice; namely, his belief that he has no moral obligations to strangers, but only obligations to friends. In his own words, "I *owe* nothing to that little girl."[29] Cash justifies his behavior on the basis of ethical particularism: the view that our strongest moral obligations are to those closest to us, family, friends, neighbors and compatriots. It is nicely encapsulated in common colloquialisms, such as "family first," and "don't talk to strangers." Not surprisingly, people who heard Cash's words were shocked. But should they have been? A brief look at a list of those to whom we do have duties to help shows that, for the most part, our legal duties are to people with whom we have relationships: spouses, parents, children, and professionals for their clients. In other words, the state encourages people to help those with whom they are close, but is silent with respect to strangers, or in the case of a mishap during rescue, punitive.[30] As I mentioned earlier in this chapter, some jurisdictions have a legal cause of action that allows victims to sue rescuers if they make things worse during the rescue. For those who justify the absence of duty to rescue law on efficiency grounds, one wonders why the same argument doesn't hold with respect to special relations. Yet many jurisdictions encourage the one, but not the other. Public outcry in the face of failure to help may signal that the norm is fragile, no longer supported by the community, ripe for the kind of norm bandwagon discussed in Chapter 2.

There are a number of arguments raised against duty to rescue laws. One of the main ones is based on the value assigned to individual autonomy: requiring people to help strangers interferes with the helper's liberty and autonomy. When people harm others, their harmful actions may be construed as consent to the limited interference of helping (righting his wrong). When, however, people have caused no harm, their consent cannot be inferred. According to Mill's harm principle, the only time the law is justified in interfering with a person's freedom of action is when the action harms another person.[31] By limiting when the law can interfere to the minimum extent necessary, we facilitate people's ability to act freely and determine their own good. As we saw in the last chapter, Mill believed that people require freedom to develop as individuals. On this reasoning, limited use of the law is necessary.

A second liberty-based argument against duty to rescue laws is made on the ground that to impose legal liability on people for failure to assist would conflate the moral with the legal and in this way interfere with the right of people to pursue diverse conceptions of the good by legislating for a particular conception: namely, that they must help others. This is similar to Mill's concerns. A third argument, one that is promoted by law and economics, states that it is economically inefficient to have duty to rescue obligations because the cost of assisting may be greater than the benefits.[32] The resounding message of the first two arguments is that negative liberty, or freedom from state interference, is more important than helping strangers in distress, even when their lives are at risk. But according to philosopher Isaiah Berlin, there is more to liberty than freedom from state interference; there is also positive liberty, the liberty that allows us to realize our aims – liberty to do something, rather than liberty from something.[33] Although the rescuer's negative liberty might be interfered with by a law that required her to assist, the positive liberty of the rescued is enhanced since she is now free to continue the business of living. Moral principles are present with respect to both the status quo (negative liberty) and duty to rescue law (beneficence, social capital). Why prefer the moral principles that underlie negative liberty over those that would support helping? With respect to the efficiency-based argument, it is important to keep in mind that efficiency is just one canon of law. My view is that the principle of social capital ought to be another one. If it were, it might outweigh the efficiency-based consideration underlying this objection to duty to rescue law. Plus, social capital might improve efficiency through increased networks and more effective cooperation. Careful analysis might reveal that duty to rescue laws are overall more efficient than their absence.

When the law fails to respond as the community expects it to, there can be considerable social harm. People feel abandoned by the state. Just as the absence of duty to rescue laws may undermine the willingness of people to engage in the dance of generalized reciprocity, so the presence of such laws could build social capital. By expressing state support for generalized reciprocity, duty to rescue law bolsters social trust and increases the willingness of people to help strangers. Given the benefits to individual well-being from helping, it may turn out that requiring people to help strangers increases the well-being of the helper as well as the person helped.[34] Directing people to help strangers may send not only a strong social signal, but may also increase bridging and global social capital as strangers become socially valued recipients of our help.

In the 2008 California case of *Van Horn v. Watson*,[35] Lisa Torti pulled her friend Alexandra from a car following an accident because she was concerned that the car would explode. Alexandra was injured in the accident and believed that Lisa exacerbated her injuries, causing damage to her spinal cord. Lisa claimed that she was immune from liability under California's Good Samaritan law. Although the trial court agreed, on appeal the California Supreme Court held that the law refers only to the provision of emergency medical care. Lisa was providing her friend with non-medical help.[36] Later, concerned with the fallout from this decision, the California legislature submitted two bills to reverse its effects: one that would provide immunity from civil liability for anyone who provides medical or non-medical aid and a second bill that targeted disaster relief aid.[37] Here again, there is evidence that we may be in the midst of a bandwagon effect and ready for a new moral principle.

There is another important way that law can take social capital into account. So far I have looked at how the expressive content of a law can affect social capital. Duty to rescue laws would foster social capital because they instantiate generalized reciprocity. They also signal state and community support for helping strangers. Law could also take social capital into account in a more direct way. Richard Daynard has identified a number of canons that the courts use in decision making in his analysis of public health law. According to Daynard, judges use implicit rules or canons that identify the kinds of arguments they make in their opinions and decisions. These have included: (a) marketplace values (that is, law and economics analysis), consumer sovereignty as a legal desideratum..., (b) individual rights as trumps..., (c) strict constructionism, (d) judicial administration, and (e) common sense.[38] The law could also include a canon or rule that identifies social capital. Similar principles or canons may already be embedded in the law. In *Jacobson v. Massachusetts*,[39] for example, the Supreme Court of Massachusetts put the interests of community before individual liberty when it stated that Massachusetts mandatory vaccination law was constitutional. Laws such as affirmative action and the ADA focus on the importance of inclusion. If courts can take marketplace values into account (which they do) surely they could include a consideration of the impact of the law on social networks, norms of reciprocity and trust.

In the absence of a duty to rescue, people are free to help others, although they may incur legal liability if something goes amiss during the rescue. When there are no duty to rescue laws, bystanders are invited to act on other values, such as self-interest, loyalty to friends, efficiency and marketplace values. In this context, people who value collaboration and cooperation are less able to realize their preferences than those who endorse rugged individualism. As we saw, Ms Torti wanted to help her friend, but found that the law did not support her efforts. Duty to rescue law can reaffirm helping behavior, and in its absence there is the potential for law to disappoint community expectations.

Emphasis on individual liberty, understood as freedom from interference, autonomy and self-determination, fosters a norm which holds individuals primarily responsible for taking care of themselves and not others. Goods that come about as a result of cooperation and collaboration are less likely to flourish in the context of negative liberty. Placing a value on negative liberty encourages people to identify their own interests separately from others. Though seemingly neutral among conceptions of the good, negative liberty favors a conception of the good that revolves around individuals and their claims to non-interference.

Destroying social capital

The workplace is an important source of social capital for many people. Employees develop close ties with co-workers and they work cooperatively and in collaboration. Unfortunately, unless otherwise specified in a contract, workers in the United States are generally governed by employment at will. Both the employer and the employee can terminate the employment relationship without cause. In a now famous passage from an early case, the court in *Payne v. Western and Atlantic Railroad* gave the following account of termination at will:

> ... men must be left, without interference to buy and sell where they please, and to discharge or retain

employees at will for good reason or for no cause, or even for bad cause without thereby being guilty of an unlawful act per se. It is a right, which an employee may exercise in the same way, to the same extent, for the same cause or want of cause as the employer.[40]

For the court, liberty for both employer and employee figures importantly in justifying termination at will. As with duty to rescue law, negative liberty is at issue here. Freedom to contract at will is for many a basic freedom. But there are other arguments in support of termination at will. According to law and economics scholar Richard Epstein, employment at will is to the mutual benefit of employer and employee.[41] It benefits firms by providing them with a cost efficient mechanism for coping with employee opportunism. Terminating employees, no questions asked, is more efficient than extending due process rights, or engaging in expensive litigation.[42] Employees are protected by public opinion: if employers terminate inappropriately, they suffer reputational losses that may carry financial consequences for the firm. Epstein also makes the point that termination at will can be used by both employer and employee to make decisions in the face of imperfect information.

The freedom-to-contract justification is based on negative liberty. Those whose conception of the good involves collaborative and cooperative interactions are not likely to fare as well as they would were the law's impact on social capital taken into account. A long-term commitment to employees would encourage generalized reciprocity, and would reduce employee opportunism. It would be good to know if, in fact, social-capital promoting practices, such as termination for cause only, are inefficient.

Organizations can choose practices that either destroy or create social capital.[43] A long-term perspective on the employment relationship is more conducive to building social capital than a short-term one.[44] Whatever other merits employment-at-will has, it is likely to undermine social capital. Unanticipated job loss carries heavy burdens for all concerned. The unemployed experience lower levels of subjective well-being. As with divorce and the death of a loved one, job loss is one of the most significant stressors in life, often leading to depression. Studies also show that the impact on well-being from job loss continues even after people resume employment. Unemployment scars people for life.[45] Job loss burdens social capital, as employees are withdrawn from the network of co-workers and colleagues they have created over the years. Families may need to relocate to accommodate a breadwinner's search for alternative employment, potentially separating families from one another, and from the community in which they are embedded. Short-term relationships are unpredictable and uncertainty about one's future may mean that social relationships that were once governed by generalized reciprocity will in the wake of unemployment be governed by *quid pro quo* transactions. Employees, feeling more vulnerable, may not trust that reciprocity will be generalized.

Individuals are not the only ones to suffer from job loss. Organizations also suffer because when they terminate employees they "diminish the connection between employees and employers, and among employees, and employees and clients."[46] Job satisfaction increases with tenure, and studies show there is greater customer satisfaction in stores with more regular employees. Termination at will may not be better for a company's bottom line. The National Bureau of Economic Research found in a study of 140,000 manufacturing plants operating between 1977 and 1987 that one third of the plants that cut employment experienced a decrease in production while the 52 percent that increased employment grew in productivity. The *Wall Street Journal* found that firms that downsize experience an initial increase in their stock price, but not after two years. The stock lagged behind those of comparable firms by up to 45 percent, and lagged behind the general market by 17–48 percent.[47] Organizations, individuals and communities suffer from unemployment. Thomas Sander and Robert Putnam report that unemployment:

> ...frays a person's ties with his community, and sometimes permanently. The unemployed are less likely to vote, petition, march, write letters to the editor or volunteer. They spend most of their time alone. Communities with high unemployment have more crime against property and more violence. Families are fragile and discipline is harsh. Mental disorders and psychological distress are more common in such communities for both the employed and the unemployed.[48]

This research shows that the impact unemployment has on social capital is deep and wide-ranging.

It undermines social capital not only in the workplace but also in the life of the unemployed, the nearby employed and the community at large.

In view of the harms that track unemployment for companies, workers and the community, termination at will can express government indifference to the interests of workers and the quality of their lives. Courts are not unfamiliar with the importance of employment policy for both employer and employee. In *Toussaint v. Blue Cross and Blue Shield of Michigan*,[49] the Michigan Supreme Court stated that employer policies create "a spirit of cooperation and friendliness," making employees "orderly, cooperative, and loyal" by giving them "peace of mind regarding job security and the belief that they will be treated fairly when termination decisions are made."[50] The court realized that employers' policies foster cooperation and loyalty. Interestingly, although social capital is not a legal canon, courts are mindful of some of its ingredients. Emphasis on cooperation, friendliness and loyalty are all qualities that can help to build social capital. A legal system mindful of the principle of social capital could ensure that termination for cause only would replace employment at will and bystanders could be encouraged by duty to rescue laws to help those who are at risk of harm.

Liberty-based concerns against such a canon are misplaced in view of the judicial commitment to other canons, such as marketplace values. Following Mill, one of the main arguments against enacting laws for the sake of social capital is that, in the absence of harm, it is morally problematic to do so. Pildes refers to this as the concern with norm manipulation and the need to protect against "the kind of oppressive state that liberalism as a political philosophy was meant to avert."[51] According to Pildes:

> ... Attention to the expressive dimensions of public policy and law should not be understood to supplant or clash with prior frameworks justifying state action and defining its boundaries. Government action is still justified only when "harm to others" occurs; once that precondition has been met, however, the most effective way of regulating that harm might well require taking account of the way laws and norms interact. But a bare governmental interest in regulating social norms intrinsically – in "making a statement" – should not in and of itself justify coercive forms of state action, such as criminalization, that would not be independently justified within the appropriate political philosophy.[52]

Using law to create social capital is not mere norm regulation, since social capital is associated with increased individual and social goods. Nonetheless, if Pildes is right, enacting duty to rescue laws might be viewed as wrong even though doing so would likely reduce social harms. The same is true for shifting employment law from termination at will to termination for cause only. Mill stated that providing people with extensive liberty and autonomy is the best way to maximize happiness. But, given what we now know about happiness and well-being and people's abilities to judge what will make them happy, a secondary principle in favor of social capital might be preferable to rigid deference to the harm principle. The two laws considered in this chapter constitute opportunities for social capital. Termination for cause would help to ensure that employee relationships are long term, sustaining levels of social capital and giving generalized reciprocity a chance to flourish. Duty to rescue law is another avenue both to help individuals at risk of harm and to build our reservoir of social capital.

In fact, one quite recent study showed a correlation between acts of kindness and happiness. According to this study, acts of kindness are correlated with happiness and as people count and reflect on these acts their happiness increases. Crafting policy and law to give people opportunities to increase their kind acts would also increase their happiness.[53] Arguably, we don't need duty to rescue laws to give people an opportunity to be kind. They are perfectly capable of that on their own. However, not all people know that kind acts will increase their happiness, and not all people know that they ought to help strangers in an emergency. People dazzled by the norm of self-interest may overrate the benefits of self-interested behavior. The combination of the duty to promote social capital and kindness counts would help to override ambivalence to helping strangers.

In my view, it is a mistake to be overly concerned with norm manipulation. Blind deference to liberty, without regard to the impact on social capital, is also norm manipulation. Either way, law supports norms. The question is which norms it supports: the status quo norm, or a new, possibly better, norm, informed by the recent findings of social scientists. I have suggested that fashioning law to serve our need for social capital would serve community and individual interests. The decision about which norms should inform the law ought not to be based on which one is there first. Rather, various principles should be weighed in any given situation to determine what will be in the public good. I am suggesting that we include social capital among those principles and canons.

A window of opportunity

International law depends on social capital, and its policies and procedures foster the creation of social capital. Because countries must *agree* to be bound by international law, it is inherently cooperative. International law is created by national governments, blocks of governments, national and transnational interest groups, government and non-government organizations.[54] Multinational corporations also participate in the creation of international law through their lobbying activities and through the contracts they negotiate with other countries and corporations, both of which can affect the domestic law of other countries. The United Nations and related organizations and agencies are the primary institutions for international law. Although national sovereignty is recognized by international law, it can become vulnerable when states join the United Nations. For example, the World Health Organization, working through the Health Assembly, can enact binding regulations to which members are obligated, unless they register a "reservation" within a specific time frame. The use of reservations, which allow countries to become a party to a treaty, but for specific provisions, encourages maximum cooperation and agreement to treaties. The United Nations General Assembly is itself a forum in which the international community comes together, articulates concerns and mobilizes around them.[55] There are countless United Nations sponsored conferences that serve as gathering places for the international community,[56] and their frequency is increasing. Custom, treaties and general principles of law are important sources of international law.[57]

Customary law, such as diplomatic immunity, based on international practice and often unwritten, is applied to countries that have indicated a willingness to comply with the custom. Such law doesn't apply to countries that have persistently objected to it. However, once a country complies, they are expected to continue to do so. "Acceptance of customary rules is the price of admission new states pay to join the international community."[58] Here the conduct of a nation indicates consent to be bound by the law. Treaties, which are written agreements between states and are only binding on those states that agree to them, are a second form of international law.[59] Some treaties are simply bilateral agreements, for example to be trading partners, but increasingly treaties are multilateral.[60]

Because international law is based on negotiation, cooperation and consent, it relies on transnational social capital and constitutes an opportunity to create social capital. Nations must interact with one another in order to come to agreements. To this end, they build countless networks. The need for agreements, which will support treaties, creates networks and trust as different countries collaborate to find mutually agreeable arrangements. Negotiation involves the kind of give and take that creates trust. This process of cooperation is even more pronounced in multilateral agreements. Prior to the General Agreement on Tariffs and Trade, bilateral agreements, which invite power exchanges to win privileges, were dominant. They often lead to conflict among trading partners. In contrast, a multilateral approach, combined with Unconditional Most Favored Nation status, as adopted by the World Trade Organization, treats all trading partners alike and invites cooperation. When the give-and-take is bilateral, it is more likely to involve tit-for-tat exchanges. According to John Ruggie, "...multilateralism is an institutional form which coordinates relations among three or more states on the basis of 'generalized' principles of conduct – that is, principles which specify appropriate conduct for a class of actions, without regard to the particularistic interests or exigencies that may exist in any specific occurrence."[61] Multilateralism facilitates trust.

Multilateralism tends to be informed by what Robert Keohane has called diffuse reciprocity, in which members arrive at a rough equivalence of benefits in the aggregate.[62] Diffuse reciprocity is similar to generalized reciprocity. Nonetheless, a great deal of international law is based on specific reciprocity, and sometimes simultaneously executed reciprocity. But there are limits to the usefulness of specific reciprocity, especially in the context of multilateral decisions.[63] According to Keohane, "Participants typically view diffuse reciprocity as an ongoing series of sequential actions which may continue indefinitely, never balancing but continuing to entail mutual concessions with the context of shared commitments and values. In personal life, groups of close friends practice diffuse reciprocity."[64] Diffuse reciprocity requires trust among participants because reciprocation can be delayed, and rather than being either simultaneous or specifically negotiated, it is based on the assumption of trust in future dealings. Keohane believes that specific reciprocity is too limiting and that complex negotiations require diffuse reciprocity "... to contribute one's share, or behave well towards others, not because of ensuing rewards from specific actors, but in the interests of continuing satisfactory overall results for the group, of which one is a part, as a whole."[65] Diffuse reciprocity among trade partners is embedded in multilateral relations, and international interactions that give rise to diffuse reciprocity have enormous potential as a source of global social capital.

Finally, although law sometimes replaces social capital, one thing is certain: law requires social capital for most efficient functioning. At best, the legal system understood broadly can provide rules to determine appropriate conduct, the judiciary and law enforcement. Nevertheless, in the absence of social capital none of these will be adequate to quell illegal activity. For that, social capital will help because when it is present people want to cooperate.

The argument of this chapter has been a modest one. I have suggested that duty to rescue law has the potential to create social capital. Helping others increases the rescuer's personal well-being as well as that of the rescued. It also expresses the state's support for helping strangers. As we saw in the Sherrice Iverson case, the absence of duty to rescue law can also be detrimental to a community, sending social capital spiraling downward. I also showed that employment at will could adversely impact social capital.

My argument is only that law should take social capital into account, and that judges, lawyers and law makers be familiar with how the law can create and destroy social capital. Affirmative action, same sex marriage law and disability rights are laws of inclusion. They recognize the value of social ties and networks and foster bridging social capital as they build social ties between in-groups and out-groups. Trust is a relatively fragile good. The more we can protect and nurture it, the better. International law is possible only because transnational actors are able to cooperate, and sometimes – as with multilateralism and Unconditional Most Favored Nation status – generalized reciprocity is present. International law will come to be ever more important in the future, and given the possibility of international conflict, the success of international law has high stakes associated with it. But it will also serve as an important source of global social capital as international actors meet, cooperate, negotiate and create agreements and law. In the absence of a moral principle to promote social capital, there is much to lose. But there is also some evidence of a bandwagon effect, as norms that impose an obligation on bystanders to help begin to accumulate, suggesting a propitious time to promote the moral principle of social capital.

6
Giving Back

Giving and helping are often first steps in the dance of generalized reciprocity, and as we have seen, when generalized reciprocity is present social capital blossoms. There are many ways to increase giving. One widely used, though morally compromised, strategy involves appealing to people's emotions with what has come to be called the "pornography of poverty." Providing people with tax deductions for their charitable contributions is another way to stimulate giving. Abundant social capital is also associated with increased giving and – unlike the pornography of poverty – is not fraught with moral compromise. We have seen how law can be used to create social capital or, in some cases, hurt it. In this chapter, I continue the analysis of law and social capital, but with a focus on two provisions in charitable tax law. I argue (1) that limiting the charitable deduction to itemizers is likely to undermine social capital and giving, and (2) that law which prejudices global giving may adversely affect the cultivation of transnational social capital. At present, the United States' Internal Revenue Code (IRC) may discourage global giving through its water's edge policy, which states that to qualify as a charitable deduction for a tax payer, the recipient of the donation must be created or organized in the United States.[1] The distant poor may receive less charitable giving because of this restriction. Since law can shape norms and values, policies of this kind can also undermine efforts to expand the scope of our moral world from a narrow, local and domestic one to a global and cosmopolitan one.[2] Global social capital is important not only to increase transnational giving but for successful international relations, transnational business and international development. Because the water's edge policy channels international giving into intermediary charitable organizations, it may undermine our efforts to create much needed transnational social capital. Global giving has increased substantially in the recent past, largely because of the Bill and Melinda Gates Foundation. Nonetheless, giving and helping are such integral parts of trust and generalized reciprocity, and transnational social capital so important for global well-being, that it is important to nurture international giving not only to meet the needs of the global poor but to build social ties that will sustain global citizenship. Much of what I say in this chapter is applicable to the law of other countries, many of which also have water's edge policies.

Sweet charity

Charitable giving is thought to increase as the stock of social capital increases people's regard for the generalized other. For Putnam, philanthropy is the result of social capital. "Social networks provide the channels through which we recruit one another for good deeds, and social networks foster norms of reciprocity that encourage attention to others' welfare."[3] Unfortunately, Putnam's studies also show that American philanthropic activity has steadily declined since 1961 – about the same time as he observed a decline in social capital.[4]

Putnam is not the only one to find that an increase in social capital is predictive of an increase in giving. Brown and Ferris found that both network-based social capital (the social capital that comes from social networks) and norm-based social capital (social capital derived from pro-social norms) were important for giving.[5] More specifically, people with high levels of norm-based social capital were found to give to secular causes and to volunteer often, while people with more network-based social capital were found to give to religious and secular-based causes.[6] In the case of network-based social capital, people who are embedded in social networks are more likely to be asked to give, and they are more likely to give.

It would not be surprising, however, if philanthropy itself had the fortuitous consequence of fostering social capital. Generalized reciprocity is, according to Putnam, the cornerstone of social capital, and giving and helping are at the heart of generalized reciprocity. Giving both reflects trust (that there will be reciprocation) and reinforces it when beneficiaries receive gifts and have their trust affirmed. To quote Putnam, "people who have received help are themselves more likely to help others, so that simple acts of kindness have a ripple effect. In short, giving, volunteering, and joining are mutually reinforcing and habit forming."[7] This has been referred to as social capital's virtuous cycle. Philanthropy mirrors generalized reciprocity insofar as the former, like some instances of the latter, constitute giving without expectation of reciprocation. If philanthropy is a form of generalized giving, and generalized giving is important for social trust and social capital, it may well be that philanthropy itself fosters social capital. This would explain the ripple effect, and the oxytocin studies in which the signal of trust created increased oxytocin and subsequent reciprocation.

In some quarters, people deny that there is a moral duty to give to others because from their perspective they alone are responsible for their personal wealth. To this, they add the idea that people are responsible for taking care of themselves. They believe their wealth belongs to them *because* they have caused it (on their own) to come into existence. Social capital challenges that paradigm. It implies that many outcomes, including financial wherewithal, may be the result not of individual talents, actions and efforts, but of cooperative and collective ones. Considered from a fairness point of view, social capital-generated outcomes would "belong" to the collective. As I noted in Chapter 3, the expression "giving back to the community," widely used by donors to explain their giving and by fundraisers to solicit it, may signal an appreciation for the role that social capital plays in personal fortunes, and of the normative implications of that fact for philanthropy.

As we saw in earlier chapters, norms and law can be fashioned to serve the interests of social capital.

Laws can be changed, norms tinkered with and biology re-engineered by new technologies that redefine our humanity. A community replete with social capital is one in which people are comfortable giving to others (without a demand for reciprocation) because they can be confident that, although they may not benefit from reciprocation now and from this beneficiary, they may be a beneficiary at some other time, or in some other way, and from some other person, or perhaps not at all. People do not track who owes what to whom because they trust their community members to take care of one another. Reciprocation is general, and in some cases may be purely hypothetical. Very often people who give to others are comforted by the thought that "he *would* do the same thing for me" and "he *would* if he could" without actually seeking or expecting reciprocation. And sometimes immediate reciprocation is regarded as positively inappropriate, as a crude effort to transform a "gift" into a consumer transaction. Timing can be everything in the dance of generalized reciprocity.

Generalized reciprocity can be an ideal way to understand giving where gifts are given to people who cannot reciprocate, such as donations to the very poor or helping a stranger. People may give to the distant poor and their neighbors reciprocate by bringing them chicken soup when they are convalescing from an illness. When reciprocation is generalized, or conjectural, to use Putnam's term, there has to be a high degree of trust that others will reciprocate because the donors may not themselves know of the reciprocation since they may not be the beneficiaries of it. Fundraisers seem to rely on the idea that people may pay forward. The widespread practice of making a donation to a foundation or NGO in another person's name may reflect the principle of generalized reciprocity. Consider an example: if I make a donation to Oxfam in my mother's name, out of appreciation for everything she has done for me, I would be paying forward. Anything we can do to diminish the influence of norms that emphasize *quid pro quo* exchanges and replace them with generalized giving and the norm of paying forward will foster social capital and giving.

Because trust facilitates generalized giving, norms that encourage it will also be helpful. Truth-telling, promise-keeping, personal integrity, fairness and altruism identify values and principles that facilitate trust. If people can be counted on to tell the truth, then those with whom they interact can be confident of their trustworthiness. The same is true for promise-keeping. Personal integrity, understood as continuity in personal traits, allows people to predict the future behavior of those with whom they interact, thus enabling trust. Pro-social norms in which one person gives to another are conducive to building an environment in which trust can flow. Recall from Chapter 2 how effective giving is in generating trust and oxytocin. Giving blood and bone marrow, giving up a seat to an elderly person, giving a lost wallet to the police, extending courtesies, such as "excuse me" when one bumps into another, and giving up your place in a queue to someone in a rush are all examples of different ways that we give to others. By contrast, leaving garbage on the street, failing to pick up after your dog and stealing parking spaces are examples of the opposite, and are firmly entrenched considerations of the interests of the self over those of others. Norms that focus on charity, such as "charity begins at home," build bonding social capital, but do little to advance social capital that creates bridges among people in different groups. The latter and not the former would be helpful to Pogge's global people who aspire to live transnationally.

Deducting our gifts

In 1917, four years after the ratification of the 16th Amendment, the United States Congress created the charitable deduction for donations to public charities and private foundations (religious, charitable, scientific and the prevention of cruelty to children and animals). Since its inception it has expanded in scope and value.[8] In the United States, tax payers who choose not to take the standard deduction, and instead itemize their deduction, are permitted to take a charitable deduction while non-itemizers are not.[9] According to the Independent Sector, a think tank and professional organization for the charitable community, non-itemizers include low- to middle-income Americans, such as students, teachers and bus drivers. Most of these people earn less than $50,000 per year, do not own their own home and do not pay a mortgage. When the charitable deduction is applied to non-itemizers, it can make a difference in giving behavior.[10] In 1985, when for a short time non-itemizers could deduct 50 percent of their charitable contribution, they contributed $9.5 billion to charity. In comparison, in 1986 when they could deduct 100 percent of it, they contributed $13.4 billion – about 40 percent more.[11]

The reasons for the deduction are multifaceted and, all things considered, none are fully satisfactory as explanations.[12] Nonetheless, Congress justified the deduction on the grounds that, although the government loses revenue from the charitable exemption, the loss can be justified because when people donate money to charity they relieve the government of a task that it would otherwise have to undertake, and there is benefit to the general welfare.[13] As with Pildes' analysis of the Takings Clause, which we considered in Chapter 5, the congressional explanation for the charitable deduction invokes a reciprocity consideration: people who make charitable donations to advance the public good relieve the government of that particular responsibility, and the government reciprocates with a tax deduction. Here, law supports the norm of reciprocity.

Non-itemizers cannot deduct their charitable contributions. Instead, any money they donate to charity is supposedly captured in the standard deduction. Administratively this is a good idea because the cost involved in monitoring many small donations would be great. Efficiency seems to be the guiding consideration. Some non-itemizers may donate more to charity than assumed by the standard deduction while others may not have made any donations at all and incur an unjustified benefit. From the perspective of the expressive theory of law, the message communicated to non-itemizers may be that their gifts "don't count" perhaps because the gift is too small. Since the predominant legal rationale for the deduction is a reciprocity consideration, failure to extend it to non-itemizers may give rise to social distrust. In some instances, the government may be unjustly enriched, while tax payers assume financial responsibility for public benefits without receiving compensation. As we saw in Chapter 5, law can destroy social capital not only by what it does, but by what it doesn't do. Since non-itemizers increased their charitable contributions by 40 percent from 1985 to 1986, following the increase in deductible amount, it is safe to assume that they are mindful of the impact of the deduction for their giving plans. They may also be mindful of its expressive content, and the unfairness implicit in it (even if that unfairness is fictional).

Because in the United States the value of a donor's charitable deduction reflects the donor's marginal tax rate, the greater a person's income, the larger the absolute tax advantage for the same gift. So those in the highest tax bracket would realize a greater tax advantage than those in a lower tax bracket. If reciprocation were to follow a tit-for-tat principle, then the value of a gift should be the same for everyone since it would be fixed by the gift itself. But when reciprocation is generalized, it doesn't matter if some people realize a greater or lesser valued reciprocation. In addition, if we want to increase giving, and increased giving will both meet social needs and increase social capital, then increasing the value of the deduction for those who can give the most may be an important consideration. By the same token we could decrease the relative value of the deduction for the affluent, and still be in keeping with the principle of generalized reciprocity.

If, as I suggested in Chapter 5, social capital were among our legal canons, law makers could consider the impact on social capital of excluding non-itemizers.

Looked at from this perspective, it probably doesn't matter how much money people give in absolute terms. If we want to increase generalized reciprocity, it is important that people are engaged, giving without an expectation of reciprocation, creating social trust and, thus, enabling cooperative activity. Excluding non-itemizers from the deduction may compromise generalized reciprocity and social capital. First, if non-itemizers do not receive a deduction for their donations, then the government may receive a benefit for which it doesn't reciprocate, perhaps contributing to social distrust. Second, taking a charitable tax deduction encourages people to keep track of how much or how little they give to others. There is some evidence that counting one's acts of kindness (and acts of giving would count) increases one's happiness, and that happy people become kinder as they count their acts of kindness.[14] Non-itemizers would not have this opportunity to count their kindnesses or to self-monitor their giving. Third, if we take social capital seriously then extending the deduction to all tax payers signals the government's approval of generalized giving and, in turn, social capital. Fourth, there is an appearance of unfairness when the deduction is extended to itemizers while withheld from non-itemizers. Although non-itemizers are free in principle to itemize, for many the cost and complexity of itemizing means that the option is but a fiction. Sometimes the costs and administrative hoops required to exercise a right are so burdensome that the right becomes virtually inaccessible.[15] Finally, there is some evidence that inequality makes it difficult for social cohesion and social capital to blossom. If so, the appearance of unequal treatment may do the same.

At present, the law fails to take advantage of an opportunity to promote social capital, and in this way to increase giving. The reasons why the charitable deduction is important are less clear than that it is important. The Independent Sector refers to the impact that itemizing has on charitable giving as the "itemizer effect." They believe the itemizer effect influences how much households give in charitable contributions – an effect that holds true regardless of income, home ownership status and other less significant household characteristics.[16] Because most people itemize to deduct home mortgage interest, they speculate that itemizers may give more because as homeowners they are more engaged in their communities, and their giving reflects this involvement. Put differently, itemizers may be more social capital rich.

But there is another more speculative factor that may explain the itemizer effect. Just as duty to rescue laws tell the apathetic bystander to intervene and help the stranger in distress when responsibility to help is diffuse (bystander effect), so it may be that itemizing tells the apathetic donor to give. The more people are prompted to give, as they are when they itemize and when they are embedded in social networks that ask them to give, the more often they give. On this explanation, itemizing functions as notice of the responsibility to give, in much the same way as norms and networks do in social capital rich communities. "Prompts" of this sort can resolve any confusion or ambivalence about who should do what. When the state offers a charitable deduction to itemizers, it puts them on notice of their responsibility, encourages pro-social behavior, rewards the performance of the responsibility and creates social trust and social capital.

On this hypothesis, the itemizer effect amounts to an override of donor apathy by assigning responsibility for charity to individual tax payers. If itemizing does serve as a "prompt" to give, then we have good reason to expand the reach of the deduction to non-itemizers because in doing so we would likely resolve their ambivalence and increase their giving. Even if this explanation of the itemizer effect is only a small part of the story, itemizing gives rise to increased giving and excluding non-itemizers may undermine social capital. If people with lower incomes give less than they would if they had an opportunity to itemize, and giving fosters social capital, non-itemizers may also lose the personal benefits of increased social capital. This would be unfortunate because they already have less social capital than the affluent, and are not as well positioned to compensate for that financially. (They cannot afford to install a security system, but instead rely on neighborhood watch.) To secure the benefits of the charitable deduction, however, we need not abandon the standard deduction altogether, thus forfeiting its administrative benefits, but we could adjust it to reflect the additional charitable deduction. In general, the charitable deduction seems to be a good way for society to increase both social capital and charitable contributions. The deduction acknowledges the importance of giving to others and signals state and community support for giving.

Charity without borders

The fruitfulness of social capital for collaboration and cooperation is clear – the need for global collaboration to solve global challenges is also clear. At present, however, the IRC may undermine both global social capital and global giving through its water's edge policy. As mentioned earlier in this chapter, according to this policy, in order for individuals or corporations to deduct their charitable gifts the recipients must be "created or organized in the United States."[17] This same restriction does not exist under gift and estate tax deductions. Although foreign charities are eligible to apply for exemption status, they are reluctant to do so because the laws are difficult and expensive for organizations in other countries to navigate.[18] There are countless charitable and not-for-profit organizations throughout the world to which donors may want to give money, and that are worthy of those donations, but for which donors would not receive a deduction, ranging from community centers for the elderly to schools for children with AIDS in some African villages. Some, but not all, of the restrictions can be circumvented by using intermediary organizations such as Oxfam and CARE. If we consider the water's edge policy through the lens of the expressive theory of law, we can gain insight into what meaning the policy might have. In a passage from the 1938 House Report some of that message is explicit:

> The exemption from taxation of money or property devoted to charitable and other purposes is based upon the theory that Government is compensated for the loss of the revenue by its relief from financial burden which would otherwise have to be met by appropriations from public funds, and by the benefits resulting from the promotion of the general

welfare. The United States derives no benefit from the gifts to foreign institutions, and the proposed limitation is consistent with the above theory.[19]

For Congress, the water's edge policy was adopted because the United States government has no duty toward foreign organizations from which tax payers could relieve the government when they make their charitable donation. More specifically, the requirement for public benefit goes as follows: "when the Government grants exemptions or allows deductions all tax payers are affected; the very fact of the exemption or deduction for the donor means that all tax payers can be said to be indirect and vicarious 'donors.' Charitable exemptions are justified because the exempt entity confers a public benefit."[20] In contrast, global giving is not regarded as a public benefit because it benefits people in other countries, and it would be unfair to compatriots (vicarious donors) because *they* forfeit the revenue. Although it is difficult to parse out the moral assumptions in this passage, the main underlying assumption is that our primary obligations are to compatriots. If one believes otherwise, that our obligations are not based on national affiliation but are cosmopolitan, then this provision is morally disconcerting.

The IRC also requires that organizations that qualify as charities for exemption purposes be consistent with public policy.[21] This requirement is nicely stated in *Bob Jones University v. The United States* in which the Supreme Court held that charitable organizations must meet a public policy requirement. At that time, Bob Jones University denied admission to anyone who was in an interracial marriage or who advocated interracial dating. According to the United States Supreme Court: "History buttresses logic to make clear that to warrant an exemption...an institution must...be in harmony with the public interest. The institution's purpose must not be so at odds with the common community conscience as to undermine any public benefits that might otherwise be conferred."[22] In addition, it is "long recognized in the law of trusts, that the purpose of a charitable trust may not be illegal or violate established public policy."[23] In the end, the Supreme Court revoked the charitable status of Bob Jones University because of its racist admission policies.

There are a few lessons to be drawn from these passages. According to law and legislative history, both reciprocity and public policy considerations justify the deduction. That rationale also serves as grounds for the water's edge policy. Because according to the standard explanation, the water's edge policy is based on the relief-of-government duty rationale, it is at risk of expressing the norm that neither the United States government, nor its citizens, has a duty to help people in other countries. It is also based on a now outdated notion of global connections. As Thomas Pogge underscores, we live in a world in which global systems are present. The suffering of people in distant countries is very often the result of structures we participate in and benefit from.[24] Today the United States and its citizens share many connections globally, while in 1917, when Congress justified the water's edge policy, there were few. Since many Americans already believe that charity begins (and ends) at home, the expressive content of the policy may only reinforce a norm to which we are already predisposed. Were the United States to lift the water's edge policy and treat foreign-based charities in much the same way it treats domestic ones, there is every reason to think that the former, like the latter, would be subject to the public policy requirement. If so, it would offer a considerable amount of protection against the possibility that the United States would end up extending exemption status to charities that are hostile to the interests of the United States.

Even if intermediary charities soften some of the impact of the water's edge policy on poor countries, the policy still consists in morally problematic expressive content that runs the risk of affirming the "charity begins at home" norm and undermining cosmopolitan ones. At the very least, the water's edge policy, combined with the congressional explanation, implies that our obligations to the distant are not the same as our obligations to our compatriots, because with respect to compatriots we stand to benefit while with respect to the distant we do not. Even if this claim were true in 1917, it is not true today in a global context; neither is it true for Pogge's global people whose lives transcend national boundaries. It is also not true insofar as "today" human beings participate in a single, global institutional scheme which draws on a system of "international law and diplomacy and a world market for capital goods and services."[25] If Pogge is right and we have one global system, then costs, benefits and obligations can no longer be assigned on the basis of nation states. If an organization's charitable status were informed by cosmopolitan ethics, the conception of community benefit would be comprehensive enough to see how helping the distant benefits us all as part of one global community.

The water's edge policy does not consist in only morally disconcerting expressive content. Although American tax payers are able to donate their money to international concerns through intermediary organizations, and to receive a deduction for those donations, some charities would not fall under the umbrella of an intermediary organization or have independent exemption status, including many that would meet the requirements of social benefit and public policy. In effect, the water's edge policy circumscribes the foreign charities to which donors can donate their money and in this way discourages global giving, and may thereby increase the likelihood that they will donate to charities organized in the United States. This is a greater hardship for some people than for others. Expatriates, for example, with emotional, cultural and filial obligations to their native countries may be uniquely burdened. They may have specific charitable organizations to which they want to donate money. The water's edge policy reduces the charitable options of transpatriates and discourages them from building social networks within multiple communities through gifting. By reducing the charitable venues to which people can donate money and build ties and bonds to other communities, it disincentivizes the creation of global social capital. Unable to deduct their gifts to non-qualifying distant charities, even when they meet the substantive requirements of exempt charities, some people may decide not to gift, or may find domestic charities where, from their perspective, their money goes further because of the deductibility of the gift.

Redrafting the water's edge policy, and placing some global giving on an equal footing with domestic giving, may result in some American money being diverted to foreign-based charities.[26] But it would also give donors more freedom to donate their charitable funds as they wish and it might induce greater giving overall as the deductible charitable options are enhanced. A substantial amount of international giving is through religious organizations and presumably that would continue. Other significant amounts of money go to environmental issues, development, humanitarian relief and human rights.[27]

More significantly, changing the water's edge policy may create a new group of donors. Those who have ties and loyalties with a number of political units, may want to give to the communities where they have those ties. At the same time, this new opportunity may facilitate additional charitable giving with an increased dollar amount. Pogge's global people, for example, may want to give directly to organizations within their multiple political milieu, and may be adept at doing so since they have established ties at the site of the charity. Our fund of global social capital would also benefit from building and reinforcing these global ties. Regardless of how trustworthy intermediary organizations are, the arm's length giving they encourage is unlikely to produce as much global social capital as direct giving through networks of multi-layered transnational relationships. Social capital is primarily the stuff of individuals and not organizations (though organizations can facilitate interactions among people). In any case, regardless of where the charitable organization is based, to qualify for exemption, it has to confer a social benefit and not a social harm, and it has to be consistent with the public policy of the United States and not the Taliban.

It might be argued that the water's edge policy is necessary because it has the potential to reduce some of the philanthropy-induced harms and at the same time to foster global social capital by making American donations especially visible.[28] But why suppose that United States based charities would be better equipped to reduce philanthropy-induced harms than those that are not? Some distant charities might well do a better job of serving their mission than qualifying charities. This might be so, for example, with respect to the environment and healthcare. Many philanthropy-related harms (such as waste and undercutting sustainable practices) have occurred under the very watch of the water's edge policy. In and of itself the water's edge policy is not a panacea against the harms associated with philanthropy, and intermediary organizations are not themselves immune from functioning as the source of those harms. Some of these harms may be the inevitable result of uncertainty and unpredictability. Others could be reduced with closer attention to the inadvertent harms that can attend philanthropy and aid.

Alternatively, one might take the position that, although the rationale for the water's edge policy is problematic, the practical implications of the policy are overall good because the policy provides the government with an opportunity to monitor foreign-based charities. Unfortunately, it isn't clear that these organizations – domestic or foreign – are carefully monitored. There are many domestic organizations such as hospitals, that enjoy tax exempt status and that don't deserve it, because they are profit oriented and offer little in the way of community benefit.[29] There are also many charities located on American soil that enjoy exemption and have had it suspended because of suspected terrorist activity. A partial list as of March 2009 includes the Al Haramain Islamic Foundation, located in Ashland Oregon, Rabbi Meir Kahane Memorial Fund, Cedarhurst New York and the Islamic American Relief Agency, Columbia Missouri.[30]

Focusing our attention on the site of an organization's origin, as the water's edge policy does, may divert it from identifying mechanisms that will solve the problem regardless of where the organization is based or organized. The solution to the problem of philanthropy's indirect harms is to give donors the tools they need to make careful and responsible decisions. There are many services that meet this need. Give Well and GlobalGiving.org are two examples. But these services need to be supplemented with something very much like a donor's checklist which would help to ensure responsible giving. To this end, a mechanism such as donor's due diligence would be helpful.[31] In the end, it really doesn't matter if more charitable dollars leave the United States, because if we take seriously Pogge's idea that we are cohabiting a "single global institutional scheme," the benefit to the distant will redound to others within that scheme.

If the United States were to modify its water's edge policy in the spirit of generalized giving, other countries may follow suit. Although it is unlikely that the United States would receive money for poverty relief (nor should it), it might receive donations for medical research and pharmaceutical innovation, to name two. Thus although some additional American funds may be sent outside the country, which would otherwise remain in the country, the United States might also receive an infusion of charitable monies from other countries that now have robust water's edge policies.

A recent case from the European Union can teach us much about amending the water's edge policy. On 27 January 2009, in an important case, *Hein Persche v. Finanzamt Ludenscheid*,[32] the Court of Justice, the highest court in the European Union, found that Germany's water's edge policy (as well as that of some other Member States) was in violation of Article 56 of the European Commission Treaty,[33] at the heart of which was a concern for the free movement of capital. The Court reasoned, among other things, that if Germany (and other Member States) did not extend a tax deduction for gifts to charities in other European Union states, it would impede donations (capital) to the other states and would undermine a guiding principle of the European Union: the free flow of capital. In this case, Hein Pershe, a German citizen and tax payer, had donated some toys and linens to a retirement home in Portugal, located close to where Mr Pershe owned a residence. When Pershe claimed the deduction on his German taxes, it was denied by the Finanzamt, largely because the recipient of the gift was not established in Germany (Germany's water's edge policy). The Court of Justice had the following to say:

> The fact remains that where a body recognized as having charitable status in a Member State satisfies the requirements imposed for that purpose by another Member State and where its object is to promote the very same interests of the general public, so that it would be likely to be recognized as having charitable status in the latter Member State, which is a matter for the national authorities of that same Member State, including its courts, to determine, the authorities of that Member State cannot deny that body the right to equal treatment solely on the ground that it is not established in that Member State.[34]

There are a few points to be gleaned from this case. First, it is noteworthy that states of the European Union are no longer permitted to preclude their tax payers from deducting a donation to a charity in another Member State solely because that charitable organization is established in the Member State. In other words, tax payers in Germany, as well as other European Union countries, can make direct contributions to charities in a number of other member countries and deduct those donations. Second, because the decision facilitates transnational giving it furthers the values inherent in cosmopolitan ethics. Third, the Court of Justice also found that the need of a Member State to "safe guard the effectiveness of fiscal supervision" of distant charities was not an adequate justification for maintaining a water's edge policy.[35] Thus the cosmopolitan thrust of the ruling is not overridden by either the need for monitoring or efficiency. The Court of Justice acknowledged that donors may be required by their tax authorities to provide evidence that the conditions of the deduction are met. Foreign charities would need to decide whether they are willing to provide the required documentation before accepting the donation. Fourth, the Court appears to believe that the legal mechanisms available to countries and their tax authorities are adequate protection against possible wrongdoing by charitable organizations, or at least that the values inherent in "the free movement of capital" are more important than any threats posed by lifting the water's edge policy. Fifth, the Court's decision provides an interesting model of the feasibility of a more open policy toward global giving. More speculatively, if we were to think about the law as a mechanism that can further global social justice, this decision can serve as an important step toward that goal.[36] There are obviously many differences between the United States and the European Union, but there are also many similarities. Following the European Union, the United States could modify its water's edge policy and broaden its use of the charitable exemption status, perhaps slowly, country by country, beginning with some of the Organization for Economic Cooperation and Development (OECD) countries. It would be morally preferable, however, to make the decision about which countries to exclude from the policy's reach on the basis of the country's need relative to other countries (with greater need giving rise to a stronger claim), and a calculation of the likelihood of successful charitable enterprises in that country. For example, a country's level of corruption and degree of political and organizational stability would be factors to take into account.

Hein Pershe shares some qualities with Pogge's global people: a citizen in one country, and a homeowner in another country, shifting wealth from one to another, thus breaking down some of the political barriers between each. Hein Pershe is not content simply to vacation in another country; he has a home in Portugal, and appears to have created social capital within the community. Insofar as giving helps to create and cement networks of trust and reciprocity among people (recall the oxytocin study), law that discourages global giving, especially global giving that stems from those relationships, unduly burdens the ability of global people to build transnational social capital and to implement a cosmopolitan conception of the good.

Consider again the rationale for the water's edge policy. According to the legislative history people, receive a tax deduction for charitable giving because they have relieved the government of a responsibility which it would otherwise have, and have conferred a social benefit. When people give to a charity that is not "created or organized" in the United States, the water's edge policy kicks in and they cannot deduct their contribution. Given this, many people would simply choose not to make the donation, and "professional donors" might simply ignore the possibility altogether, focusing their charitable dollars where they know they can deduct them. Others might seek out intermediary organizations that are created or organized in the United States and make their donation in that way. There are not, of course, mediating organizations for every charitable concern that tax payers have. And many donors may want to give to particular charitable organizations and not simply to charitable purposes. If the interests of intermediary organizations do not coincide with the donor's interests, the donor may find a domestic-based organization that will. But even if an intermediary organization can soften the impact of the water's edge policy on distant peoples in need, the rationale behind the policy will linger, be invoked by courts and help to shape future law and norms.

Social capital is created through social interaction, including one-on-one interactions and individual engagement. To create global social capital, we would have to overcome some obstacles associated with social capital within diverse groups. In an ideal world, if we want to use global giving as a way to cultivate global social capital we would, following Putnam's insights, encourage people to build networks with people from other countries, perhaps cultivate a more expansive identity so that they see themselves as members of a wider world. As their affinity with other peoples grew, so too would their transnational giving. Providing a charitable deduction that reflects and incentivizes global networks would not only facilitate global giving to the poorest members of our community but would also create social capital. Requiring an intermediary organization, on the other hand, could signal that charities which are not created or organized in the United States cannot be trusted, but require an intermediary. The more people travel, study, work and marry abroad, the more they are likely to want to contribute directly to distant countries and to control where their money goes. As they learn more about the world, experience some of the deprivations of the world as deprivations of *their* global community, their desire to give globally is likely to grow, and with that, social trust and global social capital. In the next chapter, I will consider the same line of reasoning in the context of international service. Withholding from them an opportunity to give directly to people in other countries will also reduce their opportunities to be fully engaged in the life of those people and communities. Unfortunately, the use of an intermediary organization can transform international giving into an arm's length transaction, in which we are at risk of conveying a norm of "Donor Beware."

There are some good counter arguments. I have made a number of empirical claims about the impact of various laws on social capital, and in this chapter about tax payers' beliefs. Although there are many studies about social capital, and some studies about social capital and philanthropy, there are no empirical studies to support some of the assertions about the impact of the law on social capital. On this matter, social capital is not alone, but in good company. Many claims about the impact of law on privacy, equality, liberty and the market do not have data to back them up. Nonetheless, courts do not refuse to consider empirical assertions about these norms in their determinations. Such studies could be done, and I believe that they should be done. But it would be a mistake to delay taking into account the impact of the law on social capital, and specifically global giving, until such studies are done. Global suffering is too great and the need to address it is too urgent to delay any longer. More expansive opportunities for global giving would also serve the liberty interests of American tax payers, especially for those who have cosmopolitan conceptions of the good. Although some people may not experience the water's edge policy as an interference in their liberty this may change as a more expansive conception of liberty evolves, one that coincides with a global vision.

My suggestions have been twofold. I have suggested that when a consideration of social capital is included as one canon among others in the determination of charitable tax law, there is good reason to think that the charitable deduction should be extended to non-itemizers. To my mind, the expressive content of the water's edge policy is harmful in a world in which global connections are important and global tensions high. Still, there are other considerations and other canons to take into account. It is possible that in determining whether to extend the deduction to non-itemizers and to modify the water's edge policy, other considerations would outweigh the significance of those discussed here.

In his book, *The Life You Can Save*, Peter Singer devotes an entire chapter to "Creating a Culture of Giving." He is to be applauded for recognizing the significance of culture for philanthropy. But creating a culture is a mammoth task which requires more than numerous individuals working independently committed to giving. It also requires a community in which the welfare of others is a primary concern; for that we need social capital and we need it on a global scale. To create a *culture* of global giving, we must first have a global culture in which there is some social cohesion and in which people with a cosmopolitan vision and trust care for one another enough to want to give to others. Recall the discussion in Chapter 2 of the oxytocin study in which giving signals trust in a stranger and, in turn, creates trust. Although there has been some disenchantment with micro financing, it may nonetheless be a good mechanism for creating global social capital. When people from rich countries lend money to people in poor countries for small business enterprises (solidarity groups), they signal their trust in these groups and create trust between the lender and borrower, rich country and poor country. A relationship is established.[37] The success of some micro financing may have to do with the trust and social capital that are created. Requiring an intermediary organization to stand between the donor and the receiver of money that goes directly to foreign charities can convey the message that foreign-based charities in particular need to be monitored, when the truth is that *all* charities need to be carefully monitored, and we need to develop better mechanisms for doing so.[38]

In a world in which parents still tell their children not to talk to strangers, and that charity begins at home, fear of strangers could lead to hunkering, rather than to a culture of global giving. Finally, it is helpful in thinking about the effect of law on global social capital to consider it not from the perspective of an American donor sending money across a vast ocean, but from the perspective of Pogge's global people – individuals who have a conception of the good that includes creating trust and social relationships with many people in many places. Similarly, when considering the mechanisms available to stimulate global giving it is important to consider them in comparison with the policy options most likely to be used for that purpose, such as the pornography of poverty.

7
Global People

Social networks are important for people and their communities. Throughout this book, I have suggested that social capital has a moral dimension that ought to be taken into account by individuals, organizations, governments and law. By increasing social networks, enhancing trust, cooperation and reciprocity, the principle of social capital would confer benefits such as good health, economic growth, safe neighborhoods and well-being for individuals, the community and globally. A moral commitment to promote and protect social capital would also help to weaken the hold self-interest has on our lives.

Understanding social capital as an ethical principle involves a shift in moral focus from individuals to collectives, putting "us" before "me." The question to be addressed in this chapter is: in what does "us" consist? Some of the categories on offer are small groups, such as friends, neighbors and families; large groups, such as cultures and compatriots, communities, nations and global affiliations. These are not mutually exclusive. Each of these "collections" can constitute "us." Many people have multiple networked groups to which they belong. Fortunately, because of social capital's rainmaker effect, those nearby can also enjoy the available social capital. Social capital is wonderfully versatile despite its vulnerability within diverse communities. In a global context, the moral principle of social capital can help us to become global citizens.

The potential for creating global social capital is viewed with skepticism in some quarters because of the challenge diversity poses for social capital. Nonetheless, Robert Putnam is optimistic about the possibility of creating social capital within diverse communities. In the last chapter of *Bowling Alone*, he states, "to build bridging social capital requires that we transcend social and political and professional identities to connect with people unlike ourselves."[1] Thomas Pogge provides some insight into how this might be accomplished. People living in a multilayered scheme, in which there are multiple identities, are much less likely to have prominent identifications or a single identity. Most importantly, given an array of possibilities, identities will not converge.[2] In the absence of convergence, the natural tendency to display in- and out-group bias will diminish. Whatever we can do to address both homophily and xenophobia will help to create both bridging and global social capital.

Putnam recommends team sports and art activities, such as group drawing and songfests, as a way to create social capital among diverse people within one nation.[3] I believe, however, that given the moral dimensions of social capital, and its importance for individual, community and global well-being, Putnam's approach is too modest. When we act for the sake of social capital, understood as a moral principle, we are bound to act impartially toward others. When we form social networks we would be morally required to welcome "strangers" and avoid the urge to choose our ties on the basis of homophily. A moral principle has the potential to be very effective in creating social capital because its reach is great and it would incentivize people to participate in many of the activities that Putnam and others recommend.

Laws that encourage people to help strangers, such as duty to rescue law and disability law, could help to transform our sense of what we owe to strangers. Because social capital can be built by creating a sense of *us* among people from within diverse groups, it is worth thinking about the "mechanics" of group identity and where social capital stands with respect to it.

I spoke at length about global social capital in Chapter 2. Let's return to that topic briefly, and with an emphasis on global networks. Koehn and Roseneu give the following detailed definition of global social capital:

> Our conceptualization of transnational capital encompasses both horizontal networks of civic engagement that band together by trust and reciprocation and the intercultural skills (human resources) possessed by participants. Transnational social capital – including "bridging social capital"

between government agencies, voluntary organizations and committee groups – facilitates global governance by expanding the scope of cooperative action and by minimizing transaction costs as well as the negative externalities produced when stakeholders pursuing self-interests become engaged in complex interdependencies.[4]

This definition includes networks, trust and reciprocity, familiar to us from the lean and mean definition. It adds intercultural skills and social capital among organizations. There are a number of contexts in which global social capital would be useful, and some in which it is already present. The international workforce creates and draws upon global social capital. Some of the contexts in which global people work are human rights agencies, such as those associated with the United Nations, and the Bretton Woods organizations, multinational organizations and NGOs. With respect to each of these, people from different countries work side by side, very often in a country which is unfamiliar to them, and in the global public domain. Together, people from different countries accomplish cooperative goals, create bonds, make friendships, sometimes marry, and create and exchange business and social opportunities. They go to conferences together and help one another. In global governance work, an international workforce meets frequently to work together on particular projects in order to make the world a better place.

The nature and duration of the ties that are formed vary. Some people become permanent expatriates, maintaining some ties at home and creating new ones in their chosen location. Some people relocate their families on a temporary basis to another country, maintaining ties in both places. Others, like Hein Persche, who challenged Germany's water's edge policy, maintain a primary home in one country, but spend months or weeks at a time over many years in another country. Some go to other countries to volunteer, others to study, others to work, some to vacation and others to marry. The variations are as great as one can imagine. For whatever reason people go, access to social capital is essential both while they are away and when they return, if they return. Some of this is explained by Arjun Appadurai's helpful concept of an ethnoscape:

> By ethnoscape, I mean the landscape of persons who constitute the shifting world in which we live: tourists, immigrants, refugees, exiles, guest workers and other moving groups and persons constitute the essential feature of the world, and appear to affect the politics of and between nations to a hitherto unprecedented degree. This is not to say that there are not anywhere relatively stable communities and networks, of kinship, friendship, of work and leisure, as well as of birth, residence, and other filiative forms. But this is to say that the warp of these stabilities is everywhere shot through with the woof of human motion, as more persons and groups deal with the realities of having to move, or the fantasies of wanting to move. What is more both these realities as well as these fantasies now function on larger scales, as men and women from villages in India think not just of moving to Poona or Madras,

but of moving to Dubai and Houston, and refugees from Sri Lanka find themselves in south India as well as Canada, just as the Hmong are driven to London as well as Philadelphia.[5]

These new people flows will require adjustment in how people interact with others, how they form their identities and in how we facilitate these new relations. Although there is some norm shifting under way as people begin to embrace norms that have a global reach, that shift will need support. It would be unfortunate if the many gains to be garnered from global living were to be outweighed by the losses – perhaps losses in belonging and personal happiness. Some people are concerned that global living will bring with it a loss to our sense of belonging: transpatriates may move about rudderless. Because the need to belong is great and universal, it is worth exploring whether global living necessarily involves deprivation of it.

Global belonging

In Chapter 4 we looked at the role culture plays in framing identities. There I suggested that social capital could do much of the work with respect to identity that is now assigned to culture. Here I focus on the need to belong and show that social capital can satisfy it. There are similarities in the questions raised by both belonging and identity. But the question of what role culture plays in framing our identities, and what choices we have, is conceptually different from concerns about how to satisfy our need to belong.

Let's begin with an overview of what belonging is and what it means to people. Then I will consider the implications of these insights for global belonging. In a now classic paper, Baumeister and Leary review studies on the need to belong.[6] Although there is a lot of research on this area, the conclusion to be drawn is that, because people have a strong need to belong, they put considerable effort into creating the social bonds that will meet this need. The need to belong is often satisfied by groups. People go out of their way to create groups to which they can belong. Studies on intergroup bias were designed to understand what factors create in-groups. Social psychologist Henri Tajfel set up groups based on factors so trivial that the qualities inherent in the groups themselves would not generate any favoritism. That is, groups were not based on anything potentially meaningful, such as religion or ethnicity. Tajfel found that simply being in a group, even one based on arbitrary and trivial factors such as a coin toss, was enough to generate in-group favoritism.[7] One study conducted by Locksley, Ortiz and Hepburn found that random assignment to a group was enough to generate in-group favoritism, which took the form of sharing rewards and categorizing people according to the group.[8] The consensus of a number of studies is that it takes very little for people to form attachments, though proximity is important. When there are differences among people, such as race or age, people who are counted as friends are far more likely to have lived very close by. In another study, Wilder and Thompson found that people come to have good views of whoever they are close to, even with respect to previously disliked or out-group members. Moreover, in-group bias decreased as contact with out-groups increased. Baumeister and Leary conclude as follows:

> In brief, people seem widely and strongly inclined to form social relationships quite easily in the absence of any special set of eliciting circumstances or ulterior motives. Friendships and group allegiances seem to arise spontaneously and readily, without needing evidence of material advantage or inferred similarity. Not only do relationships emerge quite naturally, but people invest a great deal of time and effort in fostering supportive relationships with others. External threat seems to increase the tendency to form strong bonds.[9]

This research suggests that it doesn't take much in the way of shared traits to create groups and the attending favoritism. Simply being assigned to a group can be enough to generate preference for the group. Threats to the group can bolster solidarity, and sometimes out-groups can be created for that very purpose. Proximity and contact are especially important for group affiliation – indeed, contact with out-group members can override bias against out-groups. It may turn out that culture and community are important because they facilitate interaction, and not because they are intrinsically meaningful. The observation that contact with "strangers" can override bias against them should give us reason to be optimistic. Homophily may be a human tendency but it does not seem to be inevitable.

As transnational people navigate multiple milieux, their bias both for their own group and against out-groups will dissipate. Rigid boundaries around groups seem to melt as people interact with strangers. According to Baumeister and Leary's belonging hypothesis, human culture is "adapted to enable people to satisfy the psychological need to live together.... We suggest that belongingness can be almost as compelling a need as food and that human culture is significantly conditioned by the pressure to provide belongingness."[10] Groups are important because they satisfy a need to belong and anchor individuals' identities as belonging to particular groups.

It is by no means obvious from the research, however, that the need to belong is best satisfied by a nation-based culture. The need to belong might be satisfied by other cultures, multiple political units, colleges, families, professional affinities, book clubs or a few friends. This overview of the social science research also suggests that people readily form groups, with in-group preferences, and that they don't need much in the way of shared qualities to do this. People are likely to build social networks wherever they are. Given this, it does not seem that transnational living must involve a loss in belonging.

Although cultures have traditionally met the need to belong, they can also give rise to problems. Because one of the ways to create in-groups is to create out-groups, excluding others may be inherent to groups. Unfortunately, in-group bias can lead to ethnocentrism. Sometimes, people discriminate against people in other groups in order to preserve their own group. Creating out-groups may be one mechanism people use to satisfy their need to belong.

According to social identity theory, people achieve a positive social identity by identifying with a group, and then ensure that their group does better than other groups.[11] Studies show that even when group members are trying to be fair in the distribution of rewards between in-groups and out-groups, they ensure that their group receives more rewards. Social psychologists view conflict as an inherent part of social categorization. They also believe that "decategorization" is the key to minimizing conflict: by reducing the salience of existing social categories, conflict between and among groups may be minimized.[12] Decategorization of this sort can be achieved through a more fluid, multilayered approach to identity.

Collectives that can meet people's belonging needs, but which do not generate conflict with respect to out-groups, would address the problems inherent in group categorization. Social capital might provide a solution. Because social capital is lodged in social networks, it has the potential to satisfy the need to belong. Yet because it emphasizes social networks per se, and not particular ones such as American, French, Jewish or Muslim, it decategorizes at the same time as it connects people to one another. The tension between the need for groups, for the sake of belonging, and the inherent difficulties associated with categorization, should make us question categorization. I believe that the networks of social capital are a morally important alternative to culturally based social identities and other potentially harmful categories. If, as I propose, we treat social capital as a moral principle and the creation of social capital a moral obligation, then we will also be obligated to create networks, trust and reciprocity impartially, without regard for nationality, religion or skin color, among others. On my view, our identities would be fluid, tied loosely to the various networks that form around our activities and lives. People would come to value others because of their place in the network and the opportunity to cooperate with them.

Given the inherent problems with categorization and the history of cultural conflict, we need to be skeptical about culture. Cultures may be a quick, ready and convenient way that people form identities and satisfy their need to belong. But they don't appear to be a morally necessary way to achieve either. Amartya Sen makes the point that most people have multiple identities, and the importance of these may vary with context.[13] No doubt if one has many identities, the importance of any one of them becomes less central to identity formation. In this way, the salience of any one category can be reduced.

A moral commitment to build global social capital would also be helpful. Putting people together, including people who are different from each other, is often enough to begin to build the social bonds that will constitute a network, satisfy the need to belong and create bridging social capital. Given the very strong desire to belong, people appear to do what it takes to form belonging relationships. This bodes well for global social capital and global citizenry. Global living need not entail a sacrifice of belonging. The human desire to belong is itself an incentive for people to create ties, even when it may be difficult to do so because of cultural difference and ethnocentrism. As the flows of global culture become more relevant to people's lives, they will create networks that span the globe.

As we saw in Chapter 4, some philosophers treat culture as morally special because of the role they believe it plays in grounding identities. Liberals value culture because it affords meaningful choices to people as they ground their identities. But what the research of the social sciences suggests is that people may identify with cultures because of their need to belong and the availability of culture. Because culture is ready made, there for the taking, people may adopt a cultural identity without much deliberation. This, incidentally, is exactly the opposite of what is imagined by liberals who support culture for the sake of autonomy and self-determination.

In a global era, people have more options, both culturally and otherwise, from which to choose to ground their identities and satisfy their belonging needs. Indeed, given what we know about in-groups and out-groups, and the risks associated with group affiliation, we would be far better off satisfying the need to belong in other ways. Multiple belongings, of the sort Pogge proposes,[14] are one way to do that because they satisfy the need to belong, while the multiplicity factor minimizes the importance of any one category, thus achieving decategorization. Multiple identities of this kind create groups of people with diverse identities, thereby mixing up in-group and out-group folks. Add to this the impact of recent demographics and the rise of multiracial identities, the notion of a single identity, as we have known it, may be a fading memory. Forging social ties, guided by the moral principle of social capital, will ensure that we do not revert to choosing our networks on the basis of homophily and ethnocentrism. In many respects, belonging, and the social connections that are created in its service, are a component of social capital – namely, networks, trust and reciprocity.

Although people form groups easily, they are sometimes reluctant to leave them. Furthermore, people appear to want only so much "belonging." Social psychologists refer to this as satiation and substitution.[15] People are satiated when the motive to create new bonds is decreased because they have their belonging needs met. With respect to satiation, studies show that people prefer a few close and good relationships to a high quantity of relationships. At a certain point, when people's need to belong is met, they no longer seek new relationships. People also substitute new relationships when the old ones don't meet their needs. One study found that when married women's need to belong was not being met by their spouse, they sought other relationships. In other words, they found substitutions. In a study of old women, researchers found that elderly women with adult children rely more heavily on their adult children for social ties. Their happiness was tied to their relationships with their offspring and not very much with other relationships. In the case of old women who did not have adult children, happiness did correlate with quality and quantity of social relations. The researchers concluded that social interaction with children is "exchangeable and interchangeable."[16] If we do not know from experience we know from common knowledge that people, for example transpatriates, migrants and refugees, leave behind old ties, and create new ones, or they maintain both. Baumeister and Leary conclude that the need to belong is satisfied when there are: (1) frequent, pleasant and positive interactions with the same person, and (2) these interactions take place in a context of long-term caring and concern.

Let's think about the implications of these findings for the prospect of both global social capital and global citizenry. The drive to create social bonds, even in the presence of cultural difference, bodes well for the possibility of global social capital. People can and do go to new countries and they can and do form new social bonds, and those bonds are a component of global social capital. The fundamental human need to "belong" ensures that people create new ties of affection. In some instances, these new transnational ties will be facilitated by the capacity of people to find substitutes for bonds that no longer exist or are inadequate to meet their need to belong. At the same time, people can become satiated with respect to their social ties, which may make it difficult to maintain many ties worldwide. The studies do not appear to indicate how much "belongingness" people need before satiation is triggered. If people need a daily dose of "belongingness" and they are living abroad, or living in multiple countries, whether they create new belonging relationships may depend on some of the details about the need. We know that belonging relationships surface in the context of frequent caring interactions. Presumably, if those interactions exist in a variety of countries, belonging relationships would as well, even if they were maintained in multiple countries simultaneously.

Social capital does not consist only in networks and social relationships. It also requires trust and reciprocity. Trust will likely surface once there are relationships in place that are persistent enough to give rise to belonging. As we saw in Chapter 2, an exchange of gifts can create trust and oxytocin. Promoting social capital as a moral principle can be helpful here. However, global social capital requires a norm that supports ties among strangers. Not only has there been a strong anti-stranger norm, encapsulated in the expression "don't talk to strangers," which must be overcome, but there has also been a strong preference for kin, encapsulated in the norm "family first." As we saw, bystanders often don't help strangers in distress, especially in the presence of a crowd of bystanders. In Chapter 5, I suggested that duty to rescue laws would support helping strangers. There are other things we could do to encourage people to help strangers. In addition to changing the default on organ donation cards so that people automatically give their organs to strangers in need unless they specifically opt out, we could create more open immigration policies, allowing people, including refugees and the global homeless, to immigrate with ease and to access healthcare once they have arrived. As Wendy Parmet points out, "by interconnecting the world's economies and cultures, globalization has necessarily increased the health interdependency of every human population on the planet."[17] International law could do more to create obligations to strangers, such as providing them with life-saving medicines.[18] In Chapter 6, I took the view that changing the water's edge policy would encourage global giving. There are many places where we treat strangers differently – and detrimentally – but where we could be more helpful and welcoming. Communicating the message that it is morally desirable to help strangers will make a difference, and including the "other" in our gatherings will be important for creating both bridging social capital and global social capital.

It is a propitious time for people to establish global social networks. There are hundreds of opportunities to help people globally. Universities abound with opportunities for students to study and intern abroad. Unfortunately, at present only those with the financial wherewithal to undertake these opportunities are able to do so. Global experiences are still reserved for elites who have the time and money to participate in them, and are relatively rare for others. Still, the demand for global experience is great and the need enormous.

To function well and morally in a global era, people need to be culturally competent with respect to multiple cultures. Tolerance and appreciation for differences will follow from international experiences and cultural competence. Civic virtues could be associated not with one nation, and love of country, but with the world, and pride could be associated with global governance institutions, such as the United Nations and the Universal Declaration of Human Rights. Stephen Castles and Alastair Davidson believe that the virtues inherent in social capital are ideal to advance globalization. According to them, "the new virtues, when combined, are the social capital that makes it possible to resolve differences by seeing what is common to all neighbors."[19] Castles and Davidson ask how to create the values inherent in social capital in the absence of a history of those civic virtues. The answer to this question lies in how we understand and treat the concept of social capital. When we view social capital as a moral principle, the values inherent in it are action guiding.

Global culture

Today, many people flourish in the midst of a global culture. Typically, culture is associated with a common language, customs and history. As we saw in Chapter 4, these shared activities can ground identities, satisfy a need to belong, provide spectacles through which people view their options, and may give meaning to their choices and lives. I have suggested that many of the good things associated with culture can be accomplished through social capital. But I am not advocating that nation-based cultures be abandoned. In addition to the possibility of multiple belongings, a vibrant global culture is emerging to which people can belong. Cultural flows, enabled by high speed transit and communications, combined with migration, have created a world in which cultural hybrids are becoming the norm. Global culture is among those hybrids.

According to Held and McGrew, cultural practices can be actively imported, or slowly and unconsciously digested through repeated contact.[20] Popular culture is global. World tours of celebrities such as Shakira and U2 are evidence of the global spread of popular culture. Held and McGrew describe the various mechanisms through which cultural flows travel. For example, in 1982 there were 12.7 billion international call minutes. By 1992 there were 42.7 billion call minutes, and by 1996 there were 67.5 billion.[21] Most of this telephone traffic exists in rich countries, in particular North America, Japan and Europe. There has also been a global explosion in cell phone use. As of 2010, there were 4.6 billion mobile phone subscriptions worldwide. More than half of the people in the developing world now have cell phones and the use of this technology is expected to continue at a remarkable pace in the developing world.[22] Internet use has also exploded enabling global communication. For many, internet call services such as Skype have replaced the telephone for international calls. By 1996 there were 12.8 million internet hosts, and by 2000 over 100,000 million users worldwide. As of June 2010, there were 1.97 billion internet users worldwide.[23] This explosion in transnational communication suggests that there is also shared language. Although English is the main individual language for global business, politics, administration, science, academia and popular culture, bilingualism and multilingualism are also prevalent. The value of access to wireless communications in poor countries should not be underestimated. Cell phones bring various global flows within the reach of people living in developing countries, including banking and better healthcare. As we saw in Chapter 2, when we considered the Twitter Revolution, cell phones are crucial for global activism.

Global entertainment, television and news are dominated by about 30 companies, which include media giants such as Time Warner, Disney, Sony and Universal, among others. They embrace different sectors: newspapers, news gathering, magazine and book publishing, television production and broadcasting, film production and distribution, video sales and rentals, and recorded music.[24] Radio and music were easily globalized because they do not depend on written or spoken language for their expressions.[25] The global music industry consists in multinational corporations that produce and market global music, including world music. Although the musical preferences of American youth and culture constitute a large part of this output, both Western and world music have some global representation.[26]

Film has also been globalized. International cooperatives produce films and distribute them internationally to many cultures. The presence of a "star" will give a film global appeal. Although Hollywood dominates the global film market, Japan, South Korea, Hong Kong and India also produce a large number of films. Combined with deregulation, this has given rise to a global market for television. Television has been more challenging to globalize because of the financial outlay needed to purchase a television. Yet televisions appear in the poorest African villages. Nonetheless, technological changes, and new websites such as Hulu, will make the need for a television irrelevant.

Many of the standard indices of culture are present in the emerging global culture. There is a common language, though also national languages. There are shared customs, such as the Olympics and the World Cup. There are also shared celebrations, such as those that revolve around International Nelson Mandela Day, International Women's Day, International Peace Day and Earth Day. There are shared industries and shared global governance institutions, for example the United Nations and international courts. There are also shared norms, such as norms about human rights, democracy, genocide and fair business practices, and norms against human trafficking, child labor and the use of child soldiers. Much of the work crafting and implementing these norms occurs in the global public domain. There is also shared law, and tribunals to enforce it. Many of the ingredients of culture are present in our global culture. Whether we like the current global culture or not, it is difficult to deny its existence.

Global living

Let's look more closely at the demands of global living to see what role social capital plays in it. National boundaries are porous and, for many people, less relevant today to what is meaningful. Arjun Appadurai's notion of global cultural flows can help us to see at a glance the different dimensions that global life takes. Appadurai has identified five *scapes* through which cultural material flows across borders. (1) Ethnoscape consists in shifting people around the world, such as workers, tourists, immigrants and refugees (and is familiar to us from an earlier discussion). (2) Technoscape consists in high speed technology that crosses boundaries and facilitates the global economic reach. (3) Financescape is the international monetary system which includes economies, markets and capital. (4) Mediascape consists in the stream of images and information through print, television, film and other media. (5) Ideoscape is the flow of values, such as norms, rights and democracy.[27] These five scapes create global pathways that generate global networks, which, in turn, require trust, reciprocity, cooperation and collaboration.

Given these scapes, the knowledge and skills that enable them are enormously important. Unfortunately, despite the increase in global communications, access to global networks and the knowledge and skills needed to negotiate them is disproportionately possessed by a white, well-educated elite.[28] Too great an emphasis on nationally fixed cultural identity, when culture is embracing global dimensions, may exacerbate unequal access to a global life. There is a risk that the poor will be left behind in culturally fixed, "nation-based" ghettos, while privileged elites enjoy the global good life.

Global living often revolves around transnational networks facilitated by shared interests, partnerships and collaborations on cooperative projects. Geographic proximity is less significant for people who enjoy global networks. People with transnational competencies will fare better than those without them. Researchers have found that transnational analytical skills give global people the ability to interpret the beliefs, practices and cultural messages of other societies. People need to be able to detect potential tensions and junctures for collaboration.[29] They must also have transnational emotional skills, which include sensitivity and identity. Emotional competence is facilitated by a desire to learn from unfamiliar cultures, a capacity to maintain respect for multiple and diverse values, beliefs and traditions, and a capacity to manage multiple identities, both of one's self and of others. Some of the identities one might need to negotiate are national, multiple political units, world citizenship, ethnicities, religious affiliations, gender, professional and organizational.[30] People with fluid and dynamic self-conceptions will be able to maintain some coherence within this variation. Self-confidence in transnational settings is also important.

Many people have many of these skills: there is a large group of transpatriates who participate in multiple transnational networks and global groups. They do not identify primarily with a sending nation or a receiving one; nor are they limited by a nation state skill set. Transpatriates retain loose contacts with many people in many places. According to Koehn and Rosenau, "transmigrant transpatriates acquire multiple-place consciousness and, thus, 'feel at home' in the globalized space where they live." They typically engage with a transcultural reference group where norms transcend national boundaries.[31] Like Pogge's global people, they have political affinities in many places. Global governance mechanisms, interacting in the global public domain, will continue to evolve to facilitate these networks and flows. To minimize the risk that global benefits will be disproportionately enjoyed by elites, Koehn and Rosenau recommend transnational social capital to expand the scope for cooperative action and minimize self-interested actions.

These goals are more likely to be achieved if we recognize and act on the moral dimension of social capital. I have suggested that transnational social capital can be important globally because it is silent about specific social ties, and is able to embrace social networks consisting in diverse people. When we understand social capital as a moral principle, it triggers the duty to act impartially with respect to creating the social ties that are at the heart of social capital. A moral obligation to consider social capital would implore people to promote social networks worldwide, build trust among diverse people and cooperate impartially. In the face of international conflict, global social capital would replace national interest with a global interest in cooperation and international harmony. Although many people now create social capital within particular, bordered communities, this can change as people find themselves drawn to distant places. Social capital is porous; it will develop globally as people do.

Intuitively, we know that social capital is morally important when we consider the good things that it facilitates, ranging from global health and well-being, to safe neighborhoods, democratic participation and effective government. Access to social capital is important for justice and global well-being. It bears repeating, given that the poor have limited access to financial and human capital, their need for social capital is great. Their deprivations will only increase if they also experience network poverty and are also excluded from social capital. A moral principle that imposes an obligation on us to create social capital impartially will make it more difficult to exclude the poor and others who are on the fringes of social networks. It implores us to find a place for them in our networks. Were we instead to add to the vulnerabilities of the poor a deprivation in global social capital, people who are already marginalized would only be more so, layering deprivation upon deprivation.

If we do not treat social capital as a moral concept, we thereby forfeit its potential as a mechanism for reducing the harms associated with social capital – the tendency to create networks based on homophily and to exclude those who are different. The question that needs to be asked is whether or not, given the harms associated with homophily and rigid boundaries, we can afford not to treat social capital as a moral principle. Leaving people to their own choices, without moral guidance, may invite entrenchment and rigid group identification, when what we most need is openness to global possibilities and fluidity with respect to individual identity.

Global citizens

Although there are a variety of ways that people negotiate global living, good citizenship practices are essential. But what exactly is a "global citizen"? By most accounts, global citizens are part of something beyond the nation state; they are part of humanity. The term "global citizen" can be understood descriptively to refer to people who are members of a global village, and it can be understood as a normative position, prescribing certain conduct. As global citizens, people have citizenship duties that extend beyond their own nation. They also have rights and entitlements. Typically, they have duties of knowledge, competency and civic engagement. These responsibilities are equally important for global citizens.

People have universal rights under the Universal Declaration of Human Rights. Do they have duties? There is an array of global moral obligations that people and institutions have, including negative duties not to cause global harm, and the corresponding obligation to rectify the harms caused.[32] There are also positive duties to assist those in need[33] and obligations of global civic engagement. An upward trend in international volunteering suggests that people believe they have international responsibilities. Many people give globally and many others volunteer their time and skills globally. In Chapter 6, we saw that, although global giving is extensive, it could be increased by modifying water's edge policies. Although controversial, micro financing is another good example of how people can help the distant poor in a way that is personally engaged. International volunteering takes individual engagement with distant strangers a step further than either charity or micro financing.

International volunteering is promising as a mechanism to promote global social capital. It is not only good for individuals but it also facilitates effective international relations. Over the years, however, the Peace Corps, the primary government venue for international service in the United States, has decreased the number of people it sends overseas to the point that in 2010 only 8,000 volunteers were sent to 77 countries. In the summer of 2010, however, the Sargent Shriver International Service Act called for a doubling of Peace Corps volunteers by 2015.[34] It also established 10,000 Global Service Fellowships in order to build international social and multilateral service opportunities in which volunteers work side by side with people from host and other countries.

Although the number of volunteers the Peace Corps sends out has declined, there has been a proliferation of privately sponsored international volunteering opportunities. In 2008, 1 million Americans participated in these. This increase reflects the rise of the first global generation. Inexpensive global transportation, global media, communications and the rise of gap years and sabbaticals have also helped. International volunteering is valued for confidence building, skills transfer, the social connections formed by volunteers, and the diversity of skills and talents of volunteers. People also seem to enjoy it. Volunteer tourism has exploded, providing people with countless opportunities to engage in morally responsible and meaningful travel during their vacations, sabbaticals and retirement years.

Just as volunteering signals the presence of social capital domestically, international service reflects the presence of global social capital. It creates links between organizations and communities, provides knowledge about globalization and development, trains people how to work effectively in a global economy and allows them to engage with people in developing countries. It builds cultural competency and fights racism and xenophobia.[35]

International ties, which are key to cooperative action and the flow of information, are also created by international service. As volunteers help people in other countries, they create and cement trust and generalized reciprocity. International service creates a "virtuous cycle" of social interaction in which volunteers engage with local people, create trust and build a sense of shared citizenship that goes beyond countries. In forging these transnational networks, building trust and generalized reciprocity among people from multiple countries, global social capital is created. The social networks created through these efforts ensure that ideas and perspectives are shared internationally. International service also facilitates an awareness of mutual rights and responsibilities, fosters transferable skills and creates a society that goes beyond the nation state and people who are comfortable working in such a society.[36] It gives people opportunities to engage globally.

Although there are enormous international benefits from international service, there are also domestic benefits. People who have participated in international volunteering return home more comfortable with different cultures than when they left. Helping people in other countries can also enhance reservoirs of bridging social capital in sending countries. People returning from international service have a new respect and appreciation for different cultures, and greater empathy for the poor and vulnerable in other countries. International volunteering creates global social capital by forging new social networks among people from different countries. It fosters generalized reciprocity among people from different countries, creates trust and cooperative activity.

There are many reasons why people volunteer. "Giving back" figures importantly for volunteers in the same way it does for people who donate money to charities. In the United States, one of the differences between service and charity is that when money is donated the donor can receive a tax deduction, while when she gives her time and skills, she does not. A similar deduction or tax credit for time spent volunteering could incentivize international service, and would signal an important message about our international obligations. Naturally this would only be true if there were no water's edge policy to block the deduction or credit.

Volunteering time, as a supplement to donating money, can create global social capital because service involves social interaction. According to the old adage, "time is money," giving time to a charity has value in much the same way that money has value. In fact, if volunteer work, which fosters transnational relationships, creates greater social capital than donating money, it may create more value than a monetary donation. If it does, and a tax deduction incentivizes service, then creating a deduction for volunteer service would be a promising strategy for international development, among other things. Some of the same rationale that justifies the charitable deduction for the donation of money would also apply to volunteering. As we discussed in Chapter 6, charitable giving is deducted on the grounds that the government is relieved of a burden it would otherwise have. International volunteers undertake tasks for global good that would otherwise fall on governments, and that very often serve to fulfill human rights, such as the right to health. International service may create even more benefits for sending countries than do charitable donations because volunteers also bring something back to their home countries. International volunteers can be viewed as ambassadors who represent their countries, create global good will and facilitate international relations. International service also promotes global knowledge, cultural competence and respect for difference – all of which are to the benefit of both the volunteer's sending country and the country where the service takes place. Even if donations to foreign-based charities are thought not to qualify for the charitable deduction because they do not relieve government of a burden it would otherwise have, international service should be considered independently because of the substantial benefits a volunteer confers on her home country.

In the United States, one of the main objections to the charitable tax deduction is that it favors the wealthy.[37] Not only are the rich most likely to take advantage of the deduction, they also receive more of a deduction given greater income. People with lower incomes might donate time instead of money, if only because they have more of one than the other. By extending a deduction or tax credit to volunteers we would further principles of reciprocity. Governments might also exempt volunteers from paying real property tax. Various states in the United States have extended tax benefits to volunteer firefighters.[38] Some combination of these with respect to international service would encourage people to volunteer to help distant strangers and build much needed global social capital. One counter argument to this proposal is based on a concern with monitoring volunteers and determining the value of their time. But this efficiency-based concern should not automatically trump considerations of reciprocity and social capital. If we take the moral value of social capital into consideration, efficiency may need to be reconsidered in light of the potential of service to build social capital. If we add to that calculation the great contribution that international service can make to our scarce, but urgently needed, reservoir of global social capital, a deduction, credit or exemption for service may well be justified. There are, of course, other things we could do to encourage international service. Students could be given course credit for international service. National governments could enact mandatory international service requirements and sponsor international volunteerism. President Barack Obama's Give Act is a good example. It promises to increase the number of volunteers from 75,000 to 250,000 and includes both domestic and international service.[39]

Martha Nussbaum believes that education can serve an important role in creating global citizens. Although she recognizes the importance of local identifications for people, she supports a cosmopolitan education in which students "learn to recognize humanity wherever they encounter it, undeterred by traits that are strange to them."[40] Nussbaum believes that the focus of our educational efforts should be world citizenship, rather than democratic or national citizenship. In this way, people would gain greater personal insight, and would begin to question their preferences and practices in a less biased fashion. It would also provide people with an opportunity to engage more fully with people from other cultures, preparing them to problem-solve when international cooperation is needed. For Nussbaum, knowledge about the world helps people to recognize their obligations to others. In the end, she believes: "We should also work to make all human beings part of our community of dialogue and concern, base our political deliberations on that interlocking commonality, and give the circle that defines our humanity special attention and respect."[41] Education is important for creating good global citizens. But we will also need massive amounts of global social capital in order to participate in a global conversation and enjoy helping our fellow human beings.

This book began with examples of urgent social problems, and evidence of indifference to them: chronic severe poverty, global and domestic homelessness and abandoned strangers in distress. I have made the case that understanding social capital as a moral principle could help to transform *indifference to others* to *concern and care* for them. Social capital identifies social relationships as important. In this way it shifts the focus from individuals and self-interest to social networks and social good. With increased social interaction comes trust, reciprocity, cooperative action and, in the end, the many benefits that social networks can produce. The emerging global culture and an increase in international volunteerism is good evidence of the existence of global citizens and of the desire to help strangers. Although there are many reasons why people volunteer internationally, including some self-interested ones, for most volunteers helping the most vulnerable members of our global community is uppermost in their minds. People who volunteer internationally trust distant others enough to live with them in their communities, befriend them, enjoy day-to-day activities with them and endure daily hardships as they work side by side. Those who invite volunteers to help them, and welcome them to their homes, show the same spirit of global citizenship. International volunteering, global giving and global lending build trust, foster generalized reciprocity and create valuable global social capital.

As Thomas Pogge has made clear, global poverty exists largely because of the global system we have created and maintained, in violation of our negative duty not to cause harm. Establishing structures, institutions and incentive mechanisms that favor the global poor will ultimately require a moral mindset that looks away from national and personal self-interest and toward transnational trust and cooperation. Taking social capital into account as a moral obligation will place it in the public's discourse, and then into the global public domain. Once there, social capital can help to ensure protection of global public goods, such as health and the environment. I have suggested that in many ways social capital is more than one principle among others. The principle of social capital is the moral sweet spot. It is difficult for human beings to watch people suffer. Shifting our moral focus to *us* brings people who were previously invisible, whether the distant poor or the local homeless, within our range of vision, making it easier to treat them morally. It is much harder to be indifferent to the suffering of those with whom we are connected than those with whom we have no connection. A moral duty to promote social capital underscores the moral value of connection to others. Focusing on social capital will invite us to value others, and what we can do together as we now value individuals. Being mindful of the moral obligation to create global social capital will be an important step toward realizing our global obligations and creating global social justice.

Because social ties are important for happiness and well-being, the social capital we create both locally and transnationally will increase our well-being. Emotional contagion ensures that our personal well-being will affect not only ourselves but those with whom we are networked. As those networks become global, so too for well-being. Promoting social capital will create other kinds of value as well, some of which is unimaginable to us now. Social networks are vital for the flow of ideas and information, both of which will create new ways to provide food and water to the global poor, and medicine to the global sick. The moral principle of social capital can increase social networks and the many good things that flow through them.

Notes

Foreword

1. Data from Branko Milanovic, principal economist in the World Bank's Development Research Group, e-mail of 25 April 2010. The data cover the period from 1988 to 2005, also showing that the share of the poorer half of humanity declined from 3.53 to 2.92 percent of global household income in 2005. Milanovic is the leading authority on the measurement of inequality, and his published work contains similar albeit somewhat less updated information. See his "True World Income Distribution, 1988 and 1993: First Calculation Based on Household Surveys Alone," *The Economic Journal* 112 (2002), 51–92; *Worlds Apart: Measuring International and Global Inequality* (Princeton, NJ: Princeton University Press 2005); and *The Haves and the Have-Nots: A Brief and Idiosyncratic History of Global Inequality* (New York: Basic Books 2011).

2. Data from the United Nations Population Division, World Population Prospects, the 2010 revision, available at http://esa.un.org/unpd/wpp/Excel-Data/fertility.htm, and from Central Intelligence Agency, The World Factbook, at https://www.cia.gov/library/publications/the-world-factbook/rankorder/2127rank.html.

3. Gunnar Heinsohn, "Exploding Population," *The New York Times*, 7 January 2008, and Central Intelligence Agency, The World Factbook, Kenya, at https://www.cia.gov/library/publications/the-world-factbook/geos/ke.html, under "People."

4. UN News Centre, "Global Population to Pass 10 Billion by 2100, UN Projections Indicate," available at http://www.un.org/apps/news/story.asp?NewsID=38253&Cr=Population&Cr1=.

5. Judith Warner, "The Charitable Giving Divide," *New York Times Magazine*, 20 August 2010.

6. Lucy Ward, "Poor Give More Generously than the Rich," *Guardian*, 21 December 2001.

213

7. Christian Barry and Gerhard Øverland, "Why Remittances to Poor Countries Should Not Be Taxed," *New York University Journal of International Law and Politics* 42:4 (2010), 1181–207.
8. This includes about $212 billion from individuals directly, $41 billion from foundations, $23 billion from bequests and $15 billion from corporations. Data from the *Giving USA 2011 Report* (June 2011), summarized at http://www.nptrends.com/nonprofit-trends/giving-usa-2011-report.htm.

Introduction

1. A. Stratton, "David Cameron Aims to Make Happiness the New GDP," *Guardian* (UK), 14 November 2010, accessed 15 March 2011, http://www.guardian.co.uk/politics/2010/nov/14/david-cameron-wellbeing-inquiry.

1 Making a Difference

1. A. Shah, "Poverty Facts and Stats," last modified 20 September 2010, http://www.globalissues.org/article/26/poverty-facts-and-stats.
2. Ibid.
3. Ibid.
4. The United Nations Refugee Agency, "UNHCR Annual Report Shows 42 Million People Uprooted Worldwide," 16 June 2009, accessed 19 February 2011, http://www.unhcr.org/4a2fd52412d.html.
5. Declaration of Human Rights, G.A. Res, 217A, at 71, U.N. GAOR, 3d Sess., 1st plen. mtg., U.N. Doc. A/810.
6. E. Posner and C. R. Sunstein, "Climate Change Justice," *The Georgetown Law Journal* 96:5 (2008): 1567.
7. K. Dumbaugh and W. Morrison, "SARS, Avian Flu, and Other Challenges for China's Political, Social, and Economic Transformation," *Congressional Research Service – The Library of Congress*, 12 February 2004, accessed 15 March 2011, http://congressional research.com/RL32227/document.php?study=SARS+Avian+ Flu +and+Other+Challenges+for+Chinas+Political+Social+ and+ Economic+Transformation.
8. S. Niwa and M. Foscarinis, "Homelessness in the United States and the Human Right to Housing," *National Law Center on*

Homelessness & Poverty, 14 January 2004, accessed 19 February 2001, http://www.nlchp.org/content/pubs/Homelessnessinthe USandRightstoHousing.pdf.

9. C. LeDuff, "Frozen in Indifference: Life Goes on around Body Found in Vacant Warehouse," *Detroit News*, 28 January 2009, accessed 19 February 2011, http://detnews.com/article/20090128/METRO08/901280491/.

10. CNN Wire Staff, "House of Horrors' Suspect Due in Court," *CNN*, 24 March 2010, accessed 19 February 2011, http://www.cnn.com/2010/CRIME/03/24/cleveland.bodies.

11. T. Pogge, "Eradicating Systemic Poverty: Brief for a Global Resource Dividend," in *The Global Justice Reader*, ed. T. Brooks (Malden, MA: Blackwell Publishing, 2008); T. Pogge, *World Poverty and Human Rights* (Cambridge, UK: Polity Press, 2002).

12. P. Singer, *The Life You Can Save: Acting Now to End World Poverty* (New York: Random House, 2009), 63.

13. R. Roth, "Pakistan Flooding Crisis Hit by 'Donor Fatigue'?" *CBS News*, 18 August 2010, accessed 25 March 2011, http://www.cbsnews.com/stories/2010/08/18/eveningnews/main6785095.shtml.

14. P. Illingworth, T. Pogge, and L. Wenar, eds, *Giving Well: The Ethics of Philanthropy* (New York: Oxford University Press, 2011).

15. Singer, *The Life You Can Save*, 76.

16. Ibid., 78.

17. R. Putnam, *Bowling Alone: The Collapse and Revival of American Community* (New York: Simon & Schuster, 2000), 32–5.

18. P. Paxton and J. Smith, "America's Trust Fall," *Greater Good Magazine*, Fall 2008, 14–17.

19. Putnam, *Bowling Alone*, 283–4.

20. H. M. Babcock, "Assuming Personal Responsibility for Improving the Environment: Moving Toward a New Environmental Norm," *Harvard Environmental Law Review* 33:1 (2009): 134.

21. K. D. Opp, "Norms," in *International Encyclopedia of the Social & Behavioral Sciences*, ed. N. J. Smelser and P. B. Baltes (Oxford, UK: Pergamon, 2011), 10714–20.

22. Ibid.

23. Babcock, "Assuming Personal Responsibility," 135.

24. Ibid., 136.

25. Ibid.

26. C. R. Sunstein, "Social Norms and Social Roles," *Columbia Law Review* 96:4 (1996): 9, emphasis in original.

27. John Ruggie, Report of the Special Representative of the Secretary-General on the Issue of Human Rights and Transnational Corporations and Other Business Enterprises, U.N. Doc A/HRC/8/5 (7 April 2008).

28. Paul Hunt, *Report of the Special Rapporteur on the Right of Everyone to the Enjoyment of the Highest Attainable Standard of Health*, U.N. Doc A/HRC/11/12/Add.2 (18 May 2009).

29. T. Pogge, "Cosmopolitanism and Sovereignty," and M. Nussbaum, "Patriotism and Cosmopolitanism," in *The Global Justice Reader*, ed. T. Brooks (Malden, MA: Blackwell Publishing, 2008); K. A. Appiah, *Cosmopolitanism: Ethics in a World of Strangers* (New York: W.W. Norton & Company Inc., 2006); P. Singer, *One World: The Ethics of Globalization* (New Haven, CT: Yale University Press, 2002).

30. Yale University: Incentives for Global Health, "The Health Impact Fund Making New Medicines Accessible for All," 30 April 2010, accessed 19 February 2011, http://www.yale.edu/macmillan/igh/.

31. C. Gould, "Transnational Solidarities," *Journal of Social Philosophy* 38 (2007): 148–64.

32. Sunstein, "Social Norms and Social Roles," 31–2.

33. Ibid., 32.

34. R. H. Thaler and C. R. Sunstein, *Nudge: Improving Decisions about Health, Wealth, and Happiness* (New York: Penguin Group Inc., 2008), 6.

35. Ibid., 5, emphasis in original.

2   The Heart of the Matter

1. The World Bank, "Overview: Social Capital," accessed 11 March 2011, http://go.worldbank.org/C0QTRW4QF0.

2. J. S. Coleman, *Foundations of Social Theory* (Cambridge, MA: Harvard University Press, 1994), 302.

3. I. Kawachi and L. F. Berkman, "Social Cohesion, Social Capital, and Health," in *Social Epidemiology*, ed. L. F. Berkman and I. Kawachi (New York: Oxford University Press, 2000), 176.

4. Ibid., 177.

5. D. Stolle, "The Sources of Social Capital," in *Generating Social Capital: Civil Society and Institutions in Comparative Perspective*, ed. M. Hooghe and D. Stolle (New York: Palgrave Macmillan, 2003), 19–20.

6. F. Fukuyama, *Trust: The Social Virtues and the Creation of Prosperity* (New York: The Free Press, 1995).

7. Ibid., 26.

8. Ibid.

9. R. Putnam, *Bowling Alone: The Collapse and Revival of American Community* (New York: Simon & Schuster, 2000), 19–21.

10. J. E. Stiglitz, A. Sen, and J. P. Fitoussi, "Report by the Commission on the Measurement of Economic Performance and Social Progress," The Commission on the Measurement of Economic Performance and Social Progress, accessed 5 April 2011, http://www.stiglitz-sen-fitoussi.fr/documents/rapport_anglais.pdf.

11. Ibid., 182–3.

12. The Saguaro Seminar, "Social Capital Primer," accessed 11 March 2011, http://www.hks.harvard.edu/saguaro/social capitalprimer.htm.

13. Putnam, *Bowling Alone*, 20.

14. L. J. Robison and J. L. Flora, "The Social Capital Paradigm: Bridging across Disciplines," *American Journal of Agricultural Economics* 85 (2003): 1208–10.

15. Putnam, *Bowling Alone*, 22.

16. K. Newton, "Social Capital and Democracy," *American Behavioral Scientist* 40:5 (1997): 575–86.

17. Putnam, *Bowling Alone*, 136.

18. Ibid.

19. P. Illingworth, *Trusting Medicine: The Moral Costs of Managed Care* (New York: Routledge, 2005), 93–4.

20. M. McPherson, L. Smith-Lovin, and J. M. Cook, "Birds of a Feather: Homophily in Social Networks," *Annual Review of Sociology* 27 (2001): 415–44.

21. The World Bank, "Overview: Social Capital."

22. Ibid.

23. C. Grootaert and T. van Bastelaer, eds, *Understanding and Measuring Social Capital: A Multidisciplinary Tool for Practitioners (Directions in Development)* (Washington, DC: World Bank, 2002), 8–9.

24. P. J. Zack, "The Neurobiology of Trust," *Scientific American Magazine*, June (2008): 88–95.

25. Ibid., 90.

26. Ibid.

27. R. Putnam, "E Pluribus Unum: Diversity and Community in the Twenty-First Century," *Scandinavian Political Studies* 30:2 (2007): 159.

28. S. Bok, *Lying: Moral Choice in Public and Private Life* (London: Quartet Books, 1978), 41.
29. J. Delhey and K. Newton, "Who Trusts? The Origins of Social Trust in Seven Societies," *European Societies* 5:2 (2003): 94.
30. Ibid., 95.
31. Ibid., 96.
32. Ibid., 98.
33. Coleman, *Foundations of Social Theory*, 305.
34. Putnam, *Bowling Alone*, 22.
35. Kawachi and Berkman, "Social Cohesion, Social Capital, and Health," 174.
36. Putnam, *Bowling Alone*, 296–7.
37. Ibid., 300.
38. Ibid., 299.
39. Ibid., 310.
40. Ibid., 318.
41. J. G. Bruhn and S. Wolf, *The Roseto Story: An Anatomy of Health* (Norman, OK: University of Oklahoma Press, 1979); S. Wolf and J. G. Bruhn, *The Power of Clan: The Influence of Human Relationships on Heart Disease* (New Brunswick, NJ: Transaction Publishers, 1993); B. Egolf, J. Lasker, S. Wolf, and L. Potvin, "The Roseto Effect: A Fifty-Year Comparison of Mortality Rates," *American Journal of Epidemiology* 15:6 (1992): 1089–92.
42. Putnam, *Bowling Alone*, 329.
43. Ibid., 327.
44. Ibid.
45. M. Hooge and D. Stolle, "Conclusion: The Sources of Social Capital Reconsidered," in *Generating Social Capital*, ed. M. Hooge and D. Stolle (New York: Palgrave Macmillan, 2003), 232.
46. Ibid., 23.
47. P. Loizos, "Are Refugees Social Capitalists?," in *Social Capital: Critical Perspectives*, ed. S. Baron, J. Field, and T. Schuller (New York: Oxford University Press, 2001), 126.
48. D. Halpern, *Social Capital* (Malden, MA: Polity Press, 2005), 250.
49. Better Together: An Initiative of the Saguaro Seminar, "150 Things You Can Do To Create Social Capital," accessed 15 April 2011, http://www.bettertogether.org/150ways.htm.
50. R. Putnam and L. Feldstein, *Better Together: Restoring the American Community* (New York: Simon and Schuster, 2003), 242.
51. *Better Together: An Initiative of the Saguaro Seminar*.
52. I. Kaul, I. Grunberg, and M. A. Stern, "Defining Global Public Goods," in *Global Public Goods: International Cooperation in the*

21st Century, ed. I. Kaul, I. Grunberg, and M. A. Stern (New York: Oxford University Press, 1999), 3–5.

53. C. R. Sunstein, "Social Norms and Social Rules," *Columbia Law Review* 96:4 (1996): 1–47.
54. Coleman, *Foundations of Social Theory*, 318.
55. Kawachi and Berkman, "Social Cohesion, Social Capital, and Health."
56. P. Illingworth and W. Parmet, *Ethical Healthcare* (Upper Saddle River, NJ: Prentice Hall, 2005).
57. Coleman, *Foundations of Social Theory*, 316.
58. A similar point was nicely made by K. Outterson in a chapter entitled "Fair Followers: Expanding Access to Generic Pharmaceuticals for Low- and Middle-Income Populations," in *The Power of Pills*, ed. J. C. Cohen, P. Illingworth, and U. Schuklenk (London: Pluto Press, 2006).
59. *Brown v. Board of Education*, 347 U.S. 483 (1954).
60. J. Helliwell, "Maintaining Social Ties: Social Capital in a Global Information Age," *Keynote address to the 75th Anniversary Conference of the University of Tilburg on Sustainable Ties in the Information Society*, 26–28 March 2003, 10.
61. Organization for Economic Cooperation and Development, *The Well-Being of Nations: The Roll of Human and Social Capital* (Paris: OECD, 2001), quoted in Helliwell, "Maintaining Social Ties," 1.
62. Ibid., 9.
63. Ibid.
64. Ibid.
65. Ibid., 10.
66. Ibid., 12.
67. T. Pogge, *World Poverty and Human Rights: Cosmopolitan Responsibilities and Reforms* (Malden, MA: Polity Press, Blackwell Publishing, 2002).
68. T. Pogge, " 'Assisting' the Global Poor," in *The Ethics of Assistance: Morality and the Distant Needy*, ed. D. K. Chatterjee (New York: Cambridge University Press, 2004), 260–88; P. Singer, *Practical Ethics* (New York: Cambridge University Press, 1993).
69. D. L. Costa and M. E. Kahn, "Civic Engagement and Community Heterogeneity: An Economist's Perspective," *Perspectives on Politics* 1:1 (2003): 103–11.
70. Ibid., 104.
71. Putnam, "E Pluribus Unum," 149.
72. Ibid., 150–1.

73. Ibid., 150.
74. T. Pogge, "Cosmopolitanism and Sovereignty," in *The Global Justice Reader*, ed. Thom Brooks (Malden, MA: Blackwell Publishing, 2008), 48.
75. Ibid., 58.
76. S. Saulny, "Counting by Race Can Throw off Some Numbers," *New York Times*, 9 February 2011, accessed 12 March 2011, http://www.nytimes.com/2011/02/10/us/10count.html.
77. Ibid.
78. S. Saluny, "Black? White? Asian? More Young Americans Choose All of the Above," *New York Times*, 29 January 2011, accessed 12 March 2011, http://www.nytimes.com/2011/01/30/us/30mixed.html.
79. L. Grossman, "Iran Protests: Twitter, the Medium of the Movement," *Time*, 17 June 2009, accessed 12 March 2011, http://www.time.com/time/world/article/0,8599,1905125,00.html.
80. J. G. Ruggie, "Reconstituting the Global Public Domain: Issues, Actors and Practices," *Corporate Social Responsibility Initiative Working Paper No. 6* (Cambridge: John F. Kennedy School of Government Harvard University, 2004), 32.

3 The Ethics of Us

1. The concept of a happy follower is loosely based on K. Outterson's notion of a "fair follower"; "Fair Followers: Expanding Access to Generic Pharmaceuticals for Low- and Middle-Income Populations," in *The Power of Pills*, ed. J.C. Cohen, P. Illingworth, and U. Schuklenk (London: Pluto Press, 2006), 164–178.
2. R. Dworkin, "The Model of Rules," *The University of Chicago Law Review* 35:1 (1967): 14–46.
3. J. S. Mill, *On Liberty* (New York: Penguin Books, 1975).
4. P. Singer, *Practical Ethics* (Cambridge, UK: Cambridge University Press, 1993).
5. S. Baron, J. Field, and T. Schuller, *Social Capital: Critical Perspectives* (New York: Oxford University Press, 2000), 35.
6. Singer, *Practical Ethics*, 11.
7. P. Keeton, *Prosser and Keeton on the Law of Torts* (St Paul: West Publishing Company, 1984), 266–7.
8. H. Simon, "Ubi and the Flat Tax," *Boston Review*, October/November 2000, 9–10.

9. AFRICAN CHARTER OF HUMAN AND PEOPLES' RIGHTS, 1981 OAU Do. CAB/Leg/67/3/Rev.5, 21 I.L.M. 58 (1982).
10. J. Rawls, *A Theory of Justice* (Cambridge, MA: Belknap Press of Harvard University Press, 1971).
11. M. Nussbaum, "Patriotism and Cosmopolitanism," in *The Global Justice Reader*, ed. T. Brooks (Malden, MA: Blackwell Publishing, 2008), 311.

4   The Moral Sweet Spot

1. J. S. Mill, *Utilitarianism*, ed. Oskar Piest (Indianapolis: Bobbs-Merrill Educational Publishing, 1977), 10–11.
2. Ibid., 45.
3. Ibid., 40.
4. Ibid., 40–1.
5. Ibid., 42–3.
6. Ibid., 39–41.
7. R. Putnam, *Bowling Alone: The Collapse and Revival of American Community* (New York: Simon and Schuster, 2000), 283.
8. Mill, *Utilitarianism*.
9. J. S. Mill, *Principles of Political Economy with Some of their Applications to Social Philosophy*, ed. S. Nathanson (Indianapolis: Hackett Publishing Company, 2004), xxx.
10. Ibid.
11. Ibid., xxxi.
12. J. S. Mill, *Three Essays*, ed. R. Wollheim (New York: Oxford University Press, 1975), 79.
13. Ibid.
14. Ibid.
15. Ibid.
16. Ibid., 70.
17. Ibid., 73.
18. M. Iacoboni, *Mirroring People: The Science of Empathy and How We Connect with Others* (New York: Picador, 2008), 126.
19. E. Diener and M. E. P. Seligman, "Very Happy People," *Psychological Science* 13 (2002): 80–3.
20. R. A. Easterlin, "Does Economic Growth Improve the Human Lot? Some Empirical Evidence," in *Nations and Households in Economic Growth*, ed. P. A. David and M. W. Reder (New York: Academic Press, 1974), 89–125; D. G. Blanchflower and A. J. Oswald, "Well-Being over Time in Britain and the USA,"

NBER Working Papers 7487 (Cambridge: National Bureau of Economic Research, 2000).

21. A. Deaton and D. Kahneman, "High Income Improves Evaluation of Life but Not Emotional Well-Being," Proceedings of the National Academy of Sciences of the United States of America, 7 September 2010.

22. M. Hooghe and D. Stolle, eds, *Generating Social Capital: Civil Society and Institutions in Comparative Perspective* (New York: Palgrave Macmillan, 2003).

23. I. Kawachi, B. P. Kennard, K. Lochner, and D. Prothrow-Stith, "Social Capital, Income Inequality, and Mortality," *American Journal of Public Health* 87:9 (1997): 1491–8.

24. J. F. Helliwell and R. Putnam, "The Social Context of Well-Being," *Philosophical Transactions of the Royal Society: Biological Sciences* 359 (2004): 1435–46.

25. Ibid.

26. Ibid.

27. Ibid., 1441.

28. Putnam, *Bowling Alone*, 332.

29. A. J. Oswald, "Happiness and Economic Performance," *Economic Journal* 107 (1997): 1815–31.

30. E. M. Uslaner, "Trust, Democracy and Governance: Can Government Policies Influence Generalized Trust?," in *Generating Social Capital*, ed. M. Hooghe and D. Stolle (New York: Palgrave Macmillan, 2003), 171–90.

31. J. Cacioppo and W. Patrick, *Loneliness: Human Nature and the Need for Social Connection* (New York: W. W. Norton and Co., 2008), 108.

32. Ibid., 98.

33. N. Christakis and J. Fowler, "Dynamic Spread Of Happiness in a Large Social Network: Longitudinal Analysis over 20 Years in the Framingham Heart Study," *British Medical Journal* 337:a2338 (2008): 1–9. See also N. Chrisakis and J. Fowler, *Connected: The Surprising Power of Our Social Networks and How They Shape Our Lives* (New York: Little, Brown and Company, 2009), 51.

34. N. Christakis and J. Fowler, "Social Networks and Happiness," *Edge*, accessed 11 March 2011, http://www.edge.org/3rd_culture/christakis_fowler08/christakis_fowler08_index.html.

35. N. Christakis and J. Fowler, *Connected: The Surprising Power of Our Social Networks and How They Shape Our Lives* (New York: Little, Brown and Company, 2009), 54.

36. Mill, *Utilitarianism*, 40–1.

37. Mill, *Three Essays*, 94.
38. D. Gilbert, *Stumbling on Happiness* (New York: Alfred A. Knopf, division of Random House, 2006).
39. D. Kahneman and R. Thaler, "Anomalies, Utility Maximization and Experienced Utility," *Journal of Economics Perspectives* 20 (2006): 221–34; D. Gilbert, *Stumbling on Happiness* (New York: Alfred A. Knopf, Random House, 2006).
40. R. Wollheim, Introduction to *Three Essays*, by J. S. Mill.
41. E. Diener and M. E. P. Seligman, "Beyond Money: Toward an Economy of Well-Being," *Psychological Science in the Public Interest* 5:1 (2004): 1–31.
42. Surgeon General, "Mental Health: A Report," accessed 11 March 2011, http://www.surgeongeneral.gov/library/mentalhealth/home.html.
43. T. B. Ustun, J. L. Ayuso-Mateos, S. Chatterji, C. Mathers, and C. J. L. Murray, "Global Burden of Depressive Disorders in the Year 2000," *British Journal of Psychiatry* 184 (2004): 386–92.
44. Center for Disease Control, National Center for Health Statistics. "Health, United States, 2004, with Chartbook on Trends in the United States," accessed 21 July 2010, http://cdc.gov/nchs/data/hus/hus04trend.pdf.
45. P. Biegler, *The Ethical Treatment of Depression: Autonomy through Psychotherapy* (Cambridge, MA: MIT Press, 2011), 184.
46. W. Kymlicka, *Multicultural Citizenship: A Liberal Theory of Minority Rights* (New York: Oxford University Press, 1995), 76.
47. Ibid.
48. Ibid.
49. R. Dworkin, *A Matter of Principle* (London, UK: Harvard University Press, 1985): 228, quoted in W. Kymlicka, *Multicultural Citizenship*, 83.
50. A. Margalit and J. Raz, "National Self-Determination," *Journal of Philosophy* 87:9 (1990): 449, quoted in W. Kymlicka, *Multicultural Citizenship*, 89.
51. D. Miller, *On Nationality* (New York: Oxford University Press, 1997), 92.
52. D. Miller, quoted in *Global Citizenship: A Critical Introduction*, ed. N. Dower and J. Williams (New York: Routledge, 2002), 86.
53. H. Tajfel, "Experiments in Intergroup Discrimination," *Scientific American* 223 (1970): 96–102.
54. Oxfam Education, "What is Global Citizenship?," *Oxfam*, accessed 15 March 2011, http://www.oxfam.org.uk/education/gc/what_and_why/what/.

55. T. Mohn, "Going Global, Stateside," *New York Times*, 8 March 2010, accessed 15 March 2011, http://www.nytimes.com/2010/03/09/business/global/09training.html.

56. R. Inglehart, "Culture and Democracy," in *Culture Matters: How Values Shape Human Progress*, ed. L. E. Harrison and S. P. Huntington (New York: Basic Books, 2000), 81.

57. R. Edgerton, "Traditional Beliefs and Practices – Are Some Better than Others?," in *Culture Matters*, ed. L. E. Harrison and S. P. Huntington (New York: Basic Books, 2000), 131.

58. C. Chiu and Y. Hong, *Social Psychology of Culture* (New York: Psychology Press, 2006), 16–17.

59. Ibid., 19.

60. Ibid., 21.

61. F. Fukuyama, *Trust: The Social Virtues and the Creation of Prosperity* (New York: Free Press, 1995), 33.

62. F. Fukuyama, "Social Capital," in *Culture Matters*, ed. L. E. Harrison and S. P. Huntington (New York: Basic Books, 2000), 99.

63. R. Putnam, "E Pluribus Unum: Diversity and Community in the Twenty-First Century," *Scandinavian Political Studies* 30:2 (2007): 159.

64. J. G. Ruggie, "Reconstituting the Global Public Domain: Issues, Actors and Practices," *KSG Faculty Research Working Paper Series* (Cambridge, MA: Harvard University, 2004), 32.

65. R. F. Baumeister and M. R. Leary, "The Need to Belong: Desire for Interpersonal Attachments as a Fundamental Human Motivation," *Psychological Bulletin* 117:3 (1995), 497.

66. G. Kendall, I. Woodward, and Z. Skrbis, *The Sociology of Cosmopolitanism* (New York: Palgrave Macmillan, 2009), 34.

67. C. Freeland, "The Rise of the New Global Elite," *The Atlantic*, January/February 2011, 51.

68. J. Kotter, *A Sense of Urgency* (Boston: Harvard Business Press, 2008).

5 With a Little Help from the Law

1. R. Pildes, "The Destruction of Social Capital through Law," *University of Pennsylvania Law Review* 144:5 (1996): 2055.

2. C. R. Sunstein, "On the Expressive Function of Law," *University of Pennsylvania Law Review* 144:5 (1996): 2046.

3. C. R. Sunstein, "Social Norms and Social Rules," *The Coase Lecture*, The University of Chicago, Autumn 1995.

4. Ibid., 2043.

5. Ibid.

6. Pildes, "Destruction of Social Capital," 2077.

7. U.S. Const. amend. V.

8. Pildes, "Destruction of Social Capital," 2071.

9. *Brown v. Board of Education*, 347 U.S. 483 (1954).

10. Americans with Disabilities Act of 1990, 42 U.S.C.A. §12101.

11. *Regents of University of California v. Bakke*, 438 U.S. 265 (1978).

12. *Goodridge v. Department of Public Health*, 798 N.E.2d 941 (Mass. 2003).

13. R. H. Thaler and C. R. Sunstein, *Nudge: Improving Decisions about Health, Wealth, and Happiness* (London, UK: Penguin Books, 2009).

14. U.S. Census Bureau, Thursday, 16 September 2010, accessed 17 April 2011, http://www.census.gov/prod/2010pubs/p60-238.pdf.

15. Universal Declaration of Human Rights, G.A. Res, 217A, at 76, U.N. GAOR, 3d Sess., 1st plen. mtg., U.N. Doc. A/810 (12 December 1948).

16. J. M. Smits, "The Good Samaritan in European Private Law: On the Perils of Principles Without a Programme and a Programme for the Future," Inaugural Lecture, Maastricht University (19 May 2000) at 4.

17. Ibid.

18. Ibid., 6.

19. Ibid., 8. This is true of the Civil Codes of France and Holland. In Dutch law the defendant has to realize that there was a danger to someone and yet not act to help. The Dutch call this an obligation to act "altruistically."

20. A few jurisdictions have enacted a general law specifying a duty to aid. Vermont, for example, has: "A person who knows that another is exposed to grave physical harm, shall, to the extent that the same can be rendered without danger or peril to himself or without interference with important duties owed to others, give reasonable assistance to the exposed person unless the assistance or care is being provided by others." Duty to Aid the Endangered Act (Good Samaritan Law), VT. STAT. ANN. tit. 12, §519 (1967).

21. D. MacKeen, "Creeps on Campus: Do Bad Guys Have a Right to Higher Education?" *Salon Ivory Tower* (1998), accessed 15 March 2011, http://www.salon.com/it/feature/1998/10/cov_09feature. html. See also M. M. Ziegler, "Comment: Nonfeasance and the Duty to Assist: The American Seinfeld Syndrome," *Dickenson Law Review* 525 (2000): 2.

22. J. S. Mill, *Three Essays*, ed. R. Wollheim (New York: Oxford University Press, 1975), 79.

23. R. H. Pildes, "Why Rights Are Not Trumps: Social meanings, Expressive Harms, and Constitutionalism," *Journal of Legal Studies* 27:S2 (June 1998): 12.

24. Sherrice Iverson Child Victim Protection Act, CAL. Penal CODE §152.3 (2001).

25. Ibid.

26. D. Mackeen, "Creeps on Campus."

27. A. McDermott, "A Silent Friend, and a Debate Over Good Samaritan Laws," CNN, 4 September 1998, accessed 15 March 2011, http://www.cnn.com/SPECIALS/views/y/1998/09/mcdermott.casino/.

28. J. M. Donley and B. Latane, "Bystander Intervention in Emergencies: Diffusion of Responsibility," *Journal of Personality and Social Psychology* 8 (1968): 377–83.

29. M. M. Ziegler, "Comment: Nonfeasance and the Duty to Assist: The American Seinfeld Syndrome."

30. OHIO REV. CODE ANN. §2919.22 (2011).

31. Mill, *Three Essays*.

32. R. Epstein, "A Theory of Strict Liability," *Journal of Legal Studies* 151 (1973): 198–9.

33. I. Berlin, "Two Concepts of Liberty" (Oxford, UK: Oxford University 1958).

34. M. F. Steger, T. B. Kashdan, and S. Oishi, "Being Good by Doing Good: Daily Eudaimonic Activity and Well-Being," *Journal of Research in Personality* 42 (2008): 22–42.

35. *Van Horn v. Watson*, 45 Cal. 4th 322 (2008).

36. Ibid.

37. CAL. CIV. CODE §1714 (2011), CAL. HEALTH & SAFETY CODE §1799.102 (2009).

38. R. Daynard, "Regulating Tobacco: The Need for a Public Health Judicial Decision-Making Canon," *Journal of Law, Medicine and Ethics* 30 (2002): 281–9.

39. *Jacobson v. Commonwealth of Massachusetts*, 197 U.S. 11 (1905).

40. *Payne v. Western & Atlantic Railroad Co.*, 81 Tenn. 507, 519–20 (1884).

41. R. Epstein, "In Defense of the Employment at Will," in *Ethical Theory and Business*, 7th edn, ed. T. L. Beauchamp and N. E. Bowie (Upper Saddle River, NJ: Prentice Hall, 2004), 274–82.

42. Ibid., 278.

43. C. R. Leana and H. J. Buren III, "Organizational Social Capital and Employment Practices," *Academy of Management Review* 24:3 (1999): 538–5.

44. Ibid., 544.

45. A. E. Clark, Y. Georgellis, and P. Sanfey, "Scarring: The Psychological Impact of Past Unemployment," *Economica* 68 (2001): 221–41.

46. Ibid.

47. J. Pfeffer, "The Real Cost of the Virtual Workforce," Stanford Business excerpt from "The Human Equation: Building Profits by Putting People First," 15 May 1998, accessed 15 March 2011, http://www.stanford.edu/group/knowledgebase/cgi-bin/1998/03/15/the-real-cost-of-the-virtual-workforce/.

48. T. H. Sander and R. Putnam, "How Joblessness Hurts Us All," *USA Today*, 10 December 2011.

49. *Toussaint v. Blue Cross & Blue Shield of Michigan,* 408 Mich 579 (1980).

50. C. J. Muhl, "The Employment at Will Doctrine: Three Major Exceptions," *Monthly Labor Review* 124:1 (2002): 8.

51. Pildes, "Destruction of Social Capital."

52. Ibid., 1996.

53. K. Otake, S. Shimai, J. Tanaka-Matsumi, K. Otsui, and B.L. Fredrickson, "Happy People Become Happier through Kindness: A Counting Kindnesses Intervention," *Journal of Happiness Studies* 7 (2006): 361–75.

54. J. M. Rochester, *Between Peril and Promise: The Politics of International Law* (Washington, DC: CQ Press, 2006), 36.

55. Ibid.

56. Ibid.

57. Ibid., 38.

58. Ibid., 39.

59. Ibid., 40.

60. J. G. Ruggie, "Multilateralism: The Anatomy of an Institution," *International Organization* 46:3 (Summer 1992): 561–86.

61. Ibid., 571.

62. Ibid., 571–2.

63. R. O. Keohane, "Reciprocity in International Relations," *International Organization* 40:1 (Winter 1986): 27.

64. Ibid., 4.
65. Ibid., 20.

6   Giving Back

1. I.R.C. §170(c)(2)(A) (2009).
2. T. Pogge, "Cosmopolitanism and Sovereignty," in *The Global Justice Reader*, ed. T. Brooks (Malden, MA: Blackwell Publishing, 2008), 51–72.
3. R. Putnam, *Bowling Alone: The Collapse and Revival of American Community* (New York: Simon and Schuster, 2000), 17.
4. Ibid., 123.
5. E. Brown, "Social Capital and Philanthropy: An Analysis of the Impact of Social Capital on Individual Giving and Volunteering," *Nonprofit and Voluntary Sector Quarterly* 36 (2007): 85–99.
6. Ibid., 96.
7. Putnam, *Bowling Alone*, 122.
8. D. E. Pozen, "Remapping the Charitable Deduction," *Connecticut Law Review* 39 (2006): 537.
9. 26 U.S.C. §170 (2008).
10. *Deducting Generosity: The Effect of Charitable Tax Incentives on Giving* (Washington, DC: Independent Sector, 2003).
11. Ibid.
12. R. Reich, "Toward a Political Theory of Philanthropy," in *Giving Well: The Ethics of Philanthropy*, ed. P. Illingworth, T. Pogge, and L. Wenar (New York: Oxford University Press, 2011), 177–95.
13. H.R. Rep. No. 1860, 75th Cong., 3d Sess. 19 (1938).
14. K. Otake, S. Shimai, J. Tanaka-Matsumi, K. Otsui, and B.L. Fredrickson, "Happy People Become Happier through Kindness: A Counting Kindnesses Intervention," *Journal of Happiness Studies* 7 (2006): 361–75.
15. C. R. Sunstein, "On the Expressive Function of Law," *University of Pennsylvania Law Review* 144 (1996): 2021.
16. *Deducting Generosity*, 27.
17. I.R.C. §170(c)(2)(A) (2009).
18. Pozen, "Remapping the Charitable Deduction," 537.
19. H.R. Rep. No. 75–1860, at 10–20 (1938).
20. *Bob Jones University v. United States*, 461 U.S. 574, 591 (1983).
21. These are 501(c)(3). The tax code defines public charities as organizations that are "religious, educational, charitable, scientific,

literary, testing for public safety, to foster national or international amateur sports competition or prevention of cruelty to animals."

22. Ibid., 592.
23. Ibid.
24. T. Pogge, "Eradicating Systemic Poverty: Brief for a Global Resource Dividend," in *The Global Justice Reader*, ed. T. Brooks (Malden, MA: Blackwell Publishing, 2008); T. Pogge, *World Poverty and Human Rights* (Cambridge, UK: Polity Press, 2002).
25. T. Pogge, "Cosmopolitanism and Sovereignty."
26. Pozen, "Remapping the Charitable Deduction," 578–9.
27. Ibid., 572.
28. L. Wenar, "Poverty is No Pond: Challenges for the Affluent," in *Giving Well: The Ethics of Philanthropy*, ed. P. Illingworth, T. Pogge, and L.Wenar (New York: Oxford University Press, 2011), 104–32.
29. *Utah County v. Intermountain Health Care, Inc.*, 709 P. 2d 275 (1985).
30. I.R.C §501(p) (2010).
31. R. E. Silverman and S. Beatty, "Doing Due Diligence on Your Donations," *Wall Street Journal*, 20 December 2007, accessed 15 March 2011, http://online.wsj.com/article/SB119 810791163740721.html.
32. Case C-318/07, *Hein Persche v. Finanzamt*, 2007 E.C.J. 95.
33. Ibid.
34. Ibid., 8.
35. Ibid., 9.
36. I have in mind here a more globalized version of Ronald Dworkin's theory of the law as an institution that gradually moves toward a more just society, while maintaining respect for precedent and coherence in the law.
37. M. Yunus and A. Jolis, *Banker to the Poor: Micro Lending and the Battle against World Poverty* (New York: Public Affairs, 1999), 235–43.
38. L. Wenar, "The Basic Structure as Object: Institutions and Humanitarian Concern," *Global Justice, Global Institutions Canadian Journal of Philosophy* 31 (2007): 253–78.

7 Global People

1. R. Putnam, *Bowling Alone: The Collapse and Revival of American Community* (New York: Simon & Schuster, 2000), 411.

2. T. Pogge, "Cosmopolitanism and Sovereignty," in *The Global Justice Reader*, ed. T. Brooks (Malden, MA: Blackwell Publishing, 2008), 70; note 19.
3. Putnam, *Bowling Alone*, 413.
4. P. H. Koehn and J. N. Rosenau, "Transnational Competence in an Emergent Epoch," *International Studies Perspective* 3 (2002): 120.
5. A. Appadurai, "Disjuncture and Difference in the Global Cultural Economy," in *Global Culture: Nationalism, Globalizations and Modernity*, ed. M. Featherstone (London, UK: Sage, 1990), 297.
6. R. F. Baumeister and M. R. Leary, "The Need to Belong: Desire for Interpersonal Attachments as a Fundamental Motivation," *Psychological Bulletin* 117:3 (1995): 497–529.
7. H. Tajfel, "Experiments in Intergroup Discrimination," *Scientific American* 223 (1970): 96–102.
8. A. Locksley, V. Ortiz, and C. Hepburn, "Social Categorization and Discriminatory Behavior: Extinguishing the Minimal Intergroup Discrimination Effect," *Journal of Personality and Social Psychology* 39 (1980): 773–83.
9. Ibid., 502.
10. Ibid., 498.
11. M. Hewstone and K. Greenland, "Intergroup Conflict," *International Journal of Psychology* 35:2 (2000): 136–44.
12. Ibid., 140.
13. A. Sen, *Identity and Violence: The Illusion of Destiny* (New York: W. W. Norton and Co., 2006), 4–5.
14. Pogge, "Cosmopolitanism and Sovereignty," 58.
15. R. F. Baumeister and M. R. Leary, "The Need to Belong," 515.
16. L. J. Beckman, "Effects of Social Interactions and Children's Relative Inputs on Older Women's Psychological Well-Being," *Journal of Personality and Social Psychology* 41 (1981): 1085.
17. W. Parmet, *Population, Public Health, and the Law* (Washington, DC: Georgetown University Press, 2009), 246.
18. T. Pogge, *Health Impact Fund*, The MacMillan Center, Yale, accessed 15 April 2011, http://www.yale.edu/macmillan/igh/.
19. S. Castles and A. Davidson, *Citizenship and Migration* (New York: Routledge, 2000), 217.
20. D. Held, A. McGrew, D. Goldblatt, and J. Perraton, *Global Transformations* (Stanford, CA: Stanford University Press, 1999), 330.
21. Ibid., 344.

22. E. Engeler, "Cell Phone Use Surging in Developing Countries," *MSNBC*, 23 February 2010, accessed 15 March 2011, http://www.msnbc.msn.com/id/35539966/ns/technology_and_science-wireless/.

23. "Internet 2010 in Numbers," *Royal Pingdom*, accessed 22 March 2011, http://royal.pingdom.com/2011/01/12/internet-2010-in-numbers/.

24. Held and McGrew, *Global Transformations*, 349.

25. Ibid., 351.

26. Ibid., 353.

27. A. Appadurai, *Modernity at Large: Cultural Dimensions of Globalization* (Minneapolis, MN: University of Minnesota Press, 1996), 33–4.

28. Ibid.

29. Ibid., 110–11.

30. Ibid., 112.

31. Ibid., 117.

32. T. Pogge, *World Poverty and Human Rights* (Malden, MA: Polity Press, 2002).

33. P. Singer, *The Life You Can Save: Acting Now to End World Poverty* (New York: Random House, 2009).

34. J. Bridgeland, H. Wofford, and D. Caprara, "Compassion across Borders," *Huffington Post*, 12 July 2010, accessed 15 March 2011, http://www.huffingtonpost.com/john-bridgeland/compassion-across-borders_b_641135.html.

35. A. M. McBride, B. J. Lough, and M. S. Sherraden, "Perceived Impacts of International Service on Volunteers: Interim Results from a Quasi-Experimental Study," The Brookings Institution, 21 June 2010, accessed 15 March 2011, http://www.brookings.edu/~/media/Files/rc/reports/2010/0621_volunteering_mcbride/0621_volunteering_mcbride.pdf.

36. Ibid.

37. R. Reich, "Toward a Political Theory of Philanthropy," In *Giving Well: The Ethics of Philanthropy*, ed. P. Illingworth, T. Pogge, and L. Wenar (New York: Oxford University Press, 2010), 183.

38. See for example, N.Y. Tax §606(e)(1) (McKinney 2010).

39. Serve America Act, Pub L. No. 111–113, 123 Stat 1460 (2009).

40. M. Nussbaum, "Patriotism and Cosmopolitanism," in *The Global Justice Reader*, ed. T. Brooks (Malden, MA: Blackwell Publishing, 2008), 309.

41. Ibid.

References

African Charter of Human and People's Rights, adopted 27 June 1981 OAU Do. CAB/Leg/3 rev. S, 21 I.L.M.S8(1982) entered into force 21 October 1986.

Americans with Disabilities Act of 1990, 42 U.S.C.A. §12101.

Appadurai, Arjun. "Disjuncture and Difference in the Global Cultural Economy." In *Global Culture: Nationalism, Globalizations and Modernity*, edited by Mike Featherstone, 295–311. London, UK: Sage, 1990.

Appadurai, Arjun. *Modernity at Large: Cultural Dimensions of Globalization*. Minneapolis, MN: University of Minnesota Press, 1996.

Appiah, Kwame Anthony. *The Ethics of Identity*. Princeton: Princeton University Press, 2005.

Appiah, Kwame Anthony. *Cosmopolitanism: Ethics in a World of Strangers*. New York, NY: W. W. Norton & Company Inc., 2006.

Appiah, Kwame Anthony. "Global Citizenship." *Fordham Law Review* 75 (2007): 2375–91.

Avineri, Shlomo, and Avner de-Shalit. *Communitarianism and Individualism*. New York: Oxford University Press, 1992.

Babcock, Hope M. "Assuming Personal Responsibility for Improving the Environment: Moving toward a New Environmental Norm." *Harvard Environmental Law Review* 33:1 (2009): 117–75.

Baron, Stephen, John Field, and Tom Schuller. *Social Capital: Critical Perspectives*. New York: Oxford University Press, 2000.

Baumeister, Roy F., and Mark R. Leary. "The Need to Belong: Desire for Interpersonal Attachments as a Fundamental Human Motivation." *Psychological Bulletin* 117:3 (1995): 497–529.

Beckman, L. J. "Effects of Social Interactions and Children's Relative Inputs on Older Women's Psychological Well-Being." *Journal of Personality and Social Psychology* 41 (1981): 1075–86.

Benhabib, Seyla. *The Claims of Culture: Equality and Diversity in the Gobal Era*. Princeton: Princeton University Press, 2002.

Berkman, Lisa F., and Ichiro Kawachi. *Social Epidemiology*. New York: Oxford University Press, 2000.

Berlin, Isaiah Sir. *Two Concepts of Liberty*. Oxford, UK: Oxford University Press, 1958.

Better Together: An Initiative of the Saguaro Seminar. "150 Things You Can Do To Create Social Capital." Accessed 15 April 2011, http://www.bettertogether.org/150ways.htm.

Biegler, Paul. *The Ethical Treatment of Depression: Autonomy through Psychotherapy*. Cambridge: MIT Press, 2011.

Blanchflower, David G., and Andrew J. Oswald. "Well-being over Time in Britain and the USA," *NBER Working Papers 7487*. Cambridge: National Bureau of Economic Research, 2000.

Bob Jones University v. United States, 461 U.S. 574, 591 (1983).

Bok, Sissela. *Lying: Moral Choice in Public and Private Life*. London, UK: Quartet Books Limited, 1978.

Borgonovi, Franesca. "Doing Well by Doing Good. The Relationship between Formal Volunteering and Self-Reported Health and Happiness." *Social Science & Medicine* 66 (2008): 2321–34.

Brewer, Marilynn B. "In-Group Bias in the Minimal Intergroup Situation: A Cognitive-Motivational Analysis." *Psychological Bulletin* 86:2 (1979): 307–24.

Bridgeland, John, Harris Wofford, and David Caprara. "Compassion Across Borders." *Huffington Post*, 12 July 2010. Accessed 15 March 2011, http://www.huffingtonpost.com/john-bridgeland/compassion-across-borders_b_641135.html.

Brock, Gillian, and Harry Brighouse, eds. *The Political Philosophy of Cosmopolitanism*. New York: Cambridge University Press, 2005.

Brooks, Thom, ed. *The Global Justice Reader*. Malden: Blackwell Publishing, 2008.

Brown, Eleanor. "Social Capital and Philanthropy: An Analysis of the Impact of Social Capital on Individual Giving and Volunteering." *Nonprofit and Voluntary Sector Quarterly* 36 (2007): 85–99.

Brown v. Board of Education, 347 U.S. 483 (1954).

Bruhn, John G., and Stewart Wolf. *The Roseto Story: An Anatomy of Health*. Norman: University of Oklahoma Press, 1979.

Cacioppo, John T., and William Patrick. *Loneliness: Human Nature and the Need for Social Connection*. New York: W. W. Norton and Company, 2008.

CAL. CIV. CODE § 1714 (2011), CAL. HEALTH & SAFETY CODE § 1799.102 (2009).

Case C-318/07, *Hein Persche v. Finanzamt*, 2007 E.C.J. 95.

Castles, Stephen, and Alastair Davidson. *Citizenship and Migration: Globalization and the Politics of Belonging*. New York: Routledge, 2000.

Centre for Educational Research and Innovation. *The Well-Being of Nations: The Role of Human and Social Capital.* 88. Paris: Organization for Economic Co-operation and Development, 2001.

Chandler, David. *International Statebuilding: The Rise of Post-Liberal Governance*, Critical Issues in Global Politics. New York: Routledge, 2010.

Cheah, Pheng, and Bruce Robbins, eds. *Cosmopolitics: Thinking and Feeling Beyond the Nation*. Minneapolis: University of Minnesota Press, 1998.

Cheung, C.-K., and C.-M. Chan. "Social-Cognitive Factors of Donating Money to Charity, with Special Attention to an International Relief Organization." *Evaluation and Program Planning* 23 (2000): 241–53.

Chiu, Chi-yue, and Ying-yi Hong. *Social Psychology of Culture*. New York: Psychology Press, 2006.

Chiu, Chi-yue, Farideh Salili, and Ying-yi Hong. *Multiple Competencies and Self-Regulated Learning: Implications for Multicultural Education, Research in Multicultural Education and International Perspectives*. Greenwich: Information Age, 2001.

Christakis, Nicholas, and James Fowler. "Dynamic Spread of Happiness in a Large Social Network: Longitudinal Analysis over 20 Years in the Framingham Heart Study." *BMJ* 337:a2338 (2008): 1–9.

Christakis, Nicholas, and James Fowler. *Connected*. New York: Little, Brown and Company, 2009.

Christakis, Nicholas, and James Fowler. "Social Networks and Happiness." *Edge*. Accessed 11 March 2011, http://www.edge.org/3rd_culture/christakis_fowler08/christakis_fowler08_index.html.

Clark, Andrew E., Yannis Georgellis, and Peter Sanfey. "Scarring: The Psychological Impact of Past Unemployment." *Economica* 68 (2001): 221–41.

Clarke, Desmond M., and Charles Jones. *The Rights of Nations: Nations and Nationalism in a Changing World*. New York: St. Martin's Press, 1999.

CNN Wire Staff. "House of Horrors' Suspect Due in Court." *CNN*, 24 March 2010. Accessed 21 May 2011, http://www.cnn.com/2010/CRIME/03/24/cleveland.bodies.

Cohen, Elizabeth. "CDC: Antidepressants Most Prescribed Drugs in U.S." *CNN*, 9 June 2007. Accessed 21 May 2011, http://articles.cnn.com/2007-07-09/health/antidepressants_1_antidepressants-high-blood-pressure-drugs-psychotropic-drugs?_s=PM:HEALTH.

Coleman, James S. *Foundations of Social Theory*. Cambridge: Harvard University Press, 1994.

Costa, Dora L., and Matthew E. Kahn. "Civic Engagement and Community Heterogeneity: An Economist's Perspective." *Perspectives on Politics* 1:1 (2003): 103–11.

Daynard, Richard A. "Regulating Tobacco: The Need for a Public Health Judicial Decision-Making Canon." *Journal of Law, Medicine & Ethics* 30:2 (2002): 281–89.

Deaton, Angus, and Daniel Kahneman. "High Income Improves Evaluation of Life but Not Emotional Well-being." Proceedings of the National Academy of Sciences of the United States of America, 7 September 2010.

Deducting Generosity: The Effect of Charitable Tax Incentive on Giving. Washington, DC: Independent Sector, 2003.

Delanty, Gerard, and Krishan Kumar, eds. *The Sage Handbook of Nations and Nationalism.* Thousand Oaks: Sage, 2006.

Delhey, Jan, and Kenneth Newton. "Who Trusts? The Origins of Social Trust in Seven Societies." *European Societies* 5:2 (2003): 93–127.

Demir, Meliksah, and Lesley A. Weitekamp. "I Am So Happy Cause Today I Found My Friend: Friendship and Personality as Predictors of Happiness." *Journal of Happiness Studies* 8 (2007): 181–211.

Diener, Ed, and Martin E.P. Seligman. "Beyond Money: Toward an Economy of Well-Being." *Psychological Science in the Public Interest* 5:1 (2004): 1–30.

Donley John M, and Bibb Latane. "Bystander Intervention in Emergencies: Diffusion of Responsibility." *Journal of Personality and Social Psychology* 8 (1968): 377–83.

Dovidio, John. "Adulthood: Prosocial Behavior and Empathy." In *International Encylopedia of the Social & Behavioral Sciences*, edited by Neil J. Smelser and Paul B. Baltes, 159–62. Oxford: Elsevier Science Ltd., 2001.

Dower, Nigel, and John Williams, eds. *Global Citizenship: A Critical Introduction.* New York: Routledge, 2002.

Dumbaugh, Kerry, and Wayne Morrison. "SARS, Avian Flu, and Other Challenges for China's Political, Social, and Economic Transformation." *Congressional Research Service – The Library of Congress*, 12 February 2004. Accessed 15 March 2011, http://congressionalresearch.com/RL32227/document.php?study= SARS+Avian+Flu+and+Other+Challenges+for+Chinas+Political+Social+and+Economic+Transformation.

Dworkin, Ronald. *Taking Rights Seriously.* Cambridge: Harvard Universit Press, 1978.

Dworkin, Ronald. *A Matter of Principle*. Cambridge: Harvard University Press, 1985.

Easterlin, Richard A. "Does Economic Growth Improve the Human Lot? Some Empirical Evidence." In *Nations and Households in Economic Growth*, edited by Paul A. David and Melvin W. Reder, 89–125. New York: Academic, 1974.

Edgerton, Robert. "Traditional Beliefs and Practices – Are Some Better than Others?" In *Culture Matters*, edited by Lawrence E. Harrison and Samuel P. Huntington, 126–40. New York: Basic Books, 2000.

Egolf, Brenda, Judith Lasker, Stewart Wolf, and Louise Potvin. "The Roseto Effect: A Fifty-Year Comparison of Mortality Rates." *American Journal of Epidemiology* 15:6 (1992): 1089–92.

Einolf, Christopher J. "Empathic Concern and Prosocial Behaviors: A Test of Experimental Results Using Survey Data." *Social Science Research* 37 (2008): 1267–79.

Engeler, Eliane "Cell Phone Use Surging in Developing Countries." *MSNBC*, 23 February 2010. Accessed 15 March 2011, http://www.msnbc.msn.com/id/35539966/ns/technology_and_science-wireless/.

Epstein, Richard A. "A Theory of Strict Liability." *Journal of Legal Studies* 2:1 (1973): 151–204.

Epstein, Richard A. "Altruism: Universal and Selective." *The Social Service Review* 67:3 (1993): 388–405.

Epstein, Richard A. "In Defense of the Employment at Will." In *Ethical Theory and Business*, 7th edition, edited by Tom L. Beauchamp and Norman E. Bowie, 247–82. Upper Saddle River, New Jersey: Prentice Hall, 2004.

Etzioni, Amitai. *The Spirit of Community: Rights, Responsibilities, and the Communitarian Agenda*. New York: Crown Publishers, Inc., 1993.

Featherstone, Mike. *Undoing Culture: Globalization, Postmodernism and Identity*. Great Britain: The Cromwell Press Ltd., 1995.

Field, John. *Social Capital*. New York: Routledge, 2003.

Fine, Ben. *Social Capital versus Social Theory: Political Economy and Social Science at the Turn of the Millennium*. New York: Routledge, 2001.

Fong, Christina M. "Empathic Responsiveness: Evidence from a Randomized Experiment on Giving to Welfare Recipients." In *Working Papers*, 1–19. 2003.

Freeland, Chrystia. "The Rise of the New Global Elite." *The Atlantic*, January/February 2011.

Fukuyama, Francis. *Trust: The Social Virtues and the Creation of Prosperity*. New York: Free Press, 1995.

Fukuyama, Francis. "Social Capital." In *Culture Matters: How Values Shape Human Progress*, edited by Lawrence E. Harrison and Samuel P. Huntington, 98–112. New York: Basic Books, 2000.

Gellner, Ernest. *Nations and Nationalism: New Perspectives on the Past*. Ithaca: Cornell University Press, 1983.

Gibbons, John M., Lynn Franco, and Linda Barrington. *I Can't Get No...Job Satisfaction, That Is*. New York: The Conference Board, 2010.

Giddens, Anthony. *The Consequences of Modernity*. Stanford, CA: Stanford University Press, 1990.

Giddens, Anthony. *Runaway World: How Globalization Is Reshaping Our Lives*. New York: Routledge, 2003.

Gilbert, Daniel. *Stumbling on Happiness*. New York: Alfred A. Knopf, Random House Inc., 2006.

Goodin, Robert E. *Protecting the Vulnerable: A Reanalysis of Our Social Responsibilities*. Chicago: University of Chicago Press, 1985.

Goodridge v. Department of Public Health, 798 N.E.2d 941 (Mass. 2003).

Gould, Carol. "Transnational Solidarities." *Journal of Social Philosophy* 38 (2007): 148–64.

Govier, Trudy. *Social Trust and Human Communities*. Montreal: McGill-Queen's University Press, 1997.

Grootaert, Christiaan, and Thierry van Bastelaer, eds. *Understanding and Measuring Social Capital: A Multidisciplinary Tool for Practitioners (Directions in Development)*. Washington, D.C.: World Bank, 2002.

Grossman, Lev. "Iran Protests: Twitter, the Medium of the Movement," *Time*, 17 June 2009. Accessed 12 March 2011, http://www.time.com/time/world/article/0,8599,1905125,00.html.

Halpern, David. *Social Capital*. Malden: Polity Press, 2005.

Hardin, Russell. *Trust*. Malden: Polity Press, 2006.

Harrison, Lawrence E., and Samuel P. Huntington, ed. *Culture Matters: How Values Shape Human Progress*. New York: Basic Books, 2000.

Harvard Kennedy School of Government. "Social Capital Primer." Accessed 20 July 2011, http://www.hks.harvard.edu/saguaro/socialcapitalprimer.htm.

Hastings, Adrian. *The Construction of Nationhood: Ethnicity, Religion, and Nationalism*. The 1996 Wiles Lectures Given at the Queen's University of Belfast. Cambridge, UK: Cambridge University Press, 1997.

Held, David, Anthony McGrew, David Goldblatt and Jonathan Perraton. *Global Transformations: Politics, Economics and Culture*. Stanford: Stanford University Press, 1999.

Helliwell, John F. "Maintaining Social Ties: Social Capital in a Global Information Age." Paper presented at the Keynote Address to the 75th Anniversary Conference of the University of Tilburg on Sustainable Ties in the Information Society, Tilburg, Netherlands, 2003.

Helliwell, John F., Haifang Huang, and Robert D. Putnam. "How's the Job? Are Trust and Social Capital Neglected Workplace Investments?" In *Social Capital: Reaching Out, Reaching In*, edited by Viva Ona Bartkus and James H. Davis. Northampton: Edward Elgar, 2009.

Helliwell, John F., and Robert D. Putnam. "The Social Context of Well-Being." *Philosophical Transactions of the Royal Society of London. Series B, Biological Sciences* 359:1449 (2004): 1435–46.

Hewstone, Miles, and Katy Greenland. "Intergroup Conflict." *International Journal of Psychology* 35:2 (2000): 136–44.

Hoffman, Martin L. "Is Empathy Altruistic?" *Psychological Inquiry* 2:2 (1991): 131–33.

Hoffman, Martin L. "Prosocial Behavior and Empathy: Developmental Processes." In *International Encyclopedia of the Social & Behavioral Sciences*, 12230–33. Oxford: Elsevier Science Ltd., 2001.

Hooghe, Marc, and Dietlind Stolle. *Generating Social Capital: Civil Society and Institutions in Comparative Perspective*. New York: Palgrave Macmillan, 2003.

Hooghe, Marc, and Dietlind Stolle. "Conclusion: The Sources of Social Capital Reconsidered." In *Generating Social Capital*, edited by Marc Hooghe and Dietlind Stolle, 231–49. New York: Palgrave Macmillan, 2003.

H.K. 1388 Serve America Act. 111 Congress 2009–2010.

H.R. Rep. No. 75–1860, at 10–20 (1938).

H.R. Rep. No. 1860, 75th Cong., 3d Sess. 19 (1938).

Iacoboni, Marco. *Mirroring People: The Science of Empathy and How We Connect with Others*. New York: Picador, 2009.

Illingworth, Patricia M. *Trusting Medicine: The Moral Costs of Managed Care*. New York: Routledge, 2005.

Illingworth, Patricia, and Wendy Parmet. *Ethical Healthcare*. Upper Saddle River: Prentice Hall, 2005.

Illingworth, Patricia, Thomas Pogge, and Leif Wenar, eds. *Giving Well: The Ethics of Philanthropy*. New York: Oxford University Press, 2011.

Inglehart, Ronald. "Culture and Democracy." In *Culture Matters: How Values Shape Human Progress*, edited by Lawrence E. Harrison and Samuel P. Huntington, 80–97. New York: Basic Books, 2000.

"Internet 2010 in Numbers." *Royal Pingdom*. Accessed 22 March 2011, http://royal.pingdom.com/2011/01/12/internet-2010-in-numbers/.

I.R.C. § 170 (2008).

I.R.C. § 170(c)(2)(A) (2009).

I.R.C § 501(p) (2010).

Jacobson v. Commonwealth of Massachusetts, 197 U.S. 11 (1905).

Kahneman, Daniel, Alan B. Krueger, David A. Schkade, Norbert Schwarz, and Arthur A. Stone. "A Survey Method for Characterizing Daily Life Experience: The Day Reconstruction Method." *Science* 306 (2004): 1776–80.

Kahneman, Daniel, and Richard Thaler. "Anomalies, Utility Maximization and Experienced Utility." *Journal of Economics Perspectives* 20:1 (2006): 221–34.

Kaul, Inge, Isabelle Grunberg, and Marc A. Stern. "Defining Global Public Goods." In *Global Public Goods: International Cooperation in the 21st Century*, edited by Inge Kaul, Isabelle Grunberg, and Marc A. Stern. New York: Oxford University Press, 1999.

Kawachi, Ichiro, Bruce P. Kennedy, Kimberly Lochner, and Deborah Prothrow-Stith, "Social Capital, Income Inequality, and Mortality," *American Journal of Public Health* 87:9 (1997): 1491–98.

Kawachi, Ichiro, and Lisa F. Berkman. "Social Cohesion, Social Capital, and Health." In *Social Epidemiology*, edited by Lisa F. Berkman and Ichiro Kawachi. New York: Oxford University Press, 2000.

Keane, John. *Global Civil Society?* Edited by Ian Shapiro. Cambridge: Cambridge University Press, 2003.

Keeton, W. Page. *Prosser and Keeton on the Law of Torts*. St. Paul: West Publishing Company, 1984.

Kendall, Gavin, Ian Woodward, and Zlatko Skrbis. *The Sociology of Cosmopolitanism*. New York: Palgrave Macmillan, 2009.

Keohane, Robert O. "Reciprocity in International Relations." *International Organization* 40:1 (1986): 1–27.

Keohane, Robert O., and Joseph S. Nye. "Introduction." In *Governance in a Globalizing World*, edited by Joseph S. Nye and John D. Donahue, 1–41. Danvers: Brookings Institution Press, 2000.

Koehn, Peter H., and James N. Rosenau. "Transnational Competence in an Emergent Epoch." *International Studies Perspective* 3 (2002): 105–27.

Kotter, John P. *A Sense of Urgency*. Boston: Harvard Business Press, 2008.

Kymlicka, Will. *Liberalism, Community and Culture*. New York: Oxford University Press, 1989.

Kymlicka, Will. *Multicultural Citizenship: A Liberal Theory of Minority Rights*. New York: Oxford University Press, 1995.

Kymlicka, Will. *Politics in the Vernacular: Nationalism, Multiculturalism, and Citizenship*. New York: Oxford University Press, 2001.

Kymlicka, Will. *Multicultural Odysseys: Navigating the New International Politics of Diversity*. New York: Oxford University Press, 2007.

Leana, Carrie R. and Harry J. van Buren III. "Organizational Social Capital and Employment Practices." *Academy of Management Review* 24:3 (1999): 538–55.

LeDuff, Charlie. "Frozen in Indifference: Life Goes on around Body Found in Vacant Warehouse." *The Detroit News*, 28 January 2009. Accessed 15 March 2011, http://detnews.com/article/20090128/METRO08/901280491/.

Locksley, Anne, Vilma Ortiz, and Christine Hepburn. "Social Categorization and Discriminatory Behavior: Extinguishing the Minimal Intergroup Discrimination Effect." *Journal of Personality and Social Psychology* 39 (1980): 773–83.

Loggia, Marco L., Jeffrey S. Mogil, and M. Catherine Bushnell. "Empathy Hurts: Compassion for Another Increases Both Sensory and Affective Components of Pain Perception." *Pain* 136 (2008): 168–76.

Loizos, Peter. "Are Refugees Social Capitalists?" In *Social Capital: Critical Perspectives*, edited by Stephen Baron, John Field, Tom Schuller, 124–41. New York: Oxford University Press, 2001.

Love, Maryann Cusimano. *Beyond Sovereignty: Issues for a Global Agenda*. Belmont: Thomson Wadsworth Learning, 2003.

Lyons, David. *Rights, The Wadsworth Series in Social Philosophy*. Belmont: Wadsworth Publishing Co., 1979.

MacKeen, Dawn. "Creeps on Campus: Do Bad Guys Have a Right to Higher Education?" *Salon Ivory Tower*, 1998. Accessed 15 March 2011, http://www.salon.com/it/feature/1998/10/cov_09feature.html.

Margalit, Avishai, and Joseph Raz. "National Self-Determination." *Journal of Philosophy* 87:9 (1990): 439–61.

Marglin, Stephen A. *The Dismal Science: How Thinking Like an Economist Undermines Community*. Cambridge: Harvard University Press, 2008.

McBride, Amanda M., Benjamin J. Lough, and Margaret S. Sherraden. "Perceived Impacts of International Service on Volunteers: Interim Results from a Quasi-Experimental Study." *The Brookings Institution*, 21 June 2010. Accessed 15 March 2011, http://www.brookings.edu/~/media/Files/rc/reports/2010/0621_volunteering_mcbride/0621_volunteering_mcbride.pdf.

McDermott, Anne. "A Silent Friend, and a Debate over Good Samaritan Laws." *CNN*, 4 September 1998. Accessed 15 March 2011, http://www.cnn.com/SPECIALS/views/y/1998/09/mcdermott.casino/.

McIntyre-Mills, Janet J. *Global Citizenship and Social Movements: Creating Transcultural Webs of Meaning in the New Millennium.* Amsterdam, The Netherlands: Harwood Academic Publishers, 2000.

McPherson, Miller, Lynn Smith-Lovin, and James M. Cook. "Birds of a Feather: Homophily in Social Networks." *Annual Review of Sociology* 27 (2001): 415–44.

Mill, John Stuart. *On Liberty.* New York: Penguin Books, 1975.

Mill, John Stuart. Three Essays: On Liberty, Representative Government, the Subjection of Women. New York, NY: Oxford University Press, 1975.

Mill, John Stuart. *Utilitarianism.* Edited by Oskar Piest. First ed. Indianapolis: The Bobbs-Merrill Company, Inc., 1977.

Mill, John Stuart. *Principles of Political Economy with Some of Their Applications to Social Philosophy.* Edited by Stephen Nathanson. Indianapolis, IN: Hackett Publishing Company, Inc., 2004.

Miller, David. *On Nationality.* New York: Oxford University Press, 1995.

Mohn, Tanya. "Going Global, Stateside," *New York Times*, 8 March 2010. Accessed 15 March 2011, http://www.nytimes.com/2010/03/09/business/global/09training.html.

Muhl, Charles J. "The Employment at Will Doctrine: Three Major Exceptions." *Monthly Labor Review* 124:1 (2002): 8.

Narayan, Uma. *Dislocating Cultures: Identities, Traditions, and Third World Feminism.* New York: Routledge, 1997.

Newton, Kenneth. "Social Capital and Democracy." *American Behavioral Scientist* 40:5 (1997): 575–86.

Ng, Yew-Kwang, and Lok-sang Ho. *Happiness and Public Policy: Theory, Case Studies and Implications.* New York: Palgrave Macmillan, 2006.

Niwa, Seiji and Maria Foscarinis. "Homelessness in the United States and the Human Right to Housing." *National Law Center on*

Homelessness & Poverty, 14 January 2004. Accessed 19 February 2001, http://www.nlchp.org/content/pubs/HomelessnessintheUS andRightstoHousing.pdf.

Nussbaum, Martha. "Patriotism and Cosmopolitanism." In *The Global Justice Reader*, edited by Thom Brooks. Malden: Blackwell Publishing, 2008.

N. Y. Tax Law Section 606: ny code – Section 606 (e–1).

OHIO REV. CODE ANN. § 2919.22 (2011).

Opp, Karl D. "Norms." In *International Encyclopedia of the Social & Behavioral Sciences*, edited by Neil J. Smelser and Paul B. Baltes, 10714–20. Oxford, UK: Pergamon, 2011.

Organization for Economic Cooperation and Development. *The Well-Being of Nations: The Roll of Human and Social Capital*. Paris: OECD, 2001.

Oskamp, Stuart. *Reducing Prejudice and Discrimination*. Mahwah: Lawrence Erlbaum Assoc. Publishers, 2000.

Oswald, Andrew J. "Happiness and Economic Performance." *Economic Journal* 107 (1997): 1815–31.

Otake, Keiko, Satoshi Shimai, Junko Tanaka-Matsumi, Kanako Otsui, and Barbara L. Fredrickson. "Happy People Become Happier through Kindness: A Counting Kindnesses Intervention." *Journal of Happiness Studies* 7 (2006): 361–75.

Outterson, Kevin. "Fair Followers: Expanding Access to Generic Pharmaceuticals for Low- and Middle-Income Populations." In *The Power of Pills*, edited by Jillian C. Cohen, Patricia Illingworth, and Udo Schuklenk, 164–78. Michigan: University of Michigan Press, 2005.

Oxfam Education, "What is Global Citizenship?," *Oxfam*. Accessed 20 July 2011, http://www.oxfam.org.uk/education/gc/what_and_ why/what/.

Parmet, Wendy E. *Populations, Public Health, and the Law*. Washington, D.C.: Georgetown University Press, 2008.

Paxton, Pamela and Jeremy Smith. "America's Trust Fall." *Greater Good Magazine*, 2008, 14–17.

Payne v. Western & Atlantic Railroad Co., 81 Tenn. 507, 519–20 (1884).

Pfeffer, Jeffrey. "The Real Cost of the Virtual Workforce." *Stanford Business*. Excerpt from "The Human Equation: Building Profits by Putting People First," 15 May 1998. Accessed 15 March 2011, http://www.stanford.edu/group/knowledgebase/ cgi-bin/1998/03/15/the-real-cost-of-the-virtual-workforce/.

Pildes, Richard. "The Destruction of Social Capital through Law." *University of Pennsylvania Law Review* 144:5 (1996): 2055–77.

Pildes, Richard. "Why Rights Are Not Trumps: Social Meanings, Expressive Harms, and Constitutionalism." *The Journal of Legal Studies* 27:2 (June 1998): 725–63.

Pogge, Thomas. *World Poverty and Human Rights: Cosmopolitan Responsibilities and Reforms.* Malden, MA: Polity Press, Blackwell Publishing Inc., 2002.

Pogge, Thomas. " 'Assisting' the Global Poor." In *The Ethics of Assistance: Morality and the Distant Needy*, edited by Deen K. Chatterjee, 260–88. New York: Cambridge University Press, 2004.

Pogge, Thomas. "Cosmopolitanism and Sovereignty." In *The Global Justice Reader*, edited by Thom Brooks. Malden, MA: Blackwell Publishing, 2008.

Pogge, Thomas. "Eradicating Systemic Poverty: Brief for a Global Resources Divided." In *The Global Justice Reader*, edited by Thom Brooks. Malden, MA: Blackwell Publishing Ltd., 2008.

Pogge, Thomas. *Health Impact Fund*, The MacMillan Center, Yale. Accessed 15 April 2011, http://www.yale.edu/macmillan/igh/.

Posner, Eric and Cass R. Sunstein. "Climate Change Justice." *The Georgetown Law Journal* 96:5 (2008): 1565–1612.

Posner, Eric and Cass R. Sunstein. *Law and Happiness.* Chicago: University of Chicago Press, 2010.

Pozen, David E. "Remapping the Charitable Deduction." *Connecticut Law Review* 39 (2006): 537.

Putnam, Robert. *Bowling Alone: The Collapse and Revival of American Community.* New York, NY: Simon & Schuster, 2000.

Putnam, Robert. "E Pluribus Unum: Diversity and Community in the Twenty-First Century." *Scandinavian Political Studies* 30:2 (2007): 159.

Putnam, Robert, and Lewis Feldstein. *Better Together: Restoring the American Community.* New York: Simon and Schuster, 2003.

Rawls, John. *A Theory of Justice.* Cambridge, MA: Belknap Press of Harvard University Press, 1971.

Regents of University of California v. Bakke, 438 U.S. 265 (1978).

Reich, Rob. "Toward a Political Theory of Philanthropy." In *Giving Well: The Ethics of Philanthropy*, edited by Patricia Illingworth, Thomas Pogge, and Leif Wenar, 177–95. New York: Oxford University Press, 2011.

Rifkin, Jeremy. "The European Dream." *Utne Reader*, September/October 2004. Accessed 20 July 2011, http://www.utne.com/2004-09-01/the-european-dream.aspx.

Robison, Lindon J., and Jan L. Flora. "The Social Capital Paradigm: Bridging across Disciplines." *American Journal of Agricultural Economics* 85 (2003): 1208–10.

Rochester, J. Martin. *Between Peril and Promise: The Politics of International Law.* Washington DC: CQ Press 2006.

Roth, Richard. "Pakistan Flooding Crisis hit by 'Donor Fatigue'?" *CBS News*, 18 August 2010. Accessed 25 March 2011, http://www.cbsnews.com/stories/2010/08/18/eveningnews/main6785095.shtml.

Ruggie, John G. "Multilateralism: The Anatomy of an Institution." *International Organization* 46:3 (Summer 1992): 561–86.

Ruggie, John G. "Reconstituting the Global Public Domain: Issues, Actors and Practices." *Corporate Social Responsibility Initiative Working Paper No. 6.* Cambridge: John F. Kennedy School of Government Harvard University, 2004.

Ruggie, John G. "Protect, Respect and Remedy: A Framework for Business and Human Rights," *Human Rights Council*, April 2008.

Rushton, J. Philippe. "Genetic and Environmental Contributions to Pro-Social Attitudes: A Twin Study of Social Responsibility." *Proceedings: Biological Sciences* 271: 1557 (2004): 2583–85.

Rutkowski, Gregory K., Charles L. Grudger, and Daniel Romer. "Group Cohesiveness, Social Norms, and Bystander Intervention." *Journal of Personality and Social Psychology* 44:3 (1983): 545–52.

Sander, Thomas H. and Robert Putnam. "How Joblessness Hurts Us All," *USA Today*, 10 December 2011.

Sandler, Ronald L. *Character and Environment: A Virtue-Oriented Approach to Environmental Ethics.* New York, NY: Columbia University Press, 2007.

Saulny, Susan. "Black? White? Asian? More Young Americans Choose All of the Above." *New York Times*, 29 January 2011. Accessed 12 March 2011, http://www.nytimes.com/2011/01/30/us/30mixed.html.

Saulny, Susan. "Counting by Race Can Throw off Some Numbers." *New York Times*, 9 February 2011, Accessed 12 March 2011, http://www.nytimes.com/2011/02/10/us/10count.html.

Schulze, Hagen. *States, Nations, and Nationalism: From the Middle Ages to the Present: The Making of Europe.* Cambridge: Wiley-Blackwell, 1998.

Sen, Amartya. *Development as Freedom.* New York: Oxford University Press, 2001.

Sen, Amartya. *Identity and Violence: The Illusion of Destiny.* New York: W.W. Norton and Co, 2006.

Sen, Amartya. *The Idea of Justice.* Cambridge: Belknap Press of Harvard University Press, 2009.

Shah, Anup. "Poverty Facts and Stats." Accessed 20 July 2011, http://www.globalissues.org/article/26/poverty-facts-and-stats.

Shapiro, Ian, Will Kymlicka, eds. *Ethnicity and Group Rights.* New York: New York University Press, 1997.

Sherrice Iverson Child Victim Protection Act, CAL. Penal CODE § 152.3 (2001).

Silverman, Rachel E. and Sally Beatty. "Doing Due Diligence on Your Donations." *Wall Street Journal*, 20 December 2007. Accessed 15 March 2011, http://online.wsj.com/article/SB1198 10791163740721.html.

Simon, Herbert. "Ubi and the Flat Tax." *Boston Review*, October/ November, 2000.

Singer, Peter. *Practical Ethics.* Cambridge: Cambridge University Press, 1993.

Singer, Peter. *One World: The Ethics of Globalization.* New Haven: Yale University Press, 2002.

Singer, Peter. *The Life You Can Save: Acting Now to End World Poverty.* New York: Random House, 2009.

Skrbiš, Zlatko. *Long-Distance Nationalism: Diasporas, Homelands and Identities: Research in Migration and Ethnic Relations Series.* Brookfield, VT: Ashgate, 1999.

Smith, Anthony D. *Nations and Nationalism in a Global Era.* Cambridge, UK: Polity Press, 1995.

Smith, Anthony D. *Nationalism and Modernism: A Critical Survey of Recent Theories of Nations and Nationalism.* New York: Routledge, 1998.

Smith, Jeremy Adam, Paxton, Pamela. "America's Trust Fall." *Greater Good*, 2008.

Smits, Jan M. "The Good Samaritan in European Private Law: On the Perils of Principles without a Programme and a Programme for the Future." Inaugural Lecture, Maastricht University, 19 May 2000.

Sommers, Samuel R., Lindsey S. Warp, and Corrine C. Mahoney. "Cognitive Effects of Racial Diversity: White Individuals' Information Processing in Heterogeneous Groups." *Journal of Experimental Social Psychology* 44 (2008): 1129–36.

Special Rapporteur of the Commission on the Human Right to the Enjoyment of the Highest Attainable Standard of Physical and Mental Health. Mission to Glaxo Smith Kline. U.N. Doc A/HRC/11/12/ADD.2. May 2009.

Spencer, Philip, and Howard Wollman. *Nations and Nationalism: A Reader.* New Brunswick: Rutgers University Press, 2005.

Steger, Michael F., Todd B. Kashdan, Shigehiro Oishi. "Being Good by Doing Good: Daily Eudaimonic Activity and Well-being." *Journal of Research in Personality* 42 (2008): 22–42.

Stephens, Christopher. "Modelling Reciprocal Altruism." *British Journal for the Philosophy of Science* 46 (1996): 533–51.

Stiglitz, Joseph E. *Making Globalization Work*. New York, NY: W.W. Norton & Company, 2006.

Stiglitz, Joseph E., A. Sen, and J.P. Fitoussi. "Report by the Commission on the Measurement of Economic Performance and Social Progress." The Commission on the Measurement of Economic Performance and Social Progress. Accessed 5 April 2011, http://www.stiglitz-sen-fitoussi.fr/documents/rapport_anglais.pdf.

Stolle, Dietlind. "The Sources of Social Capital". In *Generating Social Capital: Civil Society and Institutions in Comparative Perspective*, edited by Marc Hooghe and Dietlind Stolle. New York: Palgrave Macmillan, 2003.

Stratton, Allegra. "David Cameron Aims to Make Happiness the New GDP," *The Guardian* [UK], 14 November 2010. Accessed 15 March 2011, http://www.guardian.co.uk/politics/2010/nov/14/david-cameron-wellbeing-inquiry.

Sunstein, Cass R. "On the Expressive Function of Law." *University of Pennsylvania Law Review* 144:5 (1996): 2046.

Sunstein, Cass R. "Social Norms and Social Roles." *Columbia Law Review* 96, n4 (1996): 1–47.

Surgeon General, "Mental Health: A Report." Accessed 11 March 2011, http://www.surgeongeneral.gov/library/mentalhealth/home.html.

Tajfel, Henri. "Experiments in Intergroup Discrimination." *Scientific American* 223 (1970): 96–102.

Tajfel, Henri, and Michael Billig. "Familiarity and Categorization in Intergroup Behavior." *Journal of Experimental Social Psychology* 10 (1974): 159–70.

Tajfel, Henril, Michael G. Billig, and R. P. Bundy. "Social Categorization and Intergroup Behavior." *European Journal of Social Psychology* 1:2 (1971): 149–78.

Thaler, Richard H. and Cass R. Sunstein. *Nudge: Improving Decisions about Health, Wealth, and Happiness*. New York: Penguin Group Inc., 2008.

The Saguaro Seminar, "Social Capital Primer." Accessed 11 March 2011, http://www.hks.harvard.edu/saguaro/socialcapitalprimer.htm.

The United Nations Refugee Agency. "UNHCR Annual Report Shows 42 Million People Uprooted Worldwide," 16 June 2009. Accessed 19 February 2011, http://www.unhcr.org/4a2fd52412d.html.

The World Bank, "Overview: Social Capital." Accessed 11 March 2011, http://go.worldbank.org/C0QTRW4QF0.

Toussaint v. Blue Cross & Blue Shield of Michigan, 408 Mich 579 (1980).

Tse, Wai S., and Alyson J. Bond. "Reboxetine Promotes Social Bonding in Healthy Volunteers." Journal of Psychopharmacology 17:2 (2003): 189–95.

Universal Declaration of Human Rights, G.A. Res, 217A, at 76, U.N. GAOR, 3d Sess., 1st plen. mtg., U.N. Doc. A/810 (12 December 1948).

U.S. Census Bureau, Thursday, 16 September 2010, accessed 17 April 2011.

U.S. CONST. amend. V.

Uslaner, Eric M. "Trust, Democracy and Governance: Can Government Policies Influence Generalized Trust?" In *Generating Social Capital*, edited by Marc Hooghe and Dietlind Stolle. New York: Palgrave Macmillan, 2003.

Ustun, T. Bedirhan, Joseph L. Ayuso-Mateos, Somnath Chatterji, Colin Mathers, and Christopher J. L. Murray. "Global Burden of Depressive Disorders in the Year 2000." *British Journal of Psychiatry* 184 (2004): 386–92.

Utah County v. Intermountain Health Care, Inc., 709 P. 2d 275 (1985).

Van Horn v. Watson, 45 Cal. 4th 322 (2008).

Vasak, Karel. *The International Dimensions of Human Rights*. Edited by Philip Alston. Westport: Greenwood Press, 1982.

Vertovec, Steven, and Robin Cohen, eds. *Conceiving Cosmopolitanism: Theory Context and Practice*. New York: Oxford University Press, 2002.

Walzer, Michael. *On Toleration*. New Haven: Yale University Press, 1997.

Wenar, Leif. "Poverty Is No Pond: Challenges for the Affluent." In *Giving Well: The Ethics of Philanthropy*, edited by Patricia Illingworth, Thomas Pogge, and Leif Wenar. New York: Oxford University Press, 2011.

Wenar, Leif. "The Basic Structure as Object: Institutions and Humanitarian Concern." *Global Justice, Global Institutions Canadian Journal of Philosophy* 31 (2007): 253–278.

Wolf, Stewart, and John G. Bruhn. *The Power of Clan: The Influence of Human Relationships on Heart Disease*. New Brunswick: Transaction Publishers, 1993.

Wright, Robert. "Will Globalization Make You Happy?" *Foreign Policy*, September/October, 2000, 55–64.

Wyer, Robert S., Chi-yue Chiu, and Ying-yi Hong. *Understanding Culture: Theory, Research, and Application*. New York: Psychology Press, 2009.

Yale University: Incentives for Global Health, "The Health Impact Fund Making New Medicines Accessible for All," 30 April 2010. Accessed 19 February 2011, http://www.yale.edu/macmillan/igh/.

Yunus Muhammad, and Alan Jolis. *Banker to the Poor: Micro Lending and the Battle against World Poverty*. New York: Public Affairs, 1999.

Zack, Paul J. "The Neurobiology of Trust." *Scientific American Magazine*, June 2008, 88–95.

Ziegler, Marcia M. "Comment: Nonfeasance and the Duty to Assist: The American Seinfeld Syndrome." *Dickenson Law Review* 105 (2000): 525.

Index

Note: Page references with letter 'n' followed by locators denote note numbers.

abandoned strangers, 210
abundant social capital, 151
activism, 25
activist culture, 114
ADA, *see* Americans with
    Disabilities Act (ADA)
addictive disorders, 99
advocacy, 25
affirmative action, 125, 150
affirmative action laws, 125
Africa, xi
African Charter of Human and
    Peoples' Rights, 75, 75n9
AIDS, 13, 19, 56, 163
Al Haramain Islamic
    Foundation, 170
American Journal of Epidemiology,
    44n41
Americans with Disabilities Act
    (ADA), 123–4, 124n10
antidepressants, 100
anxiety disorders, 99–100
Appadurai, A., 184, 185n5, 199,
    199n27
Australia, x
autonomy, 27, 90
Ayuso-Mateos, J. L., 100n43

Babcock, H. M., 21n20, 22n23
bad race relations, 59
bad samaritanism, 25

bandwagons, 21–4
Baron, S., 69, 69n5
Barry, C., xiii, 214
Baumeister, R. F., 116, 116n65,
    186–8, 186n6, 192, 192n15
Beatty, S., 170n31
behavior, 21
    caring, 17–18
    cooperative, 35, 105
    healthy, 45
    opportunistic, 39
    pro-social, 27–8, 82
    self-interested, 18
    trustworthy, 40–2
belonging, 103, 188, 192–3
    in culture, 103, 105, 116, 188
    defined, 186–8
benefits
    in culture, 107–8
    of social capital, 51
Berkman, L. F., 34, 34n3, 43n35,
    51n55, 95, 192n16
Berlin, I. S., 136, 136n33
*Better Together: An Initiative of
    the Saguaro Seminar*
    (Putnam and Feldstein), 48,
    48n49, 49, 49n51
Biegler, P., 100, 101n45
bilingualism, 197
Bill and Melinda Gates
    Foundation, 152

Bill of Rights, 113
Billionaire's Club, 49
Blanchflower, D. G., 92n20
Bob Jones University, 164–5, 165
Bob Jones University v. United States, 164, 164n20
Bok, S., 41, 41n28
bonding peptide, 40
bonding social capital, 37, 55–6
Bowling Alone (Putnam), 6, 181
Bretton Woods organizations, 183
Bridgeland, J., 204n34
bridging social capital, 38
Brooks, T., 181n2
Brown, E., 153, 153n5
Brown v. Board of Education, 54n59, 123, 123n9
Bruhn, J. G., 44n41
Buffet, W., 49
Buren, H. J. III, 141n43
business contributions to social capital, 48–9
bystander effect, 127, 161

Cacioppo, J. T., 95, 95n31
Cameron, D. (Prime Minister), 11n1
capital, 33
Caprara, D., 204n34
CARE, 163
caring behavior, 17–18
cascades, 21–4
Cash, D., 130–4
cash offered to strangers, 133–4
Castles, S., 195, 195n19
categorization, 189–90
causation, 72
Cedarhurst New York and the Islamic American Relief Agency, 170

Centers for Disease Control, 100
charitable tax deductions, 208–9
charitable tax law, 151–2
charities, 152–7
    deductions and giving to, 157–79
    donor fatigue and, 16
    exemptions and, 164–5
    generalized reciprocity and, 155–6
    intermediary, 166–7
    IRC requirements for, 163–5
    laws on, 159–62
    paying forward and, 36
    philanthropy, 153–4
    public policy and, 165–6
    reciprocity and, 165–6
    trust and, 156–7
    waters edge policy on, 163–4, 167–75
Chatterji, S., 100n43
Chiu, C., 112, 112n58
choice architecture, 6, 30
Christakis, N., 95–6, 96n33, 96n34, 96n35
civic renaissance, 48
Civil Codes of France and Holland, 128n19
civil common laws, 130–1
Clark, A. E., 141n45
CNN, 133n27
CNN Wire Staff, 15n10
Cohen, J. C., 52n58, 67n1
cohesion, 38–9
    see also specific types of
Coleman, J. S., 34, 37n2, 43n33, 50, 51n54, 52, 52n57
collectives, 76, 189
common identity, 104
common sense, 138
community, social capital in, 72–3

compensation, 123
concept of social capital, 2–3,
    32–3, 35–6, 77
conditionality, 21
conduct
    ethical, 20
    ethics and, 67–8
    generalization principles of,
        148
    individual, 29, 89
    moral, 25
    suspicious, 15
conflict, 1, 108
consumer sovereignty, 138
Cook, J. M., 38n20
cooperation, vii, 4, 110–11, 120
cooperative behavior, 35, 105
cooperative interests, 53
Copenhagen Summit, 13
corruption, 25
cosmopolitan norms, 25, 60
cosmopolitanism, 60, 81–2
Costa, D. L., 58, 58n69
Court of Justice, 172–3
creation of social capital, 2,
    46–9, 181–3
criminal common laws, 130–1
cultural material flows, 199
cultural norms, 109–10
culture
    activist, 114
    belonging in, 103, 105, 116,
        188
    benefits in, 107–8
    conflict within, 1, 108
    cooperation within, 4, 110–11
    cultural norms in, 109–10
    deaf, 114
    diversity within, 115
    global identity and, 111
    green, 114
    happiness in, 114

hippie, 114
homophily and, 106–7
identity, role in, 185–6
moral values in, 107
national, 114, 118
social capital and, connection
    between, 111–13
social costs of, 108–9
societal, 103–4
tension within, 1
transnational, 114
trust in, 105–6, 110–11
values within, 84–5, 104–5
see also specific types of
Culture Wizard, 111
customary law, 147
customs, 88–92

David, P. A., 92n20
Davidson, A., 195, 195n19
Daynard, R. A., 137–8, 138n38
deaf culture, 114
death, 12–13
Deaton, A., 92, 92n21
decategroization, 189
Declaration of Human Rights,
    12n5, 57, 75, 203
deductions, 157–79
Delhey, J., 41n29
democracy, 35
demographics, 61–2, 191
destroying social capital, 139–46
Diener, E., 92n19, 98–9, 99n41
differences, appreciation for,
    195
diffuse reciprocation, 148–9
disability laws, 124–5
disability rights, 150
disruptive disorders, 100
distant strangers, 127, 204, 208
distant suffering, 16
diverse communities, 58–9

diversity, 58, 59, 115, 181–2
donations, 156
Donley, J. M., 133n28
donor fatigue, 16
donor's marginal tax rate, 159
due diligence, 24
Dumbaugh, K., 14n7
Duty to Aid the Endangered
    Act, 128n20
duty to rescue laws, 128, 135
Dworkin, R., 68n2, 104n49,
    173n36

Earth Day, 115, 198
Easterlin, R. A., 92n20
economic prosperity, 44
Edgerton, R., 112, 112n57
education, 209
egalitarian, 48, 77, 94
Egolf, B., 44n41
emotional contagion, 101–2
Engeler, E., 197n22
Epstein, R. A., 135n32, 140,
    140n41
Equatorial Guinea, x
ethical concept of social capital,
    69
ethical conduct, 20
ethical decisions, 69–70
ethical judgments, 69–70
ethical principle, social capital
    as, 180–1
ethical statements, 70–1
ethics
    conduct and, 67–8
    happiness for, importance of,
        87–8
    liberty and, concept of, 68–9
    moral obligations, 67
    morals and, 69–74
    self-interest, 66–7
    social capital and, 76–83

solidarity rights and, 75–6
    universal, 69–70
ethics entrepreneurs, 25–9
ethnic diversity, 58–9
ethnically-defined group
    hostility, 59
ethnoscape, 184–5, 199
Europe, viii
European Commission Treaty,
    171
euthanasia, 122
exclusionary social capital, 4
exemptions, 164–5
expressive function, 121–2, 129
expressive content of laws, 131–2
externalities of social capital, 3,
    50–1, 65, 183

face-to-face interaction, 71
family-level social capital, 94
Featherstone, M., 185n5
Feldstein, L., 48, 48n50
Field, J., 69, 69n5
film, 198
financescape, 199
financial capital, 33
Fitoussi, J. P., 6, 35n10
Flora, J. L., 36–7, 37n14
flows, 199
fluid sense of identity, 61
Foscarinis, M., 14n8
Fowler, J., 95–6, 96n33, 96n34,
    96n35
Fredrickson, B. L., 145n53, 160n14
free rider problem, 51, 66–7
freedom-to-contract
    justification, 140–1
Freeland, C., 118n67
friends, viii, 95–6
Fukuyama, F., 35, 35n6, 111,
    113, 113n61, 113n62

Gates, B., 49
Gates, M., 49
GDP, *see* gross domestic product
    (GDP)
General Agreement on Tariffs
    and Trade, 63, 148
general happiness, 85–6, 96–7
generalized reciprocity, 25, 58
    charities and, 155–6
    defined as, 25
    laws, impact on, 120, 123–4
    paying forward and, 36
    philanthropy and, 154
    social capital and, 34
    trust and, 40–1
Genovese, Kitty, 126–7
Georgellis, Y., 141n45
Giddens, A., 117
Gilbert, D., 98n38
Give Act, 209
Give Well, 170
giving, 151–2
    public, 18
    by upper-income Americans,
        18–19
Giving Pledge, 49
GivingWhatWeCan.org, 26
global challenges, 163
global citizenry, 60, 193, 203–12
    charitable tax deductions,
        208–9
    education, 209
    global living and, 203
    international service,
        international benefits of,
            206
    international ties, 205–6
    international volunteering,
        204–5
    universal rights, 203–4
    volunteering, 206–8
global collaboration, 162–3

global communications,
    199–200
global community, diversity in,
    59
global culture, 196–9
    in film, 198
    grounded identity in, 196
    in media, 197–8
    popular culture in, 196–7
    standard indices of, 198–9
global diversity, 59
global elite, ix, xi, xiv
global governance mechanisms,
    56
global groups, 201
global homelessness, 13
global identity, 61–2, 111
global justice, 57–8
global living, 199–203
    challenges of, 4
    cultural material flows, 199
    global citizen and, 203
    global communications,
        199–200
    in global groups, 201
    in multinational
        transnational networks,
            201
    transnational living and, 200
    transnational social capital
        and, 201–2
global norms, 57
global organizations, 56
global poverty, 5, 12, 15–16, 25,
    210–11
global public domain, 64
global scope, 56
Global Service Fellowships, 204
global social capital, 53–65, 152,
    182–3
    defined, 182–3
    dimensions of, 65

global social capital – *continued*
  ethnic diversity, 58–9
  global identity, 61–2
  global justice, 57–8
  global norms, 57
  global organizations, 56
  growth of, 53–4
  homophily, 59–61
  hunkering, 59–60
  immigration, 54–5
  international business
    relationships, 63–4
  international organizations,
    56
  international personal
    relationships, 63–4
  in public domain, 64
  refugees, 54–5
  religious diversity, 58–9
  transnational reciprocity, 57
  values of, 65
global strangers, 127
global suffering, 177
global warming, 25
GlobalGiving.org, 170
globalization, 53
Goldblatt, D., 196n20
Golden Rule, 70
good citizenship, 45–6
Good Samaritan Laws, 128,
    128n20, 133n27
*Goodridge v. Department of Public
    Health*, 125, 125n12
Google Zeitgeist Europe
    Conference, 11
Gould, C., 27n31
government action, 132
government inaction, 132
green culture, 114
Greenland, K., 189n11
Grootaert, C., 39n23
gross domestic product (GDP), 11

Grossman, L., 62n79
Ground Zero, 1
grounded identity, 117–18, 196
group identity, 182
Grunberg, I., 50n52

Haiti, 17
Halpern, D., 47n48
happiness, 85–7
  autonomy, 98
  benefits of, 97–8
  in culture, 114
  for ethics, importance of, 87–8
  friends and, 95–6
  general, 85–6, 96–7
  harmony and, 86
  impediments, 99–101
  implications for, 96
  individual, 87
  interpersonal relationships
    and, 94
  isolation and, 94–5
  kindness and, 145
  liberty and, 98–9
  loneliness and, 94–5
  maximizing, 87
  research on, 97
  social relationships and, 92–3
  social status factors and, 93
  with social ties, 86–7, 211–12
  well-being and, 93–4, 99–100
happy followers, 52, 67
harm principle, 91, 102
harmony, 86
Harvard University, 64
Health Assembly, 146
health benefits of social capital,
    44–5
Health Impact Fund, 26
healthy behavior, 45
*Hein Persche v. Finanzamt
    Ludenscheid*, 171, 171n32

Held, D., 196, 196n20, 197n24
Helliwell, J. F., 54–5, 54n60, 93, 93n24, 94
helping others, 16–17, 151–2
helping strangers, 126–39
Hepburn, C., 186, 186n8
Hewstone, M., 189n11
hippie culture, 114
HIV, 13
homelessness, 13–15
homogeneity, 58–9
homogeneous, 58–9
homophily, 59–61, 106–7
Hong, Y., 112, 112n58, 198
Hooge, M., 35n5, 46n45, 93n22, 94n30
hostility to strangers, 118
"House of Horrors, The", 15
Hulu, 198
human capital, 33
humankind, xi
human rights
    activists of, 25
    culture of, 115
    due diligence for, 24
    homelessness and, 13
    international giving and, 168
    international volunteers role in, 207
    norms about, 198
    obligations for, 58
    universal, 56, 60
    violations of, 109
human well-being, 91–2
humanity, 82
hunkering, 59–60
Hunt, P., 24n28
Hurricane Katrina, 127

Iacoboni, M., 91, 91n18
identity
    common, 104
    culture, role in, 185–6
    fluid sense of, 61
    global, 61–2, 111
    grounded, 117–18, 196
    group, 182
    racial, 61
    as sense of security, 117
    shared, 105
    single, 181
    social, 60, 115
ideoscape, 199
illegal migrants, 1
Illingworth, P., 17n14, 38n19, 51n56, 52n58, 67n1, 158n12, 169n28
imitation, 90–1
immigration, 53, 54–5
in-group bias, 188
in-group favoritism, 186
Independent Sector, 157
indifference, 13–14, 210
    caring behavior, 17–18
    within cultures, 13–14
    giving, 18–19
    helping others, 16–17
    homelessness, 13, 14
    poverty, 12–13
    self-interest, 19
    social good, 19–20
    suffering, 15–17
individual conduct, 29, 89
individual happiness, 87
individual rights, 138
individualism, 27, 66, 89–90, 101
individuals, 21
Inglehart, R., 111n56
instrumental norms, 21
intermediary charities, 166–7

internal norms, 22
Internal Revenue Code (IRC),
   152, 163, 164
   charities, requirements for,
      163–5
international business
   relationships, 63–4
International Covenant on
   Economic, Social and
   Cultural Rights, 75, 126
international giving, 168
international law, 120, 147–8,
   150
International Monetary Fund,
   63
International Nelson Mandela
   Day, 198
international organizations, 56
International Peace Day, 198
international personal
   relationships, 63–4
international service,
   international benefits of,
   206
international social capital,
   4–5
international ties, 205–6
international volunteer, 207
international volunteerism, 59,
   204–5
International Women's Day,
   115, 198
"Internet 2010 in Numbers"
   (Royal Pingdom), 197n23
interpersonal relationships, 94,
   116–17
investment in social capital, 53
IRC, *see* Internal Revenue Code
   (IRC)
Islamic Center, 1
isolation, 94–5
itemizers, xiii

itemizer effect, 161
Iverson, L., 129, 132–3

*Jacobson v. Commonwealth of
   Massachusetts*, 138n39
Jacobson v. Massachusetts, 138
John F. Kennedy School of
   Government, 64
Jolis, A., 178n37
judicial administration, 138
justice, 73–4

Kahn, M. E., 58n69
Kahneman, D., 92, 92n21,
   98n39
Kapur, Devesh, 55
Kashdan, T. B., 137n34
Kaul, I., 50n52
Kawachi, I., 34, 34n3, 43n35,
   51n55, 93, 93n23
Keeton, P., 72n7
Kendall, G., 117n66
Kennard, B. P., 93n23
Kenya, x
Keohane, R. O., 148–9, 148n63
kindness, 20, 23, 36, 112, 145,
   153, 160
Koehn, P. H., 182, 183n4, 201
Kotter, J., 118n68
Ku Klux Klan, 7, 71
Kymlicka, W., 103–4, 104n46

Lasker, J., 44n41
Latane, B., 133n28
laws, 29, 120, 144–5
   for affirmative action, 125
   charitable tax, 151–2
   on charities, 159–62
   civil common, 130–1
   criminal common, 130–1
   customary, 147
   for disabilities, 124–5

duty to rescue, 120–1, 129,
    135–6, 138–9, 182
euthanasia, for regulation of,
    122
expressive content of, 131–2
generalized reciprocity,
    impact on, 120, 123–4
Good Samaritan, 128
international, 120, 146–7
liberty and, 139
multilateralism and, 148–9
for norms, 122–3, 125–6
public health, 138
reciprocity and impact on,
    29–30
social capital, creating of, 120,
    144–5
social harm of, 136–7
as social meaning, 121–6
social networks, and impact
    on, 29–30
Taking Clause in, 123
termination at will, 121
trust, impact on, 120
value of, 121–2
lean and mean definition,
    33, 35
Leana, C. R., 141n43
Leary, M. R., 116, 116n65,
    186–7, 186n6, 192, 192n15
LeDuff, C., 15n9
legal migrants, 1
libertarian paternalism, 30
liberty, 80, 88–92
    ethics and, concept of, 68–9
    happiness and, 98–9
    laws and, 139
    negative, 140
liberty and strangers, 139
Libyan migrants, 1
Life You Can Save, The (Singer),
    18, 73, 177–8

local suffering, 16
Lochner, K., 93, 93n23
Locksley, A., 186, 186n8
Loizos, P., 47n47
loneliness, 94–5
Lough, B. J., 205n35

MacKeen, D., 130n21, 132n26
Margalit, A., 105n50
marketplace values, 138, 143–4
Mathers, C., 100n43
May Day, 115
McBride, A. M., 205n35
McDermott, A., 133n27
McGrew, A., 196, 196n20, 197n24
McPherson, M., 38n20
media, 197–8
mediascape, 199
Melinda Gates Foundation, 152
mental disorders, 100–1
Merkel, Chancellor, 1
Michigan Supreme Court, 143
migrants, 1, 54–6
Mill, J. S., 8, 68, 68n3, 85–91,
    85n1, 88n8, 88n9, 89n12,
    96–9, 101, 103, 130n22,
    135, 135n31, 143–4
Miller, D., 97n36, 97n37, 105–6,
    105n51, 106n52, 114
mirror neurons, mirroring, 91
Mohn, T., 111n55
mood disorders, 99
moral conduct, 25
moral duty, 67
moral goods, 26, 76–7
moral importance of social
    capital, 29
moral norms, 19, 21, 79–80, 82
moral obligations, 67, 134
moral principle, 49
moral values, 80–1, 107

morals
    ethics and, 69–74
    of social capital, 71
    suffering and, 16–17
Morrison, W., 14n7
Mubarak, President, 63
Muhl, C. J., 143n50
multicultural society, 1
multilateralism, 148–50
multilingualism, 197
multinational transnational
        networks, 201
multiracial identity, 191
Murray, C. J. L., 100n43

Nathanson, Stephen, 88, 89
National Bureau of Economic
        Research, 142
national culture, 114, 118
nationalism, 105
negative duties, 203
negative liberty, 6, 71, 135, 136,
        139–40
negotiation, 147–8
neighborhood effects, 44
neighborhood social capital, 44
Neighborhood Watch
        programs, 2
network-based social capital, 153
network poverty, 47, 74
Newton, K., 37n16, 41n29
NGOs, *see* non-governmental
        organizations (NGOs)
Niwa, S., 14n8
non-excludable public goods, 50
non-governmental
        organizations (NGOs), xii,
        19–20, 22
    activism of, 25
    donations to, 156
    global scope of, 56
    social capital and, 56, 81

non-itemization, 158–9
non-rivalrous public
        goods, 50
norm bandwagons, 23, 126
norm-based social capital, 153
norm cascades, 23
norm change, 22–3
norm creation, 22–3
norm entrepreneurship,
        21, 24
norm manipulation, 145–6
norms
    about human rights, 198
    characteristics of, 21
    cosmopolitan, 25, 60
    cultural, 109–10
    defined, 21
    instrumental, 21
    internal, 22
    laws for, 122–3, 125–6
    moral, 19, 21, 82
    of self-interest, 19, 51
    in social life, 28–9
    of status quo bias, 49
Nudge (Thaler and Sunstein), 30
nudges, 29–31, 91
nudging towards social capital,
        29–31
Nussbaum, M., 25, 60, 81–2,
        82n11, 209, 209n40

Obama, B., 80–1, 209
obligations, 77–8
OECD, *see* Organization for
        Economic Cooperation and
        Development (OECD)
Oishi, S., 137n34
Olympics, 198
On Liberty (Mill), 68, 89, 97, 98
Opp, K. D., 21, 21n21
opportunistic behavior, 39
oppression, 90

Organization for Economic
    Cooperation and
    Development (OECD), 32,
    55n61, 173
Ortiz, V., 186, 186n8
Oswald, A. J., 92n20, 94n29
Otake, K., 145n53, 160n14
Otsui, K., 145n53, 160n14
oughtness, 21
Outterson, K., 52n58, 67n1
Øverland, G., xiii, 214
Oxfam Education, 111n54, 163
oxytocin
    peptide, 40
    synthetic, 40
    trust and increased, 110, 154,
        156, 178

paradigm shift, 81
parens patriae duties, 116
Parent Teacher Association, 2, 77
Parmet, W. E., 51n56, 194, 194n17
Patrick, W., 95, 95n31
Paxton, P., 20n18
paying forward, 36
*Payne v. Western & Atlantic
    Railroad Co.*, 139, 140n40
peace, 76
Peace Corps, 204
Pepsi, 24
peptide oxytocin, 40
Perraton, J., 196n20
Pershe, H., 171, 174, 184
Pfeffer, J., 142n47
philanthropy, 153–4, 169
philosophers, 25–9
physical capital, 33
Pildes, R. H., 120–2, 120n1,
    123n6, 123n8, 131–2,
    132n23, 143–4, 144n51,
    158
Pogge, T., 10, 16, 16n11, 17n14,
    25, 25n29, 58n67, 58n68,

60, 60n74, 152n2, 158n12,
    165–6, 165n24, 166n25,
    169n28, 181, 181n2, 189,
    191, 191n14, 194n18,
    203n32, 210
    foreword, xvii
political engagement, 46
popular culture, 196–7
pornography of poverty, 151
Posner, E., 13n6
Potvin, L., 44n41
poverty
    death and, 12–13
    global, 12, 25, 210–11
    network, 47, 74
    pornography of, 151
    suffering and, 15–16
Pozen, D. E., 157n8, 163n18,
    168n26
Principles of Political Economy
    (Mill), 88
principle of social capital
    cosmopolitanism, 81–2
    humanity, 82
    liberty, 80
    moral good, 76–7
    moral norms, 79–80
    moral value, 80–1
    obligations, 77–8
    paradigm shift, 81
    privacy, 80
    self-interest, 78
    social trust, 79
    universalization, 82–3
privacy, 80
pro-social behavior, 27–8, 82
Prothrow-Stith, D., 93n23
public domain, 64
public giving, 18
public goods, 50
public health laws, 138
public philosophy, 25

public policy, 165–6
Putnam, R. D., 3–4, 6, 20,
   20n17, 20n19, 35–7, 35n9,
   36n13, 37n15, 38n17, 39,
   41n27, 42, 43n34, 43n36,
   44–5, 45n42, 48, 48n50,
   58–9, 59n71, 74, 87, 87n7,
   93–4, 93n24, 94n28,
   115n63, 142, 142n48, 153,
   153n3, 154n7, 181–2,
   181n1, 182n3

Queen's University, 103
quid pro quo exchanges, 73,
   156
quid pro quo transactions, 141

Rabbi Meir Kahane Memorial
   Fund, 170
racial identity, 61
rainmaker effect, 49, 66
Rawls, J., 77, 77n10
Raz, J., 104, 105n50
reciprocation, 36, 155, 193–4
   charities and, 165–6
   diffuse, 148–9
   generalized, 25, 58
   laws and impact on, 29–30
   transnational, 57
Reder, M. W., 92n20
refugees, 54–5
*Regents of the University of
   California v. Bakke*, 125,
   125n11
Reich, R., 158n12, 208n37
religious diversity, 58–9
research on social capital, 46–7
respiratory disease in
   Guangdong, 14
responsibilities of social capital,
   72
Robison, L. J., 36–7, 37n14

Rochester, J. M., 146n54
Rosenau, J. N. H., 183n4, 201
Rotary Club, 2
Roth, R., 17n13
Ruggie, J. G., 24, 24n27, 64,
   64n80, 116n64, 147n60,
   148

Saguaro Seminar, The,
   36n12
same sex marriage laws, 150
Sander, T. H., 142, 142n48
Sanfey, P., 141n45
Sargent Shriver International
   Service Act, 204
Sarkozy, President, 1
Sarkozy Report, 6, 35
SARS, *see* severe acute
   respiratory syndrome
   (SARS)
satiation, 192
Saulny, S., 61n76, 62n78
scapes, 199
Schengen Treaty, 1
Schuklenk, U., 52n58, 67n1
Schuller, T., 69, 69n5
security, 117
self-interest, 66, 78
   ethics and, 66–7
   norms of, 19, 51
   social capital and, 52
self-interested behavior, 18
Seligman, M. E. P., 92n19, 98–9,
   99n41
Sen, A., 6, 25, 35n10, 190,
   190n13
Serve America Act, 209n39
severe acute respiratory
   syndrome (SARS), 14, 82
Shah, A., 12n1
shared identity, 105
Sherraden, M. S., 205n35

Sherrice Iverson Child Victim
    Protection Act, 132, 132n24
Shimai, S., 145n53, 160n14
Silverman, R. E., 170n31
Simon, H., 73, 73n8
Singapore, x
Singer, P., 17–18, 17n12, 18n15,
    23, 25, 28, 60, 69n4, 69n6,
    73, 177, 203n33
single identity, 181
Skrbis, Z., 117n66
Skype, 197
Smith, J., 20n18
Smith-Lovin, L., 38n20
Smits, J. M., 128n16
social capital
    abundant, 151
    benefits of, 51
    bonding, 37, 55–6
    bridging, 38
    business contributions to,
        48–9
    in community, 72–3
    concept of, 2–3, 32–3, 35–6,
        77
    creation of, 2, 46–9, 181–3
    culture and, connection
        between, 111–13
    dark side of, 4, 21, 31, 38, 61,
        70, 82, 84, 119
    defined, 32, 34, 36–8
    defined as, 35
    destroying, 139–46
    ethical concept of, 69
    as ethical principle, 180–1
    ethics and, 76–83
    exclusionary, 4
    externalities of, 50–1
    family-level, 94
    generalized reciprocity and,
        34
    global, 53–65, 152, 182–3

global living and, 201–2
    health benefits of, 44–5
    international, 4–5
    investment in, 53
    laws, creating of, 120, 144–5
    lean and mean definition, 33,
        35
    measurement of, 46
    of migrants, 54–6
    moral importance of, 29
    morals of, 71
    neighborhood, 44
    network-based, 153
    non-governmental
        organizations and, 56, 81
    norm-based, 153
    nudging towards, 29–31
    Portland Oregon, 48
    principle of, 76–8, 81–3
    public good of, 50
    research on, 46–7
    responsibilities of, 72
    self-interest and, 52
    social networks and, 46
    social ties and, 36
    of strangers, 59
    sustaining, 48
    transnational, 53–65,
        201–2
    trust and, 39–40
    vulnerability of, 50–1
    see also specific topics
social cohesion, 39, 61, 115,
    160, 178
social costs of culture, 108–9
social good, 19–21, 41–2
social harm, 136–7
social identity, 60, 115
social identity theory,
    188–9
social interaction, 46
social life, 28–9

social meaning, 121–6
social nature of humans,
    102–3
social networks
    development of, 48
    laws and impact on, 29–30
    social capital and, 46
    value of, 48
social policy, 29
social qualities, 27–8
social relationships, 92–3
social solidarity, 38–9
social status factors, 93
social ties, 183–5
    happiness and, 86–7,
        211–12
    social capital and, 36
social trust, vii, 79
societal culture, 103–4
solidarity rights, 75–6
    classifications of, 75
    collectives and, 76
    ethics and, 75–6
    peace, 76
    war, 76
Sowell, A., 15
status quo bias, 49
Steger, M. F., 137n34
Stern, M. A., 50n52
Stiglitz, J. E., 6, 35n10
Stolle, D., 34, 35n5, 46n45,
    93n22, 94n30
strangers
    abandoned, 210
    cash offered to, 133–4
    distant, 127, 204, 208
    duty to rescue laws for, 128,
        135
    global, 127
    Good Samaritan laws,
        128
    helping, 126–39

hostility to, 118
legal liabilities of, 138–9
liberty and, 139
moral obligations to, 134
relationship with, 54
social capital of, 59
Stratton, S., 11n1
strict constructionism,
    138
Strohmeyer, J., 129–30
substitution, 192
suffering, 15
    distant, 16
    global, 177
    local, 16
    morals and, 16–17
    poverty and, 15–16
Sunstein, C. R., 3, 6, 13n6, 21,
    23, 23n26, 28, 28n32, 30,
    30n34, 49, 50n53, 91, 121,
    121n2, 121n3, 126n13,
    160n15
Supreme Court of
    Massachusetts, 138
Surgeon General, 99, 100n42
suspicious conduct, 15
sustaining social capital, 48
synthetic oxytocin, 40

Tajfel, H., 111n53, 186, 186n7
Takings Clause, 123, 158
Taliban, 7
Tanaka-Matsumi, J., 145n53,
    160n14
tax code, xiii
technoscape, 199
tension within culture, 1
termination at will laws, 121, 142
termination for cause, 145
Thailand, x
Thaler, R. H., 30, 30n34, 98n39,
    126n13

TheLifeYouCanSave.com, 26
thin trust, 38
third party non intervention, 127
Tiananmen Square, 76
tolerance, 195
Torti, L., 137
Toussaint v. Blue Cross & Blue Shield of Michigan, 143, 143n49
trade with migrants, 55
transnational culture, 114
transnational living, 200
transnational network, 54, 200–1, 205
transnational organizations, 56, 59
transnational reciprocation, 57
transnational social capital, 53–65
  global living and, 201–2
  see also global social capital
transpatriates, 111
trust, 193–4
  charities and, 156–7
  in culture, 105–6, 110–11
  generalized reciprocity and, 40–1
  giving, 40, 153
  laws, impact on, 29–30, 120
  oxytocin and, increased, 110
  personal factors of, 42
  social capital and, 39–40
  social factors of, 42
  as social good, 41–2
  World Value Survey, 46
trust-based networks, 55
trust game, 40
trust hormone, 40
trusting strangers, 56, 106, 110
trustworthiness, 36
trustworthy behavior, 40–2
Tunisian migrants, 1
Twitter Revolution, 62, 64

Unconditional Most Favored Nation, 148, 150
unemployment, 142–3
UNHCR, 13n4
UNICEF, *see* United Nations Children's Emergency Fund (UNICEF)
United Nations Children's Emergency Fund (UNICEF), 12
United Nations General Assembly, 147
United Nations Refugee Agency, 13n4
United States, homelessness in, 14–15
United States Supreme Court, 165
U.S. Census Bureau, 62, 126n14
U.S. State Department, 62
Universal Declaration of Human Rights, 57, 75, 115, 126n15, 195, 203
universal ethics, 69–70
universal human rights, 56, 60
universal rights, 203–4
universalization, 69, 82–3
University of Oxford, 26
upper-income Americans, giving by, 18–19
"us", focus of, 3–4
  consists in, 180
Us Before Me, 25, 31
Uslaner, E. M., 94, 94n30
Ustun, T. B., 100n43
Utah County v. Intermountain Health Care, Inc., 170n29
utilitarianism, the moral theory of (Mill), 85–6, 91, 98
utility, 88–9

values
within culture, 84–5, 104–5
economic prosperity and, 44
of global social capital, 65
good citizenship and, 45–6
of individuality, 90
of laws, 121–2
marketplace, 143–4
of social capital, 34, 42–6, 119
of social networks, 48
of "us", 1–2
in voluntary associations,
46–7
van Bastelaer, T., 39n23
Van Horn v. Watson, 137,
137n35
Vasak, K., 75
virtuous cycle, 64, 82, 154, 205
voluntary associations, 46–7
volunteering, 206–8
vulnerability of social capital,
50–1

Wall Street Journal, 142
war, 76
waters edge policy, 163–4,
167–75

well-being
global well being, 211
happiness and, 93–4, 99–100
subjective well-being, defined
as, 84
Wenar, L., 17n14, 158n12,
169n28, 178n38
Wofford, H., 204n34
Wolf, S., 44n41
Wollheim, R., 98n40
Woodward, I., 117n66
workplace, 139–40
World Bank, The, 12, 32–3,
33n1, 39, 39n21, 63
World Cup, 198
World Health Organization, 14,
146
world population, x, xi
World Poverty and Human Rights
(Pogge), 16
World Trade Organization, 63,
148
World Value Survey, 46

Yale University, 16, 26n30
Yunus, M., 178n37

Zack, P. J., 40n24
Zegler, M. M., 134n29